Student's
Guide to
College Music
Programs

THIRD
EDITION

We proudly acknowledge the following individuals who contributed their expertise in the completion of this publication. Authors Mark Thomas, Joseph J. Martinkovic and Rob Rogers. Production coordinator Michael. Rueckwald and graphic designers Laurie Chesna and Andrew Ross. Editors Christian Wissmuller and Eliahu Sussman for their assistance in compiling the information and for their proofreading skills and Randy Struckus for his assistance in assembling the database. Melanie A. Prescott for the many hours extended in helping bring this project to print and SCHOOL BAND AND ORCHESTRA Group Publisher Sidney Davis and Publisher Rick Kessel for their encouragement and support.

Cover Design by Laurie Chesna

All inquires should be addressed to:

21 Highland Circle, Suite 1
Needham, MA 02494
781-453-9310 Fax 781-453-9389
e-mail info@symphonypublishing.com

Printed in the United States of America

The Third Edition of the *Student's Guide to College Music Programs* offers an expanded state-by-state listing of more than 1,300 college and university music programs. In addition, the state "home page" features a variety of useful information for the music student, including music programs within the state, state capital and population figures.

We are grateful to the music professional contributors who assisted us in compiling information on financial aid, vocational careers, guidelines for auditions and other topics of interest to the music student.

For each of the colleges and universities in this book we present a capsule of information ranging from basic admission contacts to course requirements and music programs. We extend our thanks to the admission officers and music departments who supplied the data. While every effort has been made to verify the information contained within this book, music students are encouraged to contact their school guidance departments and college admissions officers for further information.

The *Student's Guide to College Music Programs* is affiliated with three Symphony Publishing magazines for music educators, *School Band and Orchestra, JAZZed,* and *Choral Director.* Readers are encouraged to visit our Web site at www.symphonypublishing.com for additional resources.

Ageleke Zapis
Editor

What's Expected of Incoming Freshmen

By Mark Thomas

Most high school juniors and seniors realize that the educational system they have enjoyed for the majority of their young years is nearing an end. Those familiar surroundings that have felt so comfortable are soon going to be replaced by a series of new choices. Gone will be a bell to signal a classroom change, club activities, proms, parent-teacher meetings, school bus rides, Friday night football games, and many other things that have defined the secondary school years.

After high school graduation, some students will enter the job market or decide to serve their country in the armed forces, while the majority will elect to further their education at an institution of higher learning. Students seeking a college education are urged to apply for admission early and send applications to more than one school. Applying to at least three to five institutions with programs that are appealing is quite reasonable, increasing the chances that a suitable school will make an offer.

College is Different

State laws mandate that you must attend secondary schools; whereas colleges and universities select students they wish to accept via the application process. Unlike public schools, colleges and universities – whether public or private – charge tuition to attend. Further, the college/university world is considered an adult world: students are treated accordingly. At the secondary level, it's the "boys' basketball team," or the "girls' tennis team," whereas at the university level, it's the "men's golf team" and the "women's basketball team."

A college student (or undergraduate) who experiences difficulty with a subject should not expect to arrange a parent-teacher conference to discuss the problem. The professor will discuss the problem with the student, not his/her parents. Students who earn a high grade point average after a semester can expect to be rewarded with a place on the dean or chancellor's list. Conversely, those who earn a low grade-point average can expect to be on the dean's "other list."

Self Discipline

Failure in too many subjects will soon lead to academic probation and/or expulsion from the college or university. Such failure is frequently the result of lack of self-discipline and proper time management. Students often have difficulty accepting personal responsibility for their actions. Young adults away from home for the first time no longer have someone to rouse them in the morning in time for class; indeed, class schedules often seem erratic. The English literature class may meet three times a week for 50 minutes, while a class in biology may meet twice a week for a 50-minute lecture and once a week for a two-and-a-half-hour lab. Also, a student's class schedule is likely to be different from roommates' or hall mates' schedules, since students enrolled in many disciplines room together. Evening classes and ensembles are quite normal. Undergraduates who survive the freshman year learn to use free time during the day for practice and studying.

Freedom is Double-Edged Sword

Most high schools have enrollments of 1,000-2,000, whereas a large university may have 20,000 or more. Consequently, the experience of seeing familiar faces in high school will vary drastically in college. In high school, juniors and seniors represent the upper class; in the university setting, former high school graduates are the youngest age group and freshmen again.

Many college freshmen experience loneliness in their new surroundings and bemoan the loss of their former "upper class" status. The need to find new friends and be accepted is great and can frequently lead to academic problems. Students who learn to balance their social and academic lives in the first year can avoid the disappointment and embarrassment of "flunking out" in college. Students are expected to have class assignments prepared as scheduled; excuses are unacceptable.

Music Courses

At the university level, lesson assignments are more extensive than at the high school level, and all music majors are required to have a one-hour lesson per week on his/her major instrument. Fundamentals (i.e., all forms of scales and arpeggios) must be mastered; also, professors will assign substantial etude material and repertoire appropriate for freshmen. It is never advisable to inform the private lesson professor that practice time was not available because of a paper or impending test that required extra preparation. Remember that private lessons are a class that can be failed. Private music lessons at the university level should never be considered an easy, automatic "A." Materials should be as carefully prepared for a music lesson as for any other class. Always be on time for your lessons and, should cancellation of a lesson ever be necessary, do so well in advance and only for a very valid reason. Some professors may allow for a make-up lesson. Failure to appear for your lesson will result in a grade of zero for that day.

Practice Habits

Practice sessions for most high school students can vary from one hour or more a day to none, depending on homework or school activities. The majority of private teachers try to accommodate these irregularities if they are not abused. If carried to extremes, of course, many teachers will drop such a student from their schedules.

At the college and university level, each student must find time each week for practice in order to properly prepare the music assigned. Two to four or more hours each day should be sufficient to prepare weekly assignments. Just as a student needs to spend a great deal of time reading literature or studying calculus, he or she must also spend a great deal of time practicing, not only the basics (scales, etudes) but the great literature and orchestral works for that student's instrument. The student who is well prepared in the basics will have more time to learn new things and progress more quickly.

Band, Orchestra and Ensembles

Band, orchestra, and smaller ensembles are an important part of preparing students for musical careers. These various organizations offer artistic challenges not found at the high school level, since personnel are comprised of more advanced, older players. Competition for chair seating arrangements is strong and the directors expect to take students to new musical heights. Exposure to more difficult repertoire will strengthen a sense of phrasing and intonation. As with private lesson assignments, ensemble music must also be well prepared, for numerous section rehearsals are common at the university level. Missed notes, bad intonation, and sloppy phrasing will not be tolerated. Practice time must be allocated for this music as well.

Work and Enjoy

All college and university music professors know that incoming freshmen are not seasoned artists; if they were, they would not be attending an institution of higher learning. By working together with various professors, aspiring musicians can accomplish a great deal during the college years. Students attending a college or university are seeking help in building a life-long career in music; those who enter with an open mind and are ready to learn will be successful.

Music professors have achieved acclaim in their various fields and will gladly share this expertise with students. They were once students themselves – they know what it takes to be successful. By having a positive attitude, students can achieve at this higher level. It is a time of newness and excitement. Freshmen are allowed and encouraged to have fun and enjoyment in college, but must learn to balance social activities and class work wisely. Students who do not allow "Party 101" to become the focus and the Dean's "other list" the goal can succeed in music and in life and can enjoy the many benefits and rewards a career in music has to offer. ♪

Mark Thomas is founder and honorary life president of The National Flute Association (NFA). A recitalist, soloist, conductor, and clinician, he has appeared in 20 foreign countries and 49 states. Thomas has been on the faculties of The American University, George Washington University, The University of Notre Dame, the University of North Carolina at Charlotte, Indiana University at South Bend, National Music Camp at Interlochen, and Sewanee Summer Music Center, and has lectured at many universities and conservatories.

He has numerous published flute works, including the Mark Thomas Flute Method *(SMC Publications) series. Thomas has served as a board member of National Public Radio, board President of the Elkhart County Symphony Association, and as artistic design consultant to several leading flute manufacturers. Additionally, Thomas can be heard on Golden Crest and Columbia Records.*

Tips for the College Audition

The audition process is pivotal in gaining acceptance to the music college or conservatory of your choice. We have compiled a list of tips that should help you on your way to a successful college audition.

What do I bring?

- All schools will require a performance audition, either in recorded form or in person.

What are schools looking for?

- Schools look for students who possess musical ability and sensitivity that can be shaped and polished during their academic years.

What do I have to prove at my audition?

- Students must demonstrate certain levels of technical ability, musicality, intonation and repertoire during their audition.

How should I prepare?

- Practice the school's required audition repertoire and also prepare your own etudes and solos. Know your major, minor and chromatic scales, chords, arpeggios, thirds, octaves and the like.

- Practice sight-reading every chance you get.

- Prepare a solo piece that includes a slow section that highlights tone and expression and a contrasting section that focuses on technical abilities.

- Analyze all audition pieces for style, tempo and expression markings.

- Practice for your audition by performing your pieces in front of the class. Ask for feedback, both positive and negative, after your performance.

- Don't audition on a marginal instrument.

- Before the audition, get plenty of rest and nourishment.

- Try to schedule your arrival at the school the day before your audition.

- Arrive for your audition early enough to secure a warm-up room, but do not over-practice before your performance.

- Dress nicely; an audition is a public performance and dress has bearing on how you are perceived.

- Don't forget to bow after your performance and acknowledge your accompanist if you have one. Then wait on-stage until the committee releases you.

11

Financial Aid: A Primer

Financial aid for college comes in three forms: gift aid, loan aid and work aid.

BY JOSEPH J. MARTINKOVIC

Gift aid is by far the most popular and sought-after type of financial aid. Gift aid usually takes the form of a grant or scholarship. The best part of this type of award is that it doesn't have to be paid back. If you are applying for need-based financial aid, gift aid based on need is usually called a grant. If, for example, you are musically talented and plan to pursue music as a college major or a career, you may be offered a talent scholarship. Scholarships may be based more on your ability, talent or skills than on your financial need. Some colleges and universities acknowledge students' hard work and efforts and offer academic scholarships. Both talent and academic scholarships can range from a few hundred dollars up to a full tuition scholarship and, in a few cases, may even include room and board.

Loan aid is borrowed money that has to be repaid with interest. Again, if you are applying for need-based financial aid, loans are inevitable and will most likely be a part of your financial aid package. It is also referred to as a "self-help" program. This type of financial aid is most readily available and comprises the largest source of funding within federal financial aid programs. If you are offered a loan as part of your financial aid award, you do have the right to decline the loan. Keep in mind, however, that your loan will not be replaced with gift aid. Federal Perkins Loans and subsidized Federal Stafford Loans, for instance, offer low interest rates with attractive repayment terms (including no payments against the money you borrowed while you're enrolled in college).

The final type of financial aid is work aid. Work aid is just that – you work, you get paid. Like loan aid, work aid is another self-help program and you can decline a part-time job if it's offered to you. The vast majority of colleges and universities offer some type of work opportunities either through federally-funded programs or their own on-campus programs. For the most part, however, the money you earn is not credited to your account in the business office like gift aid or loan aid would be. It is paid directly to you on a regular basis (weekly, bi-weekly or monthly). Some colleges will allow you to have all or a portion of your earnings applied against your college costs.

Primary Sources of Financial Aid

There are four primary sources of funding – the federal government; your state government; private organizations, businesses and foundations; and the colleges and universities themselves.

More than 70 percent of all sources of financial aid are federally funded. The federal government does provide funds for all three types of financial aid with the loan programs comprising the largest percentage

(about 54 percent). In order for you to be considered for these programs, you have to file the Free Application for Federal Student Aid, commonly known as the FAFSA. The FAFSA is the primary "need analysis" document that is used to determine your eligibility for federal funds and to calculate your "demonstrated" financial need. By submitting the FAFSA, you are considered for the Federal Pell Grant Program, the Federal Campus-Based Programs (Federal Supplemental Educational Opportunity Grant, Federal Perkins Loan and Federal Work-Study), and the Federal Stafford Loan Program. Even if you do not demonstrate a financial need you may be eligible for an unsubsidized Federal Stafford Loan. The major difference between a subsidized and an unsubsidized loan is who pays the interest on the loan while you're in college. If you have a subsidized loan, the federal government pays the interest; for an unsubsidized loan, you are responsible for paying the interest on the loan while enrolled. To get a better understanding of the specifics of the federal programs, you can access information at the U.S. Department of Education's Web site, www.ed.gov.

Your state government is the second source of funding. Most states do offer some form of gift aid based on a student's demonstrated financial need and may also include your scholastic performance (as measured by your class rank or standardized test scores). Since the programs do vary from state to state, it's best that you check on your respective state's program. You do need to find out if your state's grant or scholarship program is "portable" – that is, whether it can be taken out of state. Some states (such as New York and New Jersey) require you to attend a college or university in their respective state in order to be eligible for the programs. If your state does allow you to apply the grant or scholarship to an out-of-state institution, the amount of the grant or scholarship may be reduced. You also need to know whether the colleges and universities you are considering will reduce any of their own financial aid if you receive a state grant or scholarship.

Although private organizations, businesses, and foundations are the smallest players in the financial aid program, this form of gift aid or loan aid can make a significant contribution to reducing your out-of-pocket college costs. The best place to start is in your own hometown. Your high school's guidance office usually has information available on these local, regional, or national programs. What's best about these scholarship and loan programs is that you don't have to be the class valedictorian or salutatorian to be eligible for consideration for these programs.

Finally, there are the colleges and universities that offer institutional financial aid funds, primarily in the form of gift aid. When financial aid administrators review your financial situation (assuming you submitted the FAFSA), you are usually considered for all possible types of institutional financial aid. Often, families think that colleges and universities have unlimited resources. It's simply not true. Even nationally renowned institutions with nine-digit endowments have limitations on financial aid availability. Be assured, however, that financial aid administrators do their best to help you finance your education.

Merit Scholarships

Merit scholarships are talent-based and often do not take financial need into consideration. As someone who currently participates in a high school band or orchestra, you have a talent. Colleges and universities who offer degree programs in music or place special emphasis on music as an extra-curricular activity may seek you. Many of these institutions offer merit scholarships. Let your talent pay off for you and help reduce the cost of your college education.

The Application Process

The first step is to file the FAFSA form to be considered for federal financial aid programs (with the exception of the Federal PLUS Loan, a supplemental education loan program for parents). All colleges and universities must use this form for federal financial aid programs. Most states also require you to file the FAFSA in order to be considered for their state grant and scholarship programs. Likewise, the vast majority of institutions also use this form to determine your eligibility for their own need-based financial aid programs. If you plan to apply for financial aid, make sure you submit the FAFSA by the deadline dates set by the colleges and universities to which you will be applying. For entering freshmen, most colleges and universities require you to file by early or mid-February of your senior year of high school. The sooner you file the better, even if it means estimating information about you and your parents' income and assets. You can always update the information once your and your parents' federal tax returns are filed. You can apply via the Internet at www.fafsa.ed.gov.

If you are applying under a college's early admissions' decision program, you'll need to contact the college to find out what need-analysis form you may have to file. Usually, you have to submit your admissions application early in your senior year with an admissions decision some time by the end of December. Most institutions will provide you with an estimated financial aid package since you will be required to commit to attending that institution if you are admitted.

But in almost all cases, you will still have to submit the FAFSA.

Not all institutions rely solely on the results of the FAFSA when it comes to considering you for institutional financial aid. Another need-analysis form used by about 600 colleges and universities is the College Scholarship Service's (CSS) Profile. CSS charges a nominal fee for processing its need analysis form for each college you list. The purpose of this form is to supplement information not captured on the FAFSA (such as a family's home equity). The colleges and universities that require the CSS Profile factor in the additional information when determining your eligibility for institutional aid. For more information about the CSS Profile and other pertinent financial aid information, go to www.collegeboard.org.

Joseph J. Martinkovic is regional account executive at American Student Assistance (www.amsa.com) and former director of student financial assistance at the University of Hartford, West Hartford, Connecticut. Martinkovic has over 30 years of experience in college admissions and financial aid.

Conservatory or College of Music?

By Rob Rogers

Y ou've studied, practiced, performed, and prepared. You know you're ready to take your career in music to the next level. So which direction do you choose – a college of music, or a conservatory?

"In title, there's little difference. It's not like the huge difference between a university and a college," said Todd Krohne, administrative assistant to the assistant vice president for student affairs and enrollment at Berklee College of Music in Boston, Mass. "If you look at all of the aspects – location, curriculum, faculty – each has the same weight and merit."

Your choice is likely to depend on what you want out of both your music and your environment, as well as your answers to the following questions.

What Do You Want to Study?

This might seem like a simple question – you want to study music, right? However, no two schools are likely to approach this goal in the same way. Conservatories emphasize performance, encouraging and demanding excellence in an instrument or voice. Individual conservatories are known for their strength in the areas of music theory, analysis, and composition.

"Performance is the focus of what students do here," said Allison Scola, associate director of admissions at Mannes College of Music, a New York City conservatory. "The students take some humanities classes, like writing, Western civilization, and art history, that accentuate their music education, but 85 percent of what they do is music-related, including private lessons and chamber music. We want students to leave here with their ear so trained, their dictation skills and analytical techniques so well developed, that 25 years from now, they'll be able to look at a piece of music and be able to say what it's all about, what art and political history influenced it, what the writer was thinking when making key changes. That's the kind of thing we focus on here."

Music colleges – especially those located within a university – often combine a rigorous music program with a liberal arts education. This can be particularly helpful for students considering careers that require both an understanding of music and a background in business, psychology or another discipline. Many colleges offer degrees in areas such as music management, music education, instrument design, and music therapy.

"Our students study music management, production technology, and music education," said Amy Becher, director of admissions of the Hartt School in Hartford, Conn. "We also have the only undergraduate program that I am aware of in acoustics and music. Our students receive a solid conservatory training, with a strong performance background, but they also have the job security that comes with having a marketable degree."

Described as "a conservatory setting within a university," the Hartt School, which became one-third of the University of Hartford in 1957, maintains a unique middle ground between the college and conservatory experiences.

"We're still a conservatory, with a strong performing faculty," Becher said. "But we can also offer students some of the benefits of being part of a university – athletics, Greek life, opportunities to take on projects that go beyond a strictly musical focus. We invite students to incorporate music into every level of their lives, not just the performing level."

In addition, music colleges are often a choice for those students primarily interested in contemporary, rather than classical, music.

"We foster the learning of contemporary music, and it makes such a radical difference," said Krohne, a 1996 Berklee graduate. "There's an excitement, a passion about this place. The subject matter is so up-to-date, so cutting edge, that you graduate knowing what they've taught you is what the industry is doing at that time."

How Much Time Should You Devote to Your Music?

Many colleges follow the National Association of Schools of Music curriculum guidelines, which require students to spend 60 percent of their studies in music, and 40 percent on the liberal arts – creating what Amy Becher of the Hartt School calls "a well-rounded student."

However, some students may find it difficult to devote themselves to a performing career while juggling a liberal arts course load. Others may decide they simply want to spend more time practicing and studying music. For them, a conservatory might be a better choice.

"It can be a problem when, because of the amount of studies and papers you have to write, you don't have time to practice five or six hours a day," said Scola, who graduated from a music college before coming to work for a conservatory. "At my school, the English and history classes I was taking weren't related to the music curriculum at all, and things like the orchestra and chamber music were considered 'extra.' Classmates of mine who wanted to go on to master's programs had to take a year off to practice and get their chops ready before they could play at the same level as someone who had been to a conservatory."

"It's a demanding program," said Haim Avitsur, a 1999 Mannes graduate who now works in the admissions office. "It asked things of me that I never thought or dreamed I could do. I'm a trombone player, so I never thought I would have to learn the

piano. But I needed to do that to be able to graduate, and it proved to be a good thing. Now I can read scores that others cannot."

What Resources Should Your School Have?

Music colleges, especially those associated with universities, offer all the advantages of a large school – a wide range of academic subjects, an active campus life, and often significant fi-

19

nancial resources. They may also provide musical instruction for students with a wide range of abilities, and emphasize community involvement.

Depending on its size, a conservatory may have fewer resources than a university music college – but the resources at its disposal are focused on a music education.

"As an undergraduate, if I wanted to play in a woodwind quintet, I always had to make sure there were enough players," Scola said. "You don't have to worry about that in a conservatory. Also, my school had a single master class program that I knew of that took place once a year. Conservatories offer master classes on a routine basis."

Some students choose schools based on the opportunity to study with particular faculty members.

"I'm a trombone player, and I wanted to study with Per Brevig, the former principal with the Metropolitan Opera," said Avitsur, who came from Israel to study at Mannes. "He's a legend among trombone players."

Colleges and conservatories also differ in the number and kind of degree programs available. The Hartt School offers eight different bachelor of music programs, two bachelor of arts programs, and a bachelor of science in engineering in acoustics and music, as well as double majors, minors, and honors programs. Berklee offers its degree candidates a bachelor of music in 12 areas, including film scoring, music therapy, and professional music, in which a student creates a major based upon his/her

professional objectives. Mannes graduates bachelors of music and science majoring in orchestral and other instruments, voice and opera, composition, theory and conducting.

Are You Ready for the Audition?

The admissions process varies greatly for music colleges and conservatories. Most music colleges require separate applications for the school of music and the university with which the school is associated. Some require live auditions, while others will accept recordings.

Berklee College of Music offers students two options: the chance to become a degree student, incorporating liberal arts and music studies, or a diploma student, studying only music.

"There's no audition process to be admitted, only to receive scholarships," Krohne said. "The application provides us with information about how the student has done in the past, recommendations from teachers, and personal essays. We encourage students to send music along to give us a better idea about them, but it's by no means necessary for admission."

In addition, students applying to a music college may not be limited by the performance needs of a particular school.

"It's the opposite of the conservatory mode," Krohne said. "Students might apply to a conservatory that only needs a certain number of string players or oboe seats. We don't have the mindset that we need more of this or that. We accept students as musicians."

Auditions are standard for applicants to conservatories. Some schools – such as Juilliard, Mannes, and Manhattan School of Music – hold their auditions during the same time period, so students traveling to the New York area can visit all three at once. Some schools accept common applications, like that of the National Arts Learning Foundation. Mannes, for example, accepts the NALF as part one of its application, with part two including a personal statement and an assessment of the applicant's writing skills. Students at Mannes also take a placement test based on their dictation, ear training, and theory skills.

How Competitive Do You Want Your Environment to Be?

Getting into a college or conservatory is only half the battle. In addition to the long hours of practice and strict musical discipline, some students expect a competitive atmosphere when attending a top school of music – and they may be right. However, school representatives say that sense of competition often comes from the students themselves, and not their peers or institutions.

"It depends on the conservatory, but it's definitely more intensive [than a music college]," Scola said. "For one thing, there's more at stake. At least with a B.A. program, there's some-

thing to fall back on – there's more of a wide range in the job market."

However, Scola adds that the pressure to succeed tends to bring conservatory students together, rather than set them against each other.

"We rotate our players through the principal chair, second, back section and so on," Scola said. "There are other places where whatever position you end up in, you stay there, unless you're willing to challenge the first chair. That sets up a competitive atmosphere."

"You hear horror stories, but for the most part, they don't happen here," Avitsur said. "You know where you are, and you try to be a little bit better than your colleagues, but when a friend of mine gets a position with an orchestra, I smile and say congratulations. There's no talking behind someone's back, no backstabbing here. New York City is a rough city to live in, and this school is more like a home, a family."

Rob Rogers *is a journalism and English teacher in Massachusetts. He is also a freelance writer for the* Quincy Patriot Ledger *and has written for* School Band and Orchestra *in the past.*

INDEX BY STATE

Henderson State University
Hendrix College
John Brown University
Lyon College
Ouachita Baptist University
Philander Smith College
University of Arkansas at Little Rock
University of Arkansas at Monticello
University of Arkansas at Pine Bluff
University of Arkansas-Fort Smith
University of Central Arkansas
University of the Ozarks
Westark Community College
Williams Baptist College

California   *p. 59*

Ali Akbar College
Allan Hancock College
American River Community College
American School of Piano Tuning
Antelope Valley College
Azusa Pacific University
Bethany College of Assembly of God
Biola University
Cabrillo College
California Baptist University
California Institute of Technology
California Lutheran Universiy
California Polytechnic State University
    at Pomona
California Polytechnic State University at
    San Luis Obispo
California State University at Chico
California State University at Fresno
California State University at Hayward
California State University at Long Beach
California State University at Los Angeles
California State University at Northridge
California State University at San Bernardino
California State University at San Marcos
California State University at Stanislaus
California State University-Bakersfield
California State University-Dominguez Hills
Canada College
Cerritos College
Chaffey College
Chapman University
Citrus College
City College of San Francisco

Claremont Graduate University
Colburn School conservatory of Music
College of Alameda
College of Marin
College of San Mateo
College of Siskiyous
College of Siskiyous
College of the Canyons
College of the Desert
College of the Redwoods
College of the Sequoias
Colorado Christian University
Columbia College
Concordia University
Cuesta College
Cypress College
De Anza College
Diablo Valley College
Dominican University of California
East Los Angeles College
El Camino College Compton Center
Evergreen Valley College
Foothill College
Fullerton College
Gavilan College
Glendale Community College
Golden West College
Grossmont College
Hartnell College
Holy Names University
Humboldt State University
Idyllwild School of Music and the Arts
Imperial Valley College
Irvine Valley College
La Sierra University
Lake Tahoe Community College
Laney Community College
Long Beach City College
Los Angeles Harbor College
Los Angeles Pierce College
Los Angeles Recording Workshop
Los Angeles Southwest College
Los Medanos College
Loyola Marymount University
Marymount College
Masters College
Merced College
Merritt College
Mills College
Miracosta College

Trinity College
University of Bridgeport
University of Connecticut
University Of Hartford
University of New Haven
Wesleyan University
Western Connecticut State University
Yale School of Music

Delaware *p. 88*

Delaware State College
University of Delaware

District of Columbia *p. 90*

American University
Benjamin T. Rome School of Music
George Washington University
Georgetown University
Howard University
Levine School of Music
Mount Vernon College
University of the District of Columbia

Florida *p. 92*

Barry University
Bethune-Cookman College
Brenau University
Brevard Community College
Broward Community College
Chipola Junior College
Edison Community College at Lee County
Edward Waters College
Florida A&M University
Florida Atlantic University
Florida College
Florida International University
Florida Keys Community College
Florida Southern College
Florida State University
Full Sail Real World Education
Gulf Coast Community College
Harid Conservatory
Hillsborough Community College
Jacksonville University
Jeff Berlin Players School of Music
Lake City Community College

Lynn University
Miami-Dade Community College at Kendall
Oskaloosa Walton Community College
Palm Beach Atlantic College
Palm Beach Community College
Pensacola Junior College
Rollins College
Santa Fe Community College
South Florida Community College
St. Leo University
St. Petersburg College
Stetson University
University of Central Florida
University of Florida
University of Miami
University of North Florida
University of South Florida
University of Tampa
University of West Florida
Valencia Community College
Warner Southern College

Georgia *p. 99*

Agnes Scott College
Andrew College
Armstrong Atlantic State University
Augusta State University
Berry College
Brenau University
Brewton-Parker College
Clark Atlanta University
Clayton College and State University
Columbus State University
Covenant College
Darton College
Emory University at Oxford
Fort Valley State University
Georgia College and State University
Georgia Institute of Technology
Georgia Perimeter College
Georgia Southern University
Georgia Southwestern College
Georgia State University
Gordon College
Kennesaw State University
LaGrange College
Mercer University
Middle Georgia College
Morehouse College

25

Roosevelt University
Rosary College-Dominican University
Saulk Valley Community College
Sherwood Conservatory of Music
South Suburban College
Southern Illinois University at Carbondale
Southwestern Illinois College
Springfield College at Illinois
St. Xavier University
Trinity Christian College
Trinity International University
Triton College
University of Chicago
University of Illinois
University of Illinois at Chicago
University of Illinois at Urbana
University of St. Francis
VanderCook College of Music
Western Illinois University
Wheaton College
William Rainey Harper College

Indiana *p. 124*

Ancilla College
Anderson University
Associated Mennonite Biblical Seminary
Ball State University
Bethel College
Butler University
De Pauw University
Earlham College
Goshen College
Grace College
Hanover College
Huntington College
Indiana University at Bloomington
Indiana University at Purdue
Indiana University at South Bend
Indiana University at Southeast
Indiana Wesleyan University
Manchester College
Marian College
Oakland City University
St. Joseph's College
St. Mary of the Woods College
St. Mary's College
Taylor University at Upland
The University of Indianapolis
University of Evansville

University of Indianapolis
University of Notre Dame
Valparaiso University
Vincennes University
Wabash College

Iowa *p. 131*

Ashford University
Briar Cliff College
Buena Vista University
Buena Vista University
Central College
Clarke College
Coe College
Cornell College
Dort College
Drake University
Graceland University
Grandview College
Grinnell College
Indian Hills Community College
Iowa State University
Iowa Wesleyan College
Kirkwood Community College
Loras College
Luther College
Morningside College
Mount Mercy College
Mount St. Clare College
North Iowa Area Community College
Northwestern College
Simpson College
Southwestern Community College
St. Ambrose University
University of Dubuque
University of Iowa
University of Northern Iowa
Upper Iowa University
Vennard College
Waldorf College
Wartburg College
Western Iowa Tech Community College
William Penn College

Kansas *p. 136*

Allen County Community College
Baker University
Barclay College

Maryland *p. 154*

Baltimore School for the Arts
Chesapeake College
College of Notre Dame of Maryland
Columbia Union College
Community College of Baltimore City
Coppin State College
Frederick Community College
Frostburg State University
Garrett Community College
Goucher College
Hartford Community College
Hood College
McDanial Coll ege
Montgomery College
Morgan State University
Mount St. Mary's College
Peabody Conservatory of Music
Prince Georges Community College
Salisbury University
St. Mary's College of Maryland
The Peabody Institute of Johns Hopkins
University
Towson University
University of Maryland
University of Maryland Baltimore County
University of Maryland Eastern Shore
Washington Bible College
Washington College
Washington Conservatory of Music

Massachusetts *p. 159*

American International College
Amherst College
Anna Maria College
Assumption College
Berklee College of Music
Berkshire Community College
Boston College
Boston Conservatory
Boston University
Brandeis University
Bridgewater State College
Cape Cod Community College
Clark University
College of the Holy Cross
Eastern Nazarene College
Emerson College

Emmanuel College
Endicott College
Gordon College
Hampshire College
Harvard University
Holyoke Community College
Longy School of Music
Massachusetts College of Liberal Arts
Massachusetts Institute of Technology
Mount Holyoke College
New England Conservatory
North Bennet Street School
Northeastern University
Northern Essex Community College
Our Lady of the Elms College
Salem State College
Simmons College
Smith College
Springfield College
Tufts Uaniversity
University of Massachusetts at Amherst
University of Massachusetts at Boston
University of Massachusetts at Lowell
Wellesley College
Westfield State College
Wheaton College
Wheelock College
Williams College
Worcester State College

Michigan *p. 166*

Adrian College
Albion College
Alma College
Andrews University
Aquinas College
Calvin College
Central Michigan University
Cornerstone University
Delta College
Eastern Michigan University
Grand Rapids Community College
Grand Valley State University
Great Lakes Christian College
Henry Ford Community College
Hillsdale College
Hope College
Interlochen Center for the Arts
Jackson Community College

Minnesota *p. 173*

Mississippi *p. 181*

Missouri *p. 185*

Avila College
Calvary Bible College and Theological
    Seminary
Central Methodist College
Central Missouri State University
College of the Ozarks
Cottey College
Culver Stockton College
Drury College
Evangel University
Fontbonne College
Hannibal La Grange College
Jefferson College
Lindenwood University
Maryville University
Mineral Area College
Missouri Southern State College
Missouri Western State College
Northwest Missouri State University
Park University
Rockhurst College
Southeast Missouri State University
Southwest Baptist University
Southwest Baptist University
Southwest Missouri State University
St. Louis University
Stephens College
Three Rivers Community College
Truman State University
University of Missouri at Columbia
University of Missouri at Kansas City
University of Missouri at St. Louis
Washington University
Webster University Leigh Gerdine
    College of Fine Arts
William Jewell College
William Woods University

Montana *p. 192*

Dawson Community College
Montana State University at Billings
Montana State University at Bozeman
University of Montana
Western Montana College

Nebraska *p. 194*

Central Community College Platte
Chadron State College
College of St. Mary
Concordia College
Creighton University
Dana College
Doane College
Grace University
Hastings College
Midland Lutheran College
Nebraska Wesleyan University
Northeast Community College
Peru State College
Union College
University of Nebraska
University of Nebraska at Kearney
University of Nebraska at Omaha
Wayne State College
Western Nebraska Community College
York College

Nevada *p. 198*

University of Nevada at Las Vegas
University of Nevada at Reno

New Hampshire *p. 200*

Colby-Sawyer College
Dartmouth College
Franklin Pierce College
Keene State College
Plymouth State University
St. Anselm College
University of New Hampshire

New Jersey *p. 203*

Bergen Community College
Caldwell College
Camden County College
Centenary College
College of New Jersey
College of St. Elizabeth
County College of Morris
Drew University
Fairleigh Dickinson University Madison

31

Niagara County Community College
Nyack College
Onondaga Community College
Orange County Community College
Queens College
Queensborough Community College
Robert Wesleyan College
Rockland Community College
Russell Sage College
Sarah Lawrence College
Schenectady County Community College
Skidmore College
St. Bonaventure University
St. Lawrence University
Stony Brook University
Suffolk County Community College
SUNY at Adelphi University
SUNY at Albany
SUNY at Buffalo
SUNY at Cobleskill
SUNY at Cortland
SUNY at Fredonia
SUNY at Geneseo
SUNY at New Paltz
SUNY at Oneonta
SUNY at Oswego
SUNY at Plattsburgh
SUNY at Potsdam
SUNY at Purchase College
SUNY at Stony Brook
Syracuse University
Teachers College - Columbia University
The New School for Jazz and
    Contemporary Music
Tompkins Cortland Community College
Ulster County Community College
Union College
Utica College
Vassar College
Villa Maria College
Wagner College
Wells College
Westchester Conservatory of Music

North Carolina *p. 225*

Appalachian State University
Barton College
Bennett College
Brevard College

Campbell University
Catawba College
Chowan College
Coastal Carolina Community College
College of the Albemarle
Davidson College
Duke University
East Carolina University
Elizabeth City State University
Elon University
Fayetteville State University
Gaston College
Greensboro College
Guilford College
Guilford Technical Community College
Jamestown College
Johnson C. Smith University
Lees-McRae College
Lenoir Community College
Livingstone College
Mars Hill College
Meredith College
Methodist College
Mitchell Community College
Montreat College
Mount Olive College
North Carolina A and T State University
North Carolina Central University
North Carolina School of the Arts
North Carolina Wesleyan College
Peace College
Pembroke State university
Pheiffer University
Piedmont Baptist College
Queens University of Charlotte
Rockingham Community College
Salem College
Shaw University
Southeast Baptist Theology Seminary
St. Augustine's College
University of North Carolina at Asheville
University of North Carolina at Chapel Hill
University of North Carolina at Charlotte
University of North Carolina at Greensboro
University of North Carolina at Wilmington
Wake Forest University
Warren Wilson College
Western Carolina University
Wilkes Community College
Wilmington Academy of Music

Population: 33,390,141 (2007 Estimate)
Capital: Ottawa
National Bird: Common Loon
Motto: A Mari usque ad Mare (From sea to sea)
National Tree: Maple
Residents Called: Canadians
Origin of Name: a"kanata" was the Huron-Iroquois word for "village" or "settlement."
Area: 3,800,000 square miles
Largest Cities: Toronto, Montreal, Vancouver, Calgary, Edmonton

Canadian Bible College
Department of Music

630-833 4th Ave. SW
Calgary, AB T2P 3T5, Canada
403-410-2000
Fax: 403-571-2556
E-mail: enrolment@auc-nuc.ca
www.auc.ca/ministry

Medicine Hat College
Conservatory of Music

299 College Dr. SE
Medicine Hat, AB T1A 3Y6, Canada
Debbie Nielsen
403-529-3880
E-mail: dnielsen@mhc.ab.ca
www.mhc.ab.ca

Red Deer College
Department of Music

P. O. Box 5005
Red Deer, AB T4N 5H5 Canada
403-342-3300
Fax: 403-340-8940
www.rdc.ab.ca

The King's University College
Department of Music

9125 50 St.
Edmonton, AB T6B 2H3, Canada
800-661-8582
Fax: 780-465-3534
www.kingsu.net

University of Alberta
Department of Music

3-82 Fine Arts Building
Edmonton, AB T6G 2C9 Canada
780-492-3263
Fax: 780-492-9246
E-mail: music@ualberta.com
www.ualberta.ca/music

University of Calgary
Department of Music

2500 University Dr. NW, CH F217
Calgary, AB T2N IN4 Canada
403-220-5376
Fax: 403-284-0973
E-mail: music@ucalgary.ca
www.ucalgary.ca

University of Lethbridge
Department of Music

4401 University Dr.
Lethbridge, AB T1K 3M4 Canada
403-329-2126
Fax: 403-382-7127
E-mail: karen.mahar@uleth.ca
www.uleth.ca

Bachelor of Music

Douglas College
Department of Music

P.O. Box 2503
New Westminster, BC V3L 5B2 Canada
604-527-5400
Fax: 604-527-5095
www.douglas.bc.ca

Kwantlen University College
Department of Music

12666 72nd Ave.
Surrey, BC V3W 2M8 Canada
604-599-2100
E-mail: inquiry@kwantlen.ca
www.kwantlen.bc.ca

Trinity Western University
Department of Music

7600 Glover Rd.
Langley, BC V2Y 1Y1 Canada
604-888-7511
www.twu.ca

University of British Columbia
School of Music

6361 Memorial Rd.
Vancouver, BC V6T 1Z2 Canada
Admissions Secretary
604-822-3113
Fax: 604-822-4884
E-mail: music.admissions@ubc.ca
www.music.ubc.ca

University of Victoria
School of Music

P.O. Box 1700 STN CSC
Fine Arts Building 116
Victoria, BC V8W 2Y2 Canada
250-721-7755
Fax: 250-721-7748
www.uvic.ca

Vancouber Acadamy of Music
Department of Music

1270 Chestnut St.
Vancouver, BC V6J 4R9 Canada
604-734-2301
Fax: 604-731-1920
E-mail: admin@vam.bc.ca
www.vam.bc.ca

Victoria Conservatory of Music
School of Music

900 Johnson St.
Victoria, BC V8V 3N4 Canada
866-386-5311
E-mail: info@vcm.bc.ca
www.vcm.bc.ca

Brandon University
School of Music

270 18th St.
Brandon, MB R7A 6A9 Canada
204-728-9520
Fax: 204-726-4573
E-mail: admissions@brandonu.ca
www.brandonu.ca

Memorial University of Newfoundland
School of Music

P.O. Box 4200
St. John's NL A1C 5S7 Canada
Tom Gordon
709-737-7486
Fax: 709-737-4569
E-mail: music@mun.ca
www.mun.ca

Mount Allison University
Department of Music

134 Main St.
Sackville, NB E4L 1A6 Canada
506-364-2374
Fax: 506-364-2376
E-mail: music@mta.ca
www.mta.ca/music

Dalhousie University
Department of Music

6101 University Ave. DAC RM 514
Halifax, NS B3H 4R2 Canada
Lesley Brechin
902-494-2418
Fax: 902-494-2801
E-mail: music@dal.ca
www.music.dal.ca

Bachelor of Music, Bachelor of Art in Music, Bachelor of Art combined honours Music and Theatre

Located in vibrant Halifax, Nova Scotia, Dalhousie University's Music Department combines the personalized benefits of a small department with the advantages of large urban campus. We offer a variety of undergraduate training programs for prospective music professionals, as well as many elective options for the non-major. Our faculty are internationally known performers and scholars. The Dal Arts Centre is home to Symphony Nova Scotia, the best small orchestra in Canada.

St. Francis Xavier University
Department of Music

P.O. Box 5000
Antigonish NS B2G 2W5 Canada
902-867-2106
Fax: 902-867-3654
E-mail: music@stfx.ca
www.stfx.ca/academic/music

Brock University
Department of Music

500 Glenridge Ave.
St. Catharines, ON L2S 3A1 Canada
Brian Power
905-688-5550
E-mail: bpower@brocku.ca
www.brocku.ca/music

University of Regina
Department of Music

Room RC257
Riddell Center
Regina, SK S4S 0A2 Canada
306-585-5532
Fax: 306-585-5549
E-mail: music@uregina.ca
www.uregina.ca

University of Saskatchewan
Department of Music

28 Campus Dr.
Saskatoon, SK S7N 0X1 Canada
306-966-6171
Fax: 306-966-6181
E-mail: music.uofs@usask.ca
www.usask.ca/music

Bachelor of Music

Population: 4,557,808 (2005 Estimate)
Capital City: Montgomery
Bird: Yellowhammer
Motto: We Dare Defend Our Rights
Flower: Camellia
Tree: Southern Longleaf Pine
Residents Called: Alabamians
Origin of Name: Means "tribal town" in the Creek Indian language.
Area: 51,781 square miles (29th largest state)
Statehood: December 14, 1899 (22nd state)
Largest Cities: Birmingham, Mobile, Montgomery, Huntsville, Tuscaloosa, Hoover, Dothan, Decatur, Gadsen
College Band Programs: Alabama A&M University, Auburn University, Samford University, Troy State University, Trinity Presbyterian School, University of North Alabama, University of Alabama, University of Alabama-Birmingham, University of Alabama-Tuscaloosa

ALABAMA

Alabama A&M University
Department of Music

4900 Meridian St.
Normal, AL 35762
Antonio Boyle
256-372-5000
E-mail: aboyle@aamu.edu
www.aamu.edu

Alabama State University
School of Music

915 South Jackson St.
Montgomery, AL 36101
334-229-4100
E-mail: hlamar@asunet.alasu.edu
www.alasu.edu

Arkansas State University at Beebe

P.O. Box 1000
Beebe, AL 72012
Robin Hayes
501-882-3600
Fax: 501-882-8370
E-mail: rahayes@asub.edu
www.asub.edu

Associates of Arts Degree

Auburn University

Auburn University, AL 36849
334-844-4000
E-mail: webmaster@auburn.edu
www.auburn.edu

Auburn University at Montgomery

P.O. Box 244023
Montgomery, AL 36124-4023
334-244-3000
www.aum.edu

Birmingham Southern College

900 Arkadelphia Rd.
Birmingham, AL 35254
800-523-5793
www.bsc.edu

Bishop State Community College

6250 Hwy. 31 North
Tanner, AL 35671
Pat Landers
256-306-2500
www.bscc.cc.al.us

Calhoun Community College
Department of Fine Arts

P.O. Box 2216
Decatur, AL 35609
John Calhoun
256-306-2500
Fax: 256-306-2925
E-mail: pml@calhoun.edu
www.calhoun.cc.al.us

Central Alabama Community College
Department of Music

1675 Cherokee Rd.
Alexander City, AL 35010
256-234-6346
www.cacc.cc.al.us

Chattahoocheè Valley Community College
Department of Music and Drama

2602 College Dr.
P.O. Box 1000
Phenix City, AL 36869
Tom Daniel

45

334-291-4987
E-mail: tom.daniel@cv.edu
www.cvcc.cc.al.us

Enterprise-Ozark Community College
Department of Fine Arts

600 Plaza Dr.
Enterprise, AL 36330
James Snyder
334-347-2623
E-mail: rsNNder@eocc.edu
www.eocc.edu

Faulkner University
5345 Atlanta Hwy.
Montgomery, AL 36109
334-272-5820
Fax: 334-386-3323
E-mail: kmorris@faulkner.edu
www.faulkner.edu

G.C. Wallace State Community College
1141 Wallace Dr.
Dothan, AL 36303
Brenda Burns
334-983-3521
Fax: 334-983-6066
www.wcc.cc.al.us

Gadsden State Community College
Department of Music

P.O. Box 227
Gadsden, AL 35902-0227
256-549-8200
www.gadsdenst.cc.al.us

Huntingdon College Music
Department of Music

1500 East Fairview Ave.
Montgomery, AL 36106

Ronald R. Shinn
334-833-4497
E-mail: rshinn@huntingdon.edu
www.huntingdon.edu

Jacksonville State University
Department of Music

700 Pelham Rd. North
Jacksonville, AL 36265
Legare McIntosh
800-231-5291
E-mail: info@jsu.edu
www.jsu.edu

Jefferson State Community College
Department of Music

2601 Carson Rd.
Birmingham, AL 35215
Jessica Hall
205-856-7900
Fax: 205-815-8499
E-mail: jhall@jeffstateonline.com
www.jscc.cc.al.us

Judson College
Department of Music

P.O. Box 120
Bibb St.
Marion, AL 36756
Leah Washburn
334-683-5187
E-mail: admissions@judson.edu
www.judson.edu

Bachelor of Art in Music, Bachelor of Science in Music Education

Christ-centered Women's college since 1838; affiliated with AL Baptist Convention (SBC)

Northeast Alabama State Junior College
Department of Music

P.O. Box 159
Wallace Administration Building 100C
Rainsville, AL 35986
Joan Reeves
256-638-4418 x 347
E-mail: reevesj@nacc.edu
www.nacc.edu

Oakwood College
Department of Music

7000 Adventist Blvd.
Huntsville, AL 35896
Lisa Moncur
256-726-7278
Fax: 256-726-7481
E-mail: lmoncur@oakwood.edu
www.oakwood.edu/music

Bachelor of Art in Music, Bachelor of Science
in Music Education, Theory and Composition
(B.M.), Vocal Performance and Pedagogy (B.M.)

Samford University
School of Performing Arts

800 Lakeshore Dr.
Birmingham, AL 35229
Jason Black
205-726-2773
Fax: 205-726-2171
E-mail: jjblack@samford.edu
www.samford.edu

Selma College

1804 Green St.
Selma, AL 36701
334-874-5700
E-mail: webmaster@concordiaselma.edu
www.concordiaselma.edu

Shelton State Junior College
Department of Music

2714 Martin Campus
Tuscaloosa, AL 35405
Angela Gibson Wible

205-391-2937
E-mail: agivson@sheltonstate.edu
www.sheltonstate.edu

Snead State
Community College
Department of Fine Arts

220 North Walnut St.
P.O. Box 734
Boaz, AL 35957
205-593-5120
E-mail: mbrooks@snead.edu
www.snead.cc.al.us

Southeastern Bible College
Department of Music

2545 Valleydale Rd.
Birmingham, AL 35244-2083
800-749-8878
E-mail: admissions@sebc.edu
www.sebc.edu

Southern Union State
Community College

750 Roberts St.
Wadley, AL 36276
205-395-2211
Fax: 256-395-2215
www.suscc.cc.al.us

Stillman College
Department of Fine Arts

P.O. Box 1430
Tuscaloosa, AL 35403
800-841-5722
E-mail: admissions@stilman.edu
www.stillman.edu

Talladega College
Department of Humanities

627 West Battle St.
Talladega, AL 35160
256-761-6243

E-mail: tjeffers@talladega.edu
www.talladega.edu

Troy State University

University Ave
Troy, AL 36082
800-551-9716
www.troy.edu

This active school of music in a small university setting has a wide variety of solo and ensemble opportunities, including "Sound of the South" Marching Band, symphony band, chamber winds, jazz ensembles, collegiate singers, chamber choir, gospel choir, opera ensemble, trumpet ensemble and percussion ensemble.

University of Alabama at Birmingham
Department of Music

231 Hulsey Center
950 13th St. South
Birmingham, AL 35294-1260
Jeff Reynolds
205-934-7376
Fax: 205-975-1931
E-mail: jwr@uab.edu
www.music.uab.edu

Bachelor of Arts in Music, Bachelor of Arts in Music Technology, Bachelor of Arts in Music Education (with certification in choral/vocal or instrumental), as well as a Minor in Music or Music Technology.

University of Alabama at Huntsville

301 Sparkman Dr.
Huntsville, AL 35899
256-824-6436
E-mail: music@uah.edu
www.uah.edu

University of Alabama at Tuscaloosa
School of Music

Box 870366
Tuscaloosa, AL 35487-0366
Tonia Hicks
205-348-7110
Fax: 205-348-1473
E-mail: thicks@music.ua.edu
www.ua.edu

Bachelor of Arts in Music, Bachelor of Science in Music Education, Bachelor of Musi, Masters in Music

University of Mobile
College of Arts and Sciences

5735 College Pkwy.
Mobile, AL 36613
251-442-2273
www.umobile.edu

Bachelor of Arts in Music, Bachelor of Science in Music Education, Bachelor of Music in Church Music, Bachelor of Arts in Theatre, Bachelor of Music in Musical Theatre

University of Montevallo
Department of Music

Montevallo, AL 35115
Cynthis Jones
205-665-6000
E-mail: music@montevallo.edu
www.montevallo.edu/music

University of North Alabama
College of Arts and Sciences

UNA Box 5040
Florence, AL 35632-0001
James Simpson
256-765-4516
Fax: 256-765-4995
E-mail: jksimpson@una.edu
www.una.edu

University of South Alabama
Department of Music

Laidlaw Performing Arts Center, 1072
307 N. University Blvd.
Mobile, AL 36688
Greg Gruner
251-460-6136
Fax: 215-460-7328
www.southalabama.edu

University of West Alabama
Department of Fine Arts

UWA Station 23
Livingston, AL 35470
Michael A. Cooke
205-652-3457
Fax: 205-652-3717
www.uwa.edu

Wallace State College
Department of Music

P.O. Box 2000
801 Main St.
Hanceville, AL 35077
256-352-8277
www.wallacestate.edu

Population: 663,661 (2005 Estimate)
Capital City: Juneau
Bird: Ptarmigan
Motto: North to the Future
Flower: Forget-Me-Not
Tree: Sitka Spruce
Residents Called: Alaskans
Origin of Name: Based on an Aleut word "alaxsxaq" literally meaning, "object toward which the action of the sea is directed" or more simply "the mainland."
Area: 656,425 square miles (the largest state)
Statehood: January 3, 1959 (49th State)
Largest Cities: Anchorage, Juneau, Fairbanks, Sitka, Ketchikan, Kenai, Kodiak, Bethel, Wasilla, Barrow

Alaska Pacific University
Department of
Liberal Studies

4101 University Dr.
Anchorage, AK 99508-4625
907-564-8248
Fax: 907-564-8317
E-mail: admissions@alaskapacific.edu
www.alaskapacific.edu

Henderson State University
Department of Music

1100 Henderson St.
Arkadelphia, AK 71999-0001
Sharon Gardner
870-230-5000
Fax: 870-230-5144
E-mail: gardnes@hsu.edu
www.hsu.edu

Bachelor of Art in Music

Hendrix College
Department of Music
1600 Washington Ave.
Conway, AK 72032
John Krebs
501-450-1245
Fax: 501-450-1200
E-mail: krebs@hendrix.edu
www.hendrix.edu

University of Alaska
at Anchorage
Department of Music

3211 Providence Dr.
Anchorage, AK 99508
Timothy C. Smith
907-786-1595
Fax: 907-786-1799
E-mail: aftcs@uaa.alaska.edu
www.uaa.alaska.edu

University of Alaska
at Fairbanks
Department of Music

P.O. Box 757500
Fairbanks, AK 99775
Theodore Decorso
907-474-7211
Fax: 907-474-6420
E-mail: fymusic@uaf.edu
www.uaf.edu/music/department

Bachelor of Art in Music, Music Education, and
Masters of Art in Music

University of
Alaska-Fairbanks
Department of Music

P.O. Box 757500
Fairbanks, AK 99775
907-474-7211
E-mail: fymusic@uaf.edu
www.uaf.edu/music/department

Population: 5,939,292 (2005 Estimate)
Capital City: Phoenix
Bird: Cactus Wren
Motto: Ditat Deus – God Enriches
Flower: Saguaro Cactus Blossom
Tree: Palo Verde
Residents Called: Arizonans
Origin of Name: The name was probably derived from a native place name that sounded like Aleh-zon or Ali-Shonak which meant "small spring" or "place of the small spring."
Area: 113,909 square miles (6th largest state)
Statehood: February 14, 1912 (48th state)
Largest Cities: Phoenix, Tucson, Mesa, Glendale, Scottsdale, Chandler, Tempe, Gilbert Peoria, Yuma, Flagstaff
College Band Programs: Arizona State University, University of Arizona

Arizona State University
School of Music

P.O. Box 870405
Tempe, AZ 85287-0405
Karen Bryan
480-965-5069
Fax: 480-727-6544
E-mail: karen.bryan@asu.edu
www.asu.edu

Bachelor of Arts in Music, Bachelor of Music
in Music, Education, Bachelor of Music in
Jazz Performance, Bachelor of Music Therapy,
Bachelor of Music in Musical Theatre, Bachelor
of Music in Performance, Bachelor of Music in
Collaborative Piano, Bachelor of Music in Theory
and Composition

Arizona Western College
Department of Music

P.O. Box 929
Yuma, AZ 85366-0929
928-317-6000
www.awc.cc.az.us

Central Arizona College
Department of Music

Signal Peak Campus
Room P128
Coolidge, AZ 85228
Rick Moore
520-494-5399
Fax: 520-494-5435
E-mail: rick_moore@centralaz.edu
www.centralaz.edu

Cochise College
Department of Music

901 North Colombo Ave.
Sierra Vista, AZ 85635
Carol Rivera
520-515-5440
www.cochise.org

Conservatory of Recording Arts and Sciences
Department of Music

2300 East Broadway Rd.
Tempe, AZ 85282
480-858-0764
Fax: 480-829-1332
E-mail: info@cras.org
www.audiorecordingschool.com

Diploma-Master Recording Program II. The
Conservatory of Recording Arts and Sciences is
a world-class private institution for individuals
who want to pursue a career in the recording
industry. A single program is offered; the 900
clock-hour master recording program II, which
is 37 weeks in duration. This comprehensive curriculum covers multi-track music recording, live
sound, MIDI and Digital Audio, Troubleshooting,
and Music Business. The coursework is taught
using world-class state-of-the-art equipment.
The conservatory is the only school in the world
whose graduates are certified by Digidesign on
both ProTools course 135 and 235. Students are
required to complete a 280 clock-hour internship
at a location of the student's choice in order to
graduate. The institution relies on the skills of
successful professionals from the industry to develop and teach the curriculum. There are quite
a few Gold and Platinum album award winners
among our instructors. A selective enrollment
policy is practiced.

Eastern Arizona College
Department of Music

615 North Stadium Ave.
Thatcher, AZ 85552
800-678-3808
E-mail: admissions@eac.edu
www.easternarizona.com

Glendale Community College
Dept of Performing Arts

6000 West Olive Ave.

Glendale, AZ 85302
623-845-3000
www.gc.maricopa.edu

Grand Canyon University
Department of Music

3300 West Camelback Rd.
Phoenix, AZ 85017
800-486-7089
Fax: 602-589-2861
www.grand-canyon.edu

Mesa Community College
Department of Music

1833 West Southern Ave.
Mesa, AZ 85202
Sue Anne Lucius
480-461-7577
E-mail: sue.anne.lucius@mcmail.maricopa.edu
www.mc.maricopa.edu

Northland Pioneer College
Department of Music

P.O. Box 610
Holbrook, AZ 86025-0610
Benjamin Schoening
800-266-7845 ext. 6247
Fax: 928-524-7612
E-mail: bschoening@npc.edu
www.northland.cc.az.us

Phoenix College
Department of Music

1202 West Thomas Rd.
Phoenix, AZ 85013
866-766-0766
www.phoenix.edu

Pima Community College

4905 East Broadway Blvd.
Tucson, AZ 85709-1010
800-860-PIMA
E-mail: infocenter@pima.edu
www.pima.edu

Scottsdale Community College
Department of Fine Arts

9000 East Chaparral Rd.
Scottsdale, AZ 85256-2626
480-423-6000
www.sc.maricopa.edu

Yavapai College
Department of Music

1100 East Sheldon St.
Prescott, AZ 86301
800-922-6787
www2.yc.edu

Population: 2,779,154 (2005 Estimate)
Capital City: Little Rock
Bird: Mockingbird
Motto: Regnat Populus – The People Rule
Flower: Apple Blossom
Tree: Pine
Residents Called: Arkansans
Origin of Name: From the Quapaw Indians, who were called Akansea by certain other tribes. The name means "South Wind." Another possible origin is from the French interpretation of a Sioux word "acansa," meaning "downstream place."
Area: 53,225 square miles (29th largest state)
Statehood: June 15 (25th state)
Largest Cities: Little Rock, Fort Smith, North Little Rock, Fayetteville, Jonesboro, Pine Bluff, Springdale, Conway, Rogers, Hot Springs
College Band Programs: University of Arkansas at Fayetteville, Henderson State University, University of Arkansas, University of Arkansas at Pine Bluff, University of Central Arkansas

Arkansas State University
Department of Fine Arts

P.O. Box 1200
State University, AR 72467
Tom O'Connor
870-972-2094
Fax: 870-972-3932
E-mail: toconnor@astate.edu
www.astate.edu

Bachelor of Art in Music, Bachelor of Music

Arkansas Technical University

1605 Colliseum Dr.
Russellville, AR 72801
800-582-6953
www.atu.edu

East Arkansas Community College
Department of Humanities

1700 Newcastle Rd.
Forrest City, AR 72335-2204
870-633-4480
Fax: 870-633-7222
E-mail: jhaven@eacc.edu
www.eacc.cc.ar.us

Harding University
Department of Music

915 East Market Ave.
Searcy, AR 72149
Pam Jones
501-279-4343
Fax: 501-279-4086
E-mail: music@harding.edu
www.harding.edu

Bachelor of Arts, B.M.E.

Henderson State University
Department of Music

P.O. Box 7733
1100 Henderson St.
Arkadelphia, AR 71999
Jim Buckner
870-230-5000
Fax: 870-230-5424
E-mail: bucknej@hsu.edu
www.hsu.edu

Bachelor of Art in Music, Bachelor of Music

Distinguished undergraduate program focusing on teacher education. Long tradition of excellence in performance

Hendrix College
Department of Music
1600 Washington Ave.
Conway, AR 72032
800-277-9017
E-mail: adm@hendrix.edu
www.hendrix.edu

John Brown University
Department of Music

2000 West University St.
Siloam Springs, AR 72761
479-524-9500
www.jbu.edu

Lyon College
Department of Liberal Arts

2300 Highland Rd.
P.O. Box 2317
Batesville, AR 72503
870-869-4201
E-mail: admissions@lyon.edu
www.lyon.edu

Ouachita Baptist University
Bernice Young Jones School of Fine Arts

410 Ouachita St.
Arkadelphia, AR 71998

Charles Fuller
870-245-5129
E-mail: fullerc@obu.edu
www.obu.edu

Philander Smith College
One Trudie Kibbe Reed Dr.
Little Rock, AR 72202
501-370-9845
www.philander.edu

University of Arkansas at Fayetteville
Department of Music

201 Music Building
Fayetteville, AR 72701
Stephen Gates
479-575-4701
Fax: 479-575-5409
E-mail: sgates@uark.edu
www.uark.edu/depts/uamusic

University of Arkansas at Little Rock
College of Arts, Humanities, and Social Science

2801 South University Ave.
Little Rock, AR 72204
501-569-3294
E-mail: mudept@ualr.edu
www.ualr.edu/~mudept

Bachelor of Arts Music

University of Arkansas at Monticello
Department of Music

P.O. Box 3459
517 University Dr.
Monticello, AR 71656
870-460-1053
Fax: 870-460-1653
www.uamont.edu

University of Arkansas at Pine Bluff
Department of Music

1200 North University Dr.
Mail Slot 4956
Pine Bluff, AR 71601
870-575-8905
www.uapb.edu

University of Arkansas Fort Smith
Department of Music

5210 Grand Ave.
P.O. Box 3649
Fort Smith, AR 72910-3649
479-788-7000
www.uafortsmith.edu

Bachelor of Music Education, Bachelor of Arts in Music

University of Central Arkansas
Department of Music

201 Donaghey Ave.
Conway, AR 72035
Jeffrey Jarvis
501-450-3163
Fax: 501-450-5773
E-mail: jarvisj@uca.edu
www.uca.edu

Bachelor of Music in Performance, Music Education, Bachelor of Arts in Music, Master of Music in Performance, Music Theory, Conducting, and Education

University of the Ozarks
415 College Ave.
Clarksville, AR 72830
800-264-8636
www.ozarks.edu

Bachelor of Arts

Westark Community College
Department of Music

5210 Grand Ave.
P.O. Box 3649
Fort Smith, AR 72913-3649
Henry Rinne
501-788-7530
E-mail: hrinne@uafortsmith.edu
www.westark.edu

Bachelor of Music Education

Williams Baptist College
Department of Music

60 West Fulbright Ave.
Walnut Ridge, AR 72476
870-886-6741
Fax: 870-886-3924
E-mail: magee@wbcoll.edu
www.wbcoll.edu

Bachelor of Arts in Music, Bachelor of Arts
degree in Church Music, Bachelor of Science in
Education

Population: 36,132,147 (2005 Estimate)
Capital City: Sacramento
Bird: California Valley Quail
Motto: Eureka: I have found it
Flower: California Poppy
Residents Called: Californians
Area: 163,707 square miles
(3rd largest state)
Statehood: September 9, 1850 (31st state)
Largest Cities: Los Angeles, San Diego, San Jose, San Francisco, Long Beach, Fresno, Sacramento, Oakland, Santa Ana, Anaheim
College Band Programs: California Polytechnic State University, California State University, California State University-Fresno, Humboldt State University, Riverside Community College, San Diego State University, San Jose University, Stanford University, University of California-Berkley, University of California-Davis, University of California-Los Angeles, University of Southern California

Ali Akbar College

215 West End Ave.
San Rafael, CA 94901
Ali Akbar Khan
415-454-6264
Fax: 415-454-9396
E-mail: office@aacm.org
www.aacm.org

Allan Hancock College
Department of Fine Arts

800 South College Dr.
Santa Maria, CA 93454
Marcus W. Engelmann
805-922-6966
E-mail: mengelmann@hancock.cc.ca.us
www.hancock.cc.ca.us

American River Community College
Department of Fine and Applied Arts

4700 College Oak Dr.
Sacramento, CA 95841-4286
Ralph Hughes
916-484-8433
E-mail: hughesr@arc.losrios.edu
www.arc.losrios.edu

American School of Piano Tuning

17070 John Telfer Dr.
Morgan Hill, CA 95037
800-497-9793
www.piano-tuning.com

American School of Piano Tuning offers a step-by-step, 10-lesson correspondence course in Piano Tuning and Repair. Tools and parts are included. Free brochure available.

Antelope Valley College

3041 West Ave. K
Lancaster, CA 93536
661-722-6300
E-mail: info@avc.edu
www.avc.edu

Azusa Pacific University
School of Music

P.O. Box 7000
Azusa, CA 91702-7000
Colleen Kuhns
626-815-3848
Fax: 629-969-7419
E-mail: ckuhns@apu.edu
www.apu.edu/music

Bachelor of Arts in Music, Bachelor in Music

Bethany College of Assembly of God
Department of Music

800 BethaNN Dr.
Scott's Valley, CA 95066
Mark Hulse
831-438-3800
www.bethany.edu

Biola University
Band Division

13800 Ave.
La Mirada, CA 90639
Jack Schwarz
562-903-4892
Fax: 562-903-4746
E-mail: george.boespflug@truth.biola.edu
www.biola.edu

Cabrillo College
Department of Music

6500 Soquel Dr.
Aptos, CA 95003

831-479-6315
www.cabrillo.edu

A.A. in Music

California Baptist University
Department of Music

8432 Magnolia Ave.
Riverside, CA 92504
951-343-4212
E-mail: admissions@calbaptist.edu
www.calbaptist.edu

Bachelor of Arts in Liberal Studies, concentration in Music, Bachelor of Music, M.M. in Music

California Institute of Technology
Department of Music

Pasadena, CA 91125
Daryl Denning
626-395-2923
E-mail: ddenning@caltech.edu
www.music.caltech.edu

California Lutheran Universiy
Department of Music

60 West Oilsen Rd. #4000
Thousand Oaks, CA 91360
Wyant Morton
805-493-3305
Fax: 805-493-3904
E-mail: morton@callutheran.edu
www.callutheran.edu/music

Bachelor of Arts

Whether music is your life or simply a treasured part of the life you hope to create Cal Lutheran's Music Department can provide the professional training and performance experiences that maximize your abilities and enhance your love of the art. The Music Department prides itself on creating a strong musical education within a nurturing atmosphere. Faculty members are experienced professionals who are committed to teaching excellence. The music program is widely respected for its performance ensembles, its classroom teaching, its studio instruction and the musical theater productions presented in collaboration with the Drama Department.

California Polytechnic State University at Pomona
Department of Music

3801 West Temple Ave.
Pomona, CA 91768
J. Levine
909-869-3548
Fax: 909-869-4145
E-mail: ilevine@csupomona.edu
www.csupomona.edu

California Polytechnic State University at San Luis Obispo
Department of Music

1 Grand Ave.
San Luis Obispo, CA 93407-0326
W. Terrence Spiller
805-756-2406
Fax: 805-756-7464
E-mail: wspiller@calpoly.edu
www.calpoly.edu

Bachelor of Music; Music Minor

The Music Department offers a program which develops musical skills and sensitivity, encourages creativity, and cultivates vision for the future. A graduate of this program will be prepared to begin specialized study at the graduate level and to enter a wide variety of professional careers. The Bachelor of Arts in Music offered at Cal Poly introduces a student to the role of music in today,s world, helps form personal goals, and provides the discipline, skills and knowledge to accomplish those goals. The University,s polytechnic emphasis provides an excellent opportunity to explore music in conjunction with a wide range of other fields. In addition, the Music Department is a valuable resource for the non-music major. Its courses and performing ensembles are open to all students who wish to enrich their lives through music. Qualified students who wish to explore the subject in depth have the opportunity to minor in music. The Cal Poly Music Department also serves as a cultural center for both the university and the community through a program of public performances by student and faculty groups and through clinics, workshops, concerts, and lectures by outstanding individuals from outside the university. Acceptance into the music major program requires a demonstrated ability on an instrument, in voice, or other musical media, such as music composition or sound design.

California State University at Chico
Department of Music

400 Wirst First St.
Chico, CA 95929-5152
530-898-5152
Fax: 530-898-4082
E-mail: jbankhead@csuchico.edu
www.csuchico.edu

Bachelor of Arts in Music, Bachelor of Music Industry and Technology, Minor in Music

California State University at Fresno
Department of Music

2380 East Keats Ave. M/S MB77
Fresno, CA 93740-8024
559-278-2261
E-mail: musicdepartment@cvip.net
www.csufresno.edu/music

Bachelor of Music, Masters in Music

California State University at Hayward
Department of Music

25800 Carlos Bee Blvd.
Hayward, CA 94542
Mariko Abe
510-885-3135
Fax: 510-885-3461
E-mail: mariko.abe@csueasetbay.edu
www.isis.csuhayward.edu

Bachelor of Music

California State University at Long Beach
Department of Music

1250 Bellflower Blvd.
Long Beach, CA 90840-7101
Arnel Igancio
562-985-4781
Fax: 562-985-2490
E-mail: music@csulb.edu
www.csulb.edu

Bachelor of Arts, B.M., M.A., M.M.

California State University at Los Angeles
Department of Music

5151 State University Dr.
Los Angeles, CA 90032
Rene Aravena
323-343-4072
Fax: 323-343-4063
E-mail: raraven@calstatela.edu
www.calstatela.edu

California State University at Northridge
Department of Music

18111 Nordhoff St.
Northridge, CA 91330-8314
Katherine Ramos Baker
818-677-3184
Fax: 818-677-5876
E-mail: katherine.r.baker@csun.edu
www.csun.edu/-hfmus003

Bachelor of Music

California State University at San Bernardino
Department of Music

5500 University Pkwy.
San Bernardino, CA 92407
909-880-5859
Fax: 909-880-7016

www.csusb.edu

The department of music at California State University, San Bernardino is a vital and growing program, giving students the benefits of a large, full-service university and the individual attention found in a smaller, conservatory-like setting. The department faculty are highly qualified in their personal areas of expertise, dedicated to continued musical and professional growth, and integrally involved with the development of their students. The Bachelor of Arts in music degree program offers students a solid core of traditional music study, with a variety of emphasis areas tailored to suit individual student interests and needs. A variety of la_ e and small vocal and instrumental ensembles give music students ample opportunities to hone their performance skills and study traditional and modern music repertoire. The CSUSB campus is a refreshing and enlivening environment with open spaces, trees, gardens, and walkways. Campus life is vital, with a variety of ongoing social, cultural, and athletic activities. New, apartment-style residence halls make living on campus easy and enjoyable, and tuition is very reasonable when compared with similar state universities across the country.

California State University at San Marcos
Department of Visual Performing Arts

333 South Twin Oaks Valley Rd.
San Marcos, CA 92096
Lani Woods
760-750-4137
E-mail: lanwoods@csusm.edu
www.csusm.edu/a_s/vpa

California State University at Stanislaus
Department of Music

801 West Monte Vista Ave.
Turlock, CA 95380
Stephen Thomas
209-667-3421
Fax: 209-647-024

www.csustan.edu

Bachelor of Arts of Music, Bachelor of Arts of Arts Degree in Music

California State University Bakersfield
Department of Music

9001 Stockdale Hwy.
Music Building 102
Bakersfield, CA 93311
661-654-3093
www.csubak.edu

California State University Dominguez Hills
Department of Music

1000 East Victoria St.
LCH E303, LCH A349
Carson, CA 90747-3300
310-243-3543
www.cla.csudh.edu

Canada College
Department of Music

4200 Farm Hill Blvd.
Redwood, CA 94061
650-306-3336
E-mail: Canada.humanities@smccd.net
http://canadacollege.net

Cerritos College
Department of Music

11110 Alondra Blvd.
Norwalk, CA 90650
562-860-2451
E-mail: brussell@cerritos.edu
www.cerritos.edu

Chaffey College
School of Performing Arts

5885 Haven Ave.
Alta Loma, CA 91737-3002

Larry Buckley
909-941-8633
Fax: 909-466-2831
E-mail: larry.buckley@chaffey.edu
www.chaffey.edu/welcome.shtml

Chapman University
School of Music

One University Dr.
Orange, CA 92866
Mike Drummy
714-997-6871
Fax: 714-744-7671
E-mail: drummy@chapman.edu
www.chapman.edu

B.Mus. in Music Ed; B.Mus. in Performance; B.S. in Music; A.S. in Music

A department of music in a liberal arts college of the Seventh-day Adventist Church

Citrus College
Department of Fine and Performing Arts

1000 West Foothill Blvd.
Glendora, CA 91741-1899
Admissions
626-963-0323
E-mail: admissions@citruscollege.edu
www.citrus.cc.ca.us

City College of San Francisco
Department of Music

50 Phelan Ave.
San Francisco, CA 94112
415-239-3000
E-mail: mmueller@ccsf.edu
www.ccsf.edu

Claremont Graduate University
Department of Music

121 East 10th St.
Claremont, CA 91711
Patriica Easton
909-607-9440
Fax: 909-607-1221
E-mail: patricia.easton@cgu.edu
www.cgu.edu/arts/music

Master of Arts, Doctor of Church Music, Doctor of Musical Arts, Doctor of Philosophy The Music Department at Claremont Graduate University offers courses of study leading to the degrees of Master of Arts, Doctor of Church Music, Doctor of Musical Arts, and Doctor of Philosophy. In addition, three professional M.A. degrees are available that combine musicology with sub-specializations in music communications, arts administration, and information management. All programs are designed with special emphasis upon music within its interdisciplinary, cultural and intellectual context. They combine comprehensive training in music literature, historical style analysis, and study of performance practices. The Doctor of Church Music and the Master of Arts degree with a concentration in Church Music are offered in cooperation with the Claremont School of Theology. In addition, the curriculum emphasizes uses of music technology for research, teaching, and creative work. All music students have the opportunity to receive music technology instruction in several contexts, including notation, composition, performance, and film scoring techniques.

Colburn School conservatory of Music
Conservatory of Music

200 South Grand Ave.
Los Angeles, CA 90012
Kathleen Tesar
213-621-2200
Fax: 213-621-2110
E-mail: admissions@colburnschool.edu
www.colburnschool.edu

Bachelor of Music

College of Alameda
Department of Music

555 Atlantic Ave.
Alameda, CA 94501
510-522-7221
Fax: 510-769-6019
www.alameda.peralta.edu

College of Marin
Department of Music

835 College Ave.
Kentfield, CA 94904
415-457-8811
www.martin.cc.ca.us

College of San Mateo
Department of Music

1700 West Hillsdale Blvd.
San Mateo, CA 94402
650-574-6161

College of Siskiyous
Department of Music

800 College Ave.
Weed, CA 96-94-2806
800-397-4339
www.siskiyous.edu

College of Siskiyous
Department of Music

800 College Ave.
Weed, CA 96094-206
Elaine Schaefer
530-938-5315
Fax: 530-938-5227
E-mail: schaefer@siskiyous.edu
www.siskiyous.edu

AA Degree

College of the Siskiyous is a California Community College in northern California at the foot of Mt. Shasta. The music department provides all courses needed for a music major to transfer to a four year college along with an AA degree in Music.

College of the Canyons
Department of Music

26455 North Rockwell Canyon Rd.
Valencia, CA 91355
Bernado Feldman
661-362-3254
Fax: 661-259-3802
E-mail: bernardo.feldman@canyons.edu
www.canyons.edu

Associate of Arts in Music

The Department of Music offers a comprehensive curriculum to prepare songwriters, electronic minded musician, symphonic composers, and pop and jazz enthusiasts, in the path toward successful creative careers in music.

College of the Desert
Department of Music

43-500 Monterey Ave.
Palm Desert, CA 92260
Stephan E. Cragg
760-776-7344
E-mail: scragg@collegeofthedesert.edu
www.desert.cc.ca.us

Associate of Arts in Music

College of the Redwoods
Department of Music

7351 Tomkins Hill Rd.
Eureka, CA 95501
Bill Allison
707-476-4100 x3032
E-mail: bill-allison@redwoods.edu
www.redwoods.cc.ca.us

College of the Sequoias
Department of Music

915 South Mooney Blvd.
Visalia, CA 93277-2214
209-730-3700
www.cos.edu

Columbia College
Department of Music

16000 Columbia College Dr.
Sonora, CA 95370
209-588-5100
www.columbia.yosemite.cc.ca.us

Concordia University
Department of Music

1530 Concordia West
Irvine, CA 92612-3299
Peter Senkbeil
949-854-8002
www.cui.edu

Cuesta College
Department of Music

P.O. Box 8106
San Luis Obispo, CA 93403
George Stone
805-546-3100 x2792
E-mail: gstone@cuesta.edu
www.cuesta.cc.ca.us

Cypress College
Department of Music

9200 Valley View St.
Cypress, CA 90630-5805
Mark Anderman
714-484-7140
Fax: 714-952-9602
E-mail: manderman@cypress.cc.ca.us
www.cypresscollege.edu

De Anza College
Department of Music

21250 Stevens Creek Blvd.
Cupertino, CA 95014
Pat Fifield
408-864-8832
Fax: 408-864-8492
E-mail: canternancy@fhda.edu
www.deanza.fhda.edu

A.A.

Outstanding, All-Steinway institution. Most noted: theory and instrumental programs with emphasis on the study of vocal and instrumental jazz, piano, guitar, electronic music. Great facilities for study and performing

Diablo Valley College
Department of Music

321 Golf Club Rd.
Pleasant Hill, CA 94523-1529
925-685-1230
www.dvc.edu

Dominican University of California
Department of Music

50 Acacia Ave.
San Rafael, CA 94901
Craig Singleton
415-485-3275
E-mail: singleton@dominican.edu
www.dominican.edu

East Los Angeles College
Department of Music

1301 Avenida Cesar Chavez
Monterey Park, CA 91754
Robert Dawson
323-265-8931
E-mail: dawsonrb@elac.edu
www.elac.cc.ca.us

El Camino College Compton Center
Department of Music

1111 East Artesia Blvd.
Music Building, Room 101
Compton, CA 90221-5314
Kristi Blackburn
310-660-3715
E-mail: kblackburn@elcamino.edu

Associate in Arts Degree in Music

Evergreen Valley College
Department of Music

3095 Yerba Buena Rd.
San Jose, CA 95235-1513
408-274-7900
Fax: 408-223-9351
www.evc.edu

Foothill College
Department of Music

12345 El Monte Rd.
Los Altos Hills, CA 94022
Music Department
650-949-7262
Fax: 650-949-7375
www.foothill.fhda.edu

Fullerton College
Department of Music

321 East Chapman Ave.
Fullerton, CA 92832-2095
714-992-7303
E-mail: jtebay@fullcoll.edu
www.fullcoll.edu

Gavilan College
Department of Music

5055 Santa Teresa Blvd.
Gilroy, CA 95020-9578
408-848-4800
www.gavilan.edu

Glendale Community College

Department of Music
1500 North Verdrigo Rd.
Glendale, CA 91208-2894
Kristine Hanna
818-240-1000
www.glendale.cc.ca.us

AA in Music

Golden West College
Department of Performing and Visual Arts

15744 Golden West St.
P.O. Box 4718
Huntington Beach, CA 92647-2748
Henrietta Carter
714-895-8772
E-mail: hcarter@gwc.cccd.edu
www.gwc.cccd.edu

AA degree

Golden West College is a 2 year community junior college, located in Huntington Beach close to the Pacific Ocean. Academic programs include college transfer and general education, and vocational programs include recording arts and entertainment technology.

Grossmont College
Department of Music

8800 Grossmont College Dr.
El Cajon, CA 92020-1799
619-644-7000
E-mail: steve.baker@gcccd.net
www.grossmont.net/music

The Grossmont College Music Department offers an Associate in Arts degree in music. It is a traditional two-year music program consisting of four semesters of music theory and ear-training, class piano and performance studies with required recital performance and jury examinations before the music faculty. The music department currently serves more than 50 music majors, plus more than 1,500 general music education students each semester. The school has seven student performance ensembles including the Grossmont Symphony Orchestra, Grossmont College Master Chorale, chamber singers, jazz ensemble, jazz vocal ensemble, concert band and classical guitar ensemble. In addition, the school offers three four-semester courses of classroom instruction in piano, guitar, and voice. Along with the theatre arts department, a transfer degree in musical theatre is offered. Also, the school is currently developing a jazz studies transfer program as well as a music technology program. The facility consists of a two-story complex that includes two large rehearsal rooms, two keyboard/music technology rooms, 11 practice rooms with pianos, and a 240-seat recital hall. In addition, the budget allows for six to 10 yearly concerts in the 1,200-seat East County Performing Arts Center. Scholarships that provide financial support for private lessons for declared full-time music majors are available.

Hartnell College
Department of Music

156 Homestead Ave.
Salinas, CA 93901
Kathleen Rose
831-755-6905
E-mail: krose@hartnell.edu
www.hartnell.cc.ca.us

Holy Names University
Department of Music

3500 Mountain Blvd.
Oakland, CA 94619
510-436-1000
www.hnu.edu

Bachelor of Arts in Music, Bachelor of Music, Minor in Music

Humboldt State University
Department of Music

1 Harp St.
Arcata, CA 95521
Ken Ayoob
707-826-5448
Fax: 707-826-3528
E-mail: kpal@humboldt.edu
www.humboldt.edu

Idyllwild School of Music and the Arts
Department of Music

P.O. Box 38
52500 Temecula Rd.
Idyllwild, CA 92549

Karen R. Porter
909-659-2171
E-mail: kporter@idyllwildarts.org
www.idyllwildarts.org

Imperial Valley College
Department of Music

380 East Ira Aten Rd.
P.O. Box 158
Imperial, CA 92251
Van Decker
760-355-6205
E-mail: van.decker@imperial.edu
www.imperial.cc.ca.us

Irvine Valley College
Department of Music

5500 Irvine Center Dr.
Irvine, CA 92618
Karima Benremouga
949-451-5336
E-mail: kbenremouga@ivc.edu
www.ivc.cc.ca.us

La Sierra University
Department of Music

4500 Riverwalk Pkwy.
Riverside, CA 92515
Kimo Smith
909-785-2036
Fax: 909-785-2070
E-mail: ksmith@lasierra.edu
www.lasierra.edu

Lake Tahoe Community College
Department of Music

One College Dr.
South Lake Tahoe, CA 96150
Mark Williams
530-541-4660 x382
E-mail: williams@ltcc.edu
www.ltcc.cc.ca.us

Laney Community College
Department of Music

900 Fallon St.
Oakland, CA 94607
Jay Lehmann
510-464-3463
E-mail: jlehmann@peralt.edu
www.laney.peralta.edu

Long Beach City College
Department of Music, Radio and TV

4901 East Carson St.
Long Beach, CA 90808
Gary Scott
562-938-4314
www.lbcc.cc.ca.us

Los Angeles Harbor College
Department of Music

1111 Figueroa Place
Wilmington, CA 90744
310-233-4429
E-mail: moorelp@lahc.edu
www.lahc.edu

Los Angeles Pierce College
Department of Music

6201 Winnetka Ave.
Woodland Hills, CA 91371
818-719-6476
www.piercecollege.com

Los Angeles Recording Workshop
Department of Music

6690 Sunset Blvd.
North Hollywood, CA 90028
888-688-5277
E-mail: info@larecordingschool.com
www.recordingcareer.com

Los Angeles Southwest College
Department of Music

1600 West Imperial Hwy.
Los Angeles, CA 90047
323-241-5320
www.lasc.cc.ca.us

Los Medanos College
Department of Music and Recording Arts

2700 East Leland Rd.
Pittsburgh, CA 94565
John Maltester
925-439-2181 x3209
www.losmedanos.net

Loyola Marymount University
Department of Music

One LMU Dr.
MS 8347
Los Angeles, CA 90045-2659
Fax: 310-338-6046
E-mail: lmusic@lmu.edu
www.lmu.edu

Marymount College
Department of Music

30800 Palos Verdes Dr. East
Rancho Palos Verdes, CA 90275-6299
310-377-5501
Fax: 310-377-6223
www.marymountpv.edu

Masters College
Department of Music

21726 Placerita Canyon Rd. #13
Santa Clarita, CA 91321
800-568-6248
www.masters.edu

Bachelor of Arts, B.M.

CALIFORNIA

Merced College
Department of Music

3600 M St.
Merced, CA 95348
209-384-6000
www.merced.cc.ca.us

Merritt College
Department of Music

12500 Campus Dr.
Oakland, CA 94619
510-436-2419
E-mail: ryoung@peralta.edu
www.merritt.edu

Mills College
Department of Music

5000 MacArthur Blvd.
Oakland, CA 94613
David Bernstein
510-430-2171
Fax: 510-430-3228
E-mail: davidb@mills.edu
www.mills.edu

BA, MFA, MA

For well over half a century, the Music Department at Mills College has enjoyed an international reputation. Because of its strong faculty and history of innovation, the department is in a unique position to enable its students to participate in some of the most exciting areas of development for music-making in our time. All music students at Mills, whether they are music majors, music minors, or those who simply wish to take music courses, benefit from this stimulating, creative atmosphere. The curricular emphasis of the Music Program is twofold: First, in keeping with the liberal arts mission of the College, courses for non-majors not only expose students to a wide variety of styles and repertory, but also place musical activity within the broader context of intellectual history and global culture. Second, the Music Department offers a unique undergraduate major in music that promotes a dynamic interaction between performance and improvisation, historical and theoretical studies, composition, and music technology. The music student at Mills also learns that Western musical culture is only one of the world's many musical traditions a fact accentuated by the cultural diversity of the Bay Area as well as its position on the Pacific Rim. The Music major revolves around a core curriculum of music history, theory, and performance that provides knowledge and skills basic to all musicians. In addition, music majors select one of four areas of emphasis: performance, theory/history, composition, or composition with an emphasis in media technology or electronic music. Performance students work with top San Francisco Bay area musicians and perform in various musical groups, such as the Early Music, Performance Collective (Chamber), Vocal, Gamelan, Kongolese Drumming, Music Improvisation, and Contemporary Performance Ensembles. Our program in composition provides undergraduate women the opportunity to assume roles in music technology, recording engineering, and composition that have traditionally been inaccessible to them. All music students at Mills can also work at Mills' Center for Contemporary Music, a world-renowned facility for electronic and computer music that has played an influential role in the development of contemporary musical culture and is an important link in a long tradition of musical innovation at Mills. Finally, just as all musical activities should be interrelated, music should not be isolated from other disciplines in the arts, humanities, and sciences. The Music Department therefore offers several interdisciplinary courses and is committed to creating interdisciplinary programs that fit the needs of students with special interests. Prospective students: See the catalog Financial Aid, Music Awards for reference to information regarding the Carroll Donner Commemorative Scholarship in Music and the Barbara Hazelton Floyd Scholarship.

Miracosta College
Department of Music

1 Bernard Dr.
T300
Oceanside, CA 92056
David Megill
760-757-2121 x6438
E-mail: dwmegill@miracosta.edu
www.miracosta.cc.ca.us

Mission College
Department of Music
3000 Mission College Blvd.
Santa Clara, CA 95054
Joseph Ordaz
408-855-5276
E-mail: joseph_ordaz@wvmccd.cc.ca.us
www.missioncollege.org

Modesto Junior College
Department of Music and Arts Division
435 College Ave.
Modesto, CA 95350
209-575-6081
www.gomjc.org

Monterey Peninsula College
Department of Music
Monterey, CA 93940
Dan Schamber
408-646-4200
www.mpc.edu

Moorpark College
Department of Music and Dance
7075 Campus Rd.
Moorpark, CA 93021
Outreach Office
805-378-1400
E-mail: mcoutreach@vcccd.edu
www.moorparkcollege.net

A.A. in Music

Two year community college music program designed to transfer into most four year colleges and universities

Mount San Antonio College
Department of Music
1100 N Grand Ave.
Walnut, CA 91789

909-594-5611
E-mail: info@mtac.edu
www.mtsac.edu

Mount St. Mary's College
Department of Music
12001 Chalon Rd.
Los Angeles, CA 90049-1709
Teresita Espinosa
310-954-4266
Fax: 310-954-1709
E-mail: tespinosa@msmc.la.edu
www.msmc.la.edu

Music Academy of the West
Department of Music
1070 Fairway Rd.
Santa Barbara, CA 93108-2899
805-969-4726
Fax: 805-969-0686
www.musicacademy.org

Musicians Institute
Department of Music
1655 McCadden Place
Hollywood, CA 90028
Director of Admissions
800-255-7529
Fax: 323-462-1575
E-mail: admissions@mi.edu
www.mi.edu

Napa Valley College
Department of Music
2277 Napa Vallejo Hwy.
Napa, CA 94558
Eve-Anne Wilkes
707-253-3204
E-mail: ewilkes@napavalley.edu
www.nvc.cc.ca.us

Notre Dame de Namur University
Department of Music

1500 Ralston Ave.
Belmont, CA 94002
Debra Lampert
650-508-3594
E-mail: dlambert@ndnu.edu
www.music.ndnu.edu

Occidental College
Department of Music

1600 Campus Rd.
Los Angeles, CA 90041
Irene Girton
323-259-2785
Fax: 323-341-4983
E-mail: music@oxy.edu
www.oxy.edu

Ohlone College
Department of Music

43600 Mission Blvd.
Fremont, CA 94539
Sylvia Impert
714-432-5536
E-mail: simpert@occ.cccd.edu
www.ohlone.cc.ca.us

Orange Coast College
Department of Music

2701 Fairview Rd.
P.O. Box 5005
Costa Mesa, CA 92628-5005
www.orangecoastcollege.com

Oxnard College
Department of Music

4000 South Rose Ave.
Oxnard, CA 93033
Christie Morla
805-986-5800 x1929

E-mail: Cmorla@vcccd.net
www.oxnardcollege.edu

Pacific Union College
Department of Music

1 Angwin Ave.
Angwin, CA 94508-9797
707-965-6201
Fax: 707-965-6336
E-mail: lwheeler@puc.edu
www.puc.edu

B.Mus. in Music Ed; B.Mus. in Performance; B.S. in Music; A.S. in Music

A department of music in a liberal arts college of the Seventh-day Adventist Church.

Palo Verde Junior College
Department of Music

811 West Chanslor Way
Blythe, CA 92225
William Davila
714-922-6168
Fax: 714-922-0230
www.paloverde.cc.ca.us

Palomar College
Department of Performance Arts and Music

1140 West Mission Rd.
San Marcos, CA 92069
Micael Mufson
760-744-1150 x2321
E-mail: mmufson@palomar.edu
www.palomar.edu

Pasadena City College
Division of Music

1570 East Colorado Blvd.
Pasadena, CA 91106
Paul Kilian
626-585-7208
Fax: 626-585-7949
E-mail: pkilian@pasadena.edu
www.pasadena.edu

Patten College
Department of Music

2433 Coolidge Ave.
Oakland, CA 94601
Don Benham
877-4PATTEN
Fax: 510-534-4344
E-mail: admissions@patten.edu
www.patten.edu

Pepperdine University at Malibu
Department of Music

24255 Pacific Coast Hwy.
Malibu, CA 90265
Danah Sanders
310-456-4462
Fax: 310-456-4077
E-mail: danah.snaders@pepperdine.edu
www.pepperdine.edu

Pitzer College
Music Program at Scripps College

1050 North Mills Ave.
Claremont, CA 91711
909-621-8000
www.pitzer.edu

Point Loma Nazarene University
Department of Music

3900 Lomaland Dr.
San Diego, CA 92117
Chip Killingsworth
619-849-2445
Fax: 619-849-2668
E-mail: ChipKillingsworth@ptloma.edu
www.ptloma.edu

BA in Music, BA in Music Education, BA in Music and Ministry, BMus in Performance and BMus in Composition

Point Loma Nazarene University exists to provide higher education in a vital Christian community where minds are engaged and challenged, character is modeled and formed, and service becomes an expression of faith. Being of Wesleyan heritage, we aspire to be a learning community where grace is foundational, truth is pursued, and holiness is a way of life

Pomona College
Department of Music

340 North College Ave.
Claremont, CA 91711
Cathy Endress
909-621-8155
Fax: 909-621-8645
E-mail: cathy.endress@pomona.edu
www.music.pomona.edu

Sacramento City College
Department of Music

3835 Freeport Blvd.
Sacramento, CA 95822
Chris Iwata
916-558-2551
www.scc.losrios.edu

San Diego City College
Department of Music

1425 Russ Blvd.
San Diego, CA 92101
Alicia Rincon
619-388-3563
www.city.sdccd.cc.ca.us

San Diego State University
School of Music

San Diego, CA 92182
Sandra Konar
619-594-6031
Fax: 619-594-1692
E-mail: music.dance@sdsu.edu
www.music.sdsu.edu

San Francisco Conservatory of Music
Department of Music

1201 Ortega St.
San Francisco, CA 94122
Alex Brose
800-899-7326
Fax: 415-503-6299
E-mail: admit@sfcm.edu
www.sfcm.edu

San Francisco State University
Department of Music

1600 Holloway Ave.
San Francisco, CA 94132
George DeGraffenreid
415-338-1431
Fax: 415-338-3294
E-mail: georgede@sfsu.edu
www.sfsu.edu/~music

San Joaquin Delta College
Department of Music

5151 Pacific Ave.
Stockton, CA 95207
Brian Kendrick
209-954-5209
E-mail: bkendrick@deltacollege.edu
www.deltacollege.edu

San Jose City College
Department of Music

2100 Moorpark Ave.
San Jose, CA 95128
408-298-2181
www.sjcc.edu

San Jose State University
School of Music and Dance

One Washington Square
San José, CA 95192-0088

408-924-4300
E-mail: music@email.sisu.edu
www.sjsu.edu

Bachelor of Arts, Music, Preparation for Teaching, Music, Concentration in Composition, B.M., Music, Concentration in Electro-Acoustic Music, B.M., Music, Concentration in Performance, Minor, Music M.A., Music.

Santa Barbara City College
Department of Music

721 Cliff Dr.
Santa Barbara, CA 93109
805-965-0581
www.sbcc.cc.ca.us

Associate in Arts Degree, Music

Santa Clara University
Department of Music

500 El Camino Real
Santa Clara, CA 95053
408-554-4428
www.scu.edu

Santa Monica College
Department of Music

1900 Pico Blvd.
Santa Monica, CA 90405
310-424-4000
www.wmc.edu

Santa Rosa Junior College
Department of Music

1501 Mendocino Ave.
Santa Rosa, CA 95401
Elona Russell
707-527-4249
Fax: 707-521-7988
E-mail: erussell@santarosa.edu
www.santarosa.edu

Scripps College
Department of Music

1030 Columbia Ave.
Claremont, CA 91711
Music Department
909-607-3266
www.scrippscol.edu

Scripps Womens College
Department of Music

1030 Columbia Ave.
Claremont, CA 91711
909-607-3266
Fax: 909-621-8323
www.scrippscol.edu

Shasta College
Department of Music

P.O. Box 496006
Redding, CA 96049-6006
530-225-4946

www.shastacollege.edu

The Shasta College Music Department enthusiastically offers a wide variety of music classes and is vibrantly dedicated to serving all student clientele, including music majors, pre-music majors, general college students, and community/adult students. Department enrollment within all music courses is approximately 1,500 per year. The Music Department offers an associate degree in music, a certificate in music, music transfer program, and general studies (humanities) requirements. All interested students are strongly encouraged to participate within the Music Department's activities. The Music Department maintains a supportive and congenial atmosphere. Facilities include a theater, band room, choir room, central classrooms, practice rooms with pianos, and a computer/electronic laboratory. Performance opportunities are provided by a variety of ensembles including the concert band, symphony orchestra, chorale, concert choir, jazz band, jazz/rock ensemble, and vocal jazz ensemble. Available full-term classroom courses include a series of six music theory classes, keyboard classes, the history of jazz and rock, music appreciation, general studies, beginning voice,

beginning guitar, and a variety of short term courses. Applied music is normally available for declared full-time music majors.

Simpson College
Department of Music

2211 College View Dr.
Redding, CA 96003
Maria DiPalma
515-961-1570
Fax: 515-961-1498
E-mail: maria.dipalma@simpson.edu
www.simpson.edu

Solano College
Department of Music

4000 Suisun Valley Rd.
Fairfield, CA 94534-3197
Donna Meyer
707-864-7114
Fax: 707-863-7892
E-mail: Donna.Meyer@solano.edu
www.solano.edu

Sonoma State University
Department of Music

1801 East Cotati Ave.
Rohnert Park, CA 94928
Julie Blankenship
707-664-2235
E-mail: blankenj@sonoma.edu
www.sonoma.edu

Southern California Conservatory of Music
Department of Music

8230 Fallbrook Ave.
West Hills, CA 91304
Braille Music Division
818-704-3819
E-mail: braillemusic@sccm.us
www.sccm.us

Southwestern College
Department of Performing Arts

900 Otay Lakes Rd.
Chula Vista, CA 91910
619-482-6372
www.swc.cc.ca.us

St. Mary's College of California
Department of Performing Arts

1928 St. Mary's Road
Moraga, CA 94575
www.stmarys-ca.edu

Stanford University
Department of Music

Braun Music Center
541 Lasuen Mall
Stanford, CA 94305
Nette Worthey
650-723-3811
Fax: 650-725-2686
E-mail: ugmusicinquiries@stanford.edu
www.stanford.edu

Bachelor of Arts, concentrations in Performance, Composition, Conducting, Music History and Theory, MST (Music, Science, and Technology)

Taft College
Division of Liberal Arts

29 Emmons Park Dr.
Taft, CA 93268
661-763-7700
Fax: 661-763-7705
www.taft.cc.ca.us

UCLA
Department of Music

2443 Schoenberg Music Building
Box 951623
Los Angeles, CA 90095-1623
Music Department
310-206-5187
Fax: 310-206-9203
www.ucla.edu

University of California at Berkeley
Department of Music

104 Morrison Hall #1200
Berkeley, CA 94720-1200
510-642-2678
Fax: 510-642-8480
E-mail: music@berkeley.edu
www.ls.berkeley.edu/Dept/Music

University of California at Irvine
Claire Trevor School of the Arts

303 Music and Media Building
Irvine, CA 92697-2775
949-824-6615
Fax: 949-824-4914
E-mail: music@uci.edu
www.arts.uci.edu/music

BA, BM, MFA

The Department of Music offers a curriculum that combines a thorough training in instrumental and vocal performance with wide-ranging studies in music history, music theory, composition, jazz, and computer music. Opportunities for musical performance include membership in the UCI Symphony, UCI Jazz Orchestra, various chamber and wind ensembles, UCI Anteater Band, and numerous choral ensembles

University of California at L.A.
Department of Music

2539 Schoenberg Music Building
Box 951616
Los Angeles, CA 90095-1616

Ian Krouse
310-825-4761
Fax: 310-206-4738
E-mail: ikrouse@arts.ucla.edu
www.music.ucla.edu

University of California at Riverside
Department of Music

Department of Music-061
Riverside, CA 92521-0325
Walter Clark
951-827-2114
Fax: 909-787-4651
E-mail: walter.clark@ucr.edu
www.ucr.edu

A spectacular new arts building now houses studio art, art history, dance, theatre, and music. Inter-arts endeavors will be fostered by the proximity of departments, faculty and students. Music students enjoy wonderful rehearsal rooms with variable acoustics and the latest sound technology. Music composition is taught in a wide variety of styles and world music ensembles and classes are a growing specialty of the department. Standard ensembles, such as wind ensemble, orchestra, chamber music, early music ensemble, choral society, and jazz ensemble, among others, are enjoying rapid growth in size and quality. The total campus enrollment is projected to increase from 13,000 to 20,000 by 2010 or before.

University of California at San Diego
Department of Music

Mandeville Room 111
9500 Gilman Dr. MC 0326
La Jolla, CA 92093-0326
858-534-3230
Fax: 858-534-8502
E-mail: info@music.ucsd.edu
www.ucsd.edu

University of California at Santa Barbara
Department of Music

1315 Music Building
Santa Barbara, CA 93106-6070
805-893-3261
Fax: 805-893-7194
E-mail: music@music.ucsb.edu
www.ucsb.edu

University of California at Santa Cruz
Division of the Arts

1156 High St.
Santa Cruz, CA 95064
Paul Nauert
831-459-2292
E mail: dogshark@ucsc.edu
www.music.ucsc.edu

University of La Verne
Department of Music

1950 3rd St.
La Verne, CA 91750
909-593-3511
E-mail: gratzr@ulv.edu
www.ulv.edu/music

BA Music

The University of La Verne Music Department is a small, vital part of a growing west coast university. ULV,and particularly the Music Department focuses on the individual and each student's needs and life directions. The department concentrates on choral and vocal performance, piano, guitar, bass, and drums. There is an active West African Drum Ensemble and collaborations with the Theater Department are common and dynamic. The University is located on the east end of Los Angeles County, near the Los Angeles County Fairgrounds and at the bottom of Mount Baldy.

University of Redlands
School of Music

1200 E. Colton Ave.
Redlands, CA 92373
Kimberley Wolf
909-335-4014
Fax: 909-748-6343
E-mail: music@redlands.edu
www.redlands.edu

University of Southern California Thornton School of Music
Office of Admissions

University Park - UUC 218
Los Angeles, CA 90089-2991
800-872-2213
Fax: 213-740-8995
E-mail: uscmusic@usc.edu
www.usc.edu

BS, BM, BA, MM, MA, DMA, PhD, Graduate Certificate

A large department with a wide variety of undergraduate and graduate programs in performance, composition, education, and music industry.

University of the Pacific Conservatory of Music
Conservatory of Music

3601 Pacific Ave.
Stockton, CA 95211
Carolyn Eads
209-946-2417
Fax: 209-946-2770
E-mail: conservatory@pacific.edu
www.uop.edu

Vanguard University
Department of Music

55 Fair Dr.
Costa Mesa, CA 92626
James Melton

714-556-3610
Fax: 714-662-5229
E-mail: jmelton@vanguard.edu
www.vanguard.edu

Bachelor of Arts

Vanguard University is a private, coeducational, comprehensive university of liberal arts and professional studies that believes its Pentecostal/charismatic Christian community provides a supportive and challenging environment in which to pursue a quality education. The Department of Music offers majors with emphases in Music Education, Music Ministry, Music Composition, or Performance, as well as a minor in Music.

Ventura College
Department of Music

4667 Telegraph Rd.
Ventura, CA 93003
805-654-6400
Fax: 805-654-6466
www.venturacollege.edu

Victor Valley College
Department of Music

18422 Bear Valley Rd.
Victorville, CA 92392
760-245-4271
www.vvc.edu

West Los Angeles College
Department of Music

900 Overland Ave.
Culver City, CA 90230
Carlos Ramos
310-287-4200
www.wlac.cc.ca.us

Westmont College
Department of Music

955 La Paz Rd.
Santa Barbara, CA 93108
805-565-6040

E-mail: music@westmont.edu
www.westmont.edu

Whittier College
Department of Music

13406 Philadelphia St.
Whittier, CA 90608
562-907-4237
www.whittier.edu

Whittier College's primary mission is to educate
students in a small college atmosphere where
they can learn, acquire skills and form attitudes
and values appropriate for leading and serving
in a global society. The music department offers
instruction in composition, conducting, music
education, music literature and materials, music
performance and theory. Students may also develop areas of specialization or individual projects
under faculty supervision in related fields such
as organ and church music, management and
music industries, musicology, ethnomusicology, and musical theatre. All students will find
in music a varied and enriching program in
performance and study. Those with a background
in an instrument or in voice are encouraged to
consider a major. Exceptional opportunities for
both solo and ensemble performance are available, and all students are eligible to audition for
membership in the college choir, jazz ensemble,
string ensemble or wind ensemble. Individual
instruction in voice and instruments is offered at
all levels of proficiency by an outstanding artist
faculty. Class instruction is also available in piano
and voice. The music faculty is active in a wide
range of educational, community, and professional activities, including composition, adjudication,
performance, musical theatre, jazz and popular
music production.

Yuba College
Department of Music

2088 N. Beale Rd.
Marysville, CA 95901
530-741-6761
www.yuba.cc.ca.us

Population: 4,665,177 (2005 Estimate)
Capital City: Denver
Bird: Lark Bunting
Motto: Nil sine Numine – Nothing without Providence
Flower: Rocky Mountain Columbine
Tree: Colorado Blue Spruce
Residents Called: Coloradans
Origin of Name: Taken from the Spanish for the "color red" and was applied to the Colorado river.
Area: 104,100 square miles (8th largest state)
Statehood: August 1, 1876 (38th state)
Largest Cities: Denver, Colorado Springs, Aurora, Lakewood, Fort Collins, Arvada Pueblo, Westminster, Boulder, Thornton
College Band Programs: Colorado State University, University of Colorado, University of Northern Colorado

Adams State College
Department of Music

208 Edgemont Blvd.
Alamosa, CO 81102
William Lipke
719-587-7621
E-mail: ascmuisc@adams.edu
www.music.adams.edu

Bachelor of Arts in Music Education, B.A. in
Music, Bachelor of Arts in Music, Emphasis in
Composition or Liberal Arts

Arapahoe Community College
Department of Music

5900 South Santa Fe Dr.
Littleton, CO 80160
Hidemi Matsushita
303-797-5867
E-mail: hidemi.matsushita@arapahoe.edu
www.arapahoe.edu

Aspen Music Festival and School
Office of Student Services

2 Music School Rd.
Aspen, CO 81611
David Zinman
970-925-3254
E-mail: school@aspenmusic.org
www.aspenmusicfestival.com

Colorado Christian University
School of Music, Theatre and Art

8787 West Alameda Ave.
Lakewood, CO 80226
800-44-FAITH
Fax: 303-963-3001
E-mail: questions@ccu.edu
www.ccu.edu

Colorado Christian University
School of Music

8787 West Alameda Ave.
Lakewood, CO 80226
Janet Serfoss
303-963-3135
Fax: 303-963-3131
E-mail: jserfoss@ccu.edu
www.ccu.edu

BA in Music (Sound Recording Technology,
Performance), BM (Music Education, Music
Ministry)

Colorado Christian University exists to help
students pursue a Christ-centered undergraduate and graduate education. It is an institution of
higher learning that integrates biblical concepts
with the arts and sciences and prepares graduates
for leadership and service within their selected
careers and communities. Colorado Christian
University is carrying out a commitment to
higher education implicit in America,s national
heritage of Christian faith. The university integrates diverse fields of study with biblical truth.
Each academic discipline (e.g., philosophy; business; education; psychology; music; the physical,
social, and behavioral sciences) is taught by instructors who have clear biblical presuppositions
for their disciplines. Music at Colorado Christian
University offers a well-rounded exposure to
diverse styles of music including Classical, Jazz,
Contemporary Christian, and World Music.
Programs include the Bachelor of Arts (BA) in
Music (with elective areas of study available in
Sound Recording Technology or Performance),
the Bachelor of Music (BM) with areas of study
in Music Education and Music Ministry and the
Music Minor and Music Ministry Minor.

Colorado State University
Department of Music, Theatre, and Dance

Fort Collins, CO 80523-1778
Michael Thaut
970-491-5529
Fax: 970-491-7541

E-mail: mtdinfo@colostate.edu
www.colostate.edu/Depts/Music

Colorado State University-Pueblo
Department of Music

2200 Bonforte Blvd.
Room 175
Pueblo, CO 81001-4901
Mark Hudson
719-549-2552
Fax: 719-549-2969
E-mail: music@colostatepueblo.edu
www.chass.colostate-pueblo.edu

Community College of Aurora
Department of Music

16000 East Centre Tech Pkwy.
Aurora, CO 80011-9057
Richard Italiano
303-361-7425
E-mail: rich.italiano@ccaurora.edu
www.ccaurora.edu

Fort Lewis College
Department of Music

1000 Rim Dr.
Durango, CO 81301-3999
Rochelle Mann
970-247-7447
Fax: 970-247-7520
E-mail: mann_r@fortlewis.edu
www.fortlewis.edu

Fort Range Community College
Department of Music

3645 West 112th Ave.
East Service Center
Westminster, CO 80031
303-466-8811
Fax: 303-466-1623
www.frcc.cc.co.us

Lamar Community College
Department of Music

2401 South Main St.
Lamar, CO 81052
719-336-2248
www.lcc.cccoes.edu

Mesa State College
Department of Music

1100 North Ave.
Grand Junction, CO 81501
Calvin Hofer
970-248-1233
Fax: 970-248-1159
E-mail: chofer@mesastate.edu
www.mesastate.edu

Metropolitan State College of Denver
Department of Music

P.O. Box 173362
Denver, CO 80217-3362
303-556-3058
Fax: 303-556-6345
www.mscd.edu

Bachelor of Arts, B.M. Music

Naropa University
Department of Music

2130 Arapahoe Ave.
Boulder, CO 80302
Emily Harrison
303-245-4833
Fax: 303-245-4829
E-mail: eharrison@naropa.edu
www.naropa.edu

Bachelor of Arts Music

Northeastern Junior College
Department of Music

100 College Dr.
E.S. French Hall 175
Sterling, CO 80751
Celeste Pelton-Delgado
970-521-6777
E-mail: celeste.delgado@njc.edu
www.njc.edu

University of Colorado Boulder
Department of Music

Campus Box 30
Boulder, CO 80209-0017
James Austin
303-492-6352
Fax: 303-492-5619
E-mail: ugradmus@colorado.edu
www.colorado.edu

University of Colorado Boulder
College of Music

College of Music Building
18th and Euclid 301 UCB
Boulder, CO 80309-0301
303-492-6352
E-mail: ugradmus@colorado.edu
www.colorado.edu

University of Northern Colorado
Department of Music

Campus Box 10
Greeley, CO 80639
Valerie Anderson
970-351-2679
Fax: 970-351-1923
E-mail: valerie.anderson@unco.edu
www.unco.edu

Western State College of Colorado
Department of Music

600 North Adams St.
Gunnison, CO 81231
Martha Violett
970-943-3054
E-mail: mviolett@western.edu
www.western.edu

Population: 3,510,297 (2005 Estimate)
Capital City: Hartford
Bird: Robin
Motto: Qui transtulit sustinet – He who transplanted still sustains
Flower: Mountain Laurel
Tree: White Oak
Residents Called: Nutmeggers
Origin of Name: Based on Mohican and Algonquin Indian words for a "place beside a long river."
Area: 5,544 square miles (48th largest state)
Statehood: January 9, 1788 (5th state)
Largest Cities: Bridgeport, New Haven, Hartford, Stamford, Waterbury, Norwalk, Danbury, New Britain, West Hartford, Greenwich
College Band Programs: Sacred Heart University, University of Connecticut, Yale University

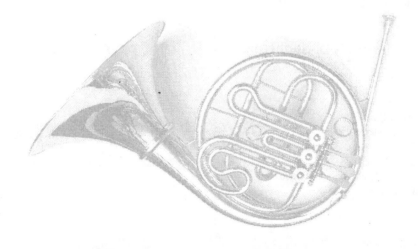

Central Connecticut State University
Department of Music

1615 Stanley St.
New Britain, CT 06050
Daniel D'Addio
860-832-2912
Fax: 860-832-2902
E-mail: inglism@ccsu.edu
www.ccsu.edu

Connecticut College
Department of Music

270 Mohegan Ave.
New London, CT 06320
Terry Wisniewski
860-439-2720
Fax: 860-439-5382
E-mail: tawis@conncoll.edu
www.camel.conncoll.edu

Eastern Connecticut State University
Dept of Music and Fine Arts

83 Windham St.
Willimantic, CT 06226
Kathy Parmalee
860-465-5325
Fax: 860-465-5764
E-mail: parmaleek@easternct.edu
www.ecsu.ctstateu.edu

Gateway Community Technical College
Department of Music

60 Sargent Dr.
New Haven, CT 06511
Douglas Salyer
203-789-7053
E-mail: gw_salyer@commnet.edu
www.gwctc.commnet.edu

Hartford College for Women
Department of Music
1265 Asylum Ave.
Hartford, CT 06105
Irene Conley
860-768-4957
Fax: 860-768-4441
E-mail: conley@hartford.edu
www.hartford.edu

B.A. in Music, Bachelor of Arts. Bachelor of Arts of Fine Arts, BA of Science in Engineering, Masters of Music and Music Education.

Mitchell College
Department of Music

437 Pequot Ave.
New London, CT 06320
800-443-2811
Fax: 860-444-1209
www.mitchell.edu

National Guitar Workshop
Admissions

NGW
Box 222
Lakeside, CT 06758
800-234-6479
www.guitarworkshop.com

Northwestern College
Department of Music

3003 Snelling Avnue North
St. Paul, MN 55113-1598
888-878-5514
E-mail: music@nwc.edu
www.nwc.edu

Bachelor of Music, Music Education and Arts

Sacred Heart University
Department of Music

5151 Park Ave.

Fairfield, CT 06825-1000
John Michniewicz
203-371-7735
Fax: 203-365-7609
E-mail: michniewiczj@sacredheart.edu
www.sacredheart.edu

Minor only in Music.

Southern Connecticut State University
Department of Music

501 Crescent St.
New Haven, CT 06515
Richard Gerber
203-392-6625
E-mail: gerberr1@southernct.edu
www.southernct.edu

Bachelor of Arts in Music

The Hartford Conservatory
Diploma School
Music Department

834 Asylum Ave.
Hartford, CT 06154
Jerry Prell
860-246-2588
Fax: 860-249-6330
E-mail: jprell@hartfordconservatory.org
www.hartfordconservatory.org

Accredited Artist Diploma

Two-year accredited diploma program in Jazz & Pop Performance or Music Pedagogy. Conservatory total immersion model, no gen ed classes and no SATs. Other majors, dance performance, dance pedagogy, musical theater, and recording arts. Seeking motivated students with passion and potential. Rolling admissions.

Trinity College
Department of Music

300 Summit St.
Hartford, CT 06106-3100
Patricia Kennedy
860-297-5122
E-mail: patricia.kennedy
www.trincoll.edu/pub

University of Bridgeport
Department of Music

126 Park Ave.
Bridgeport, CT 06604
800-392-3582
E-mail: response@bridgeport.edu
www.bridgeport.edu

University of Connecticut
Department of Music

1295 Storrs Rd., Unit 1012
Storrs, CT 06269-1012
Deborah Trahan
860-486-3728
Fax: 860-486-3796
E-mail: musicc@uconn.edu
www.music.uconn.edu

Bachelor of Science in Music Education, Bachelor of Music in Music Theory, Performance. Bachelor of Arts with a major in Music, in Music History, Bachelor of Arts in Jazz

University Of Hartford
The Hartt School

200 Bloomfield Ave.

West Hartford, CT 06117
860-768-4255
Fax: 860-768-5724
www.hartford.edu

University of New Haven
Department of Music

300 Boston Post Rd.
West Haven, CT 06516
203-342-5864
Fax: 203-932-6080
E-mail: cas@newhaven.edu
www.newhaven.edu

BA in Music, Music Industry, Music and
Sound Recording

Wesleyan University
Department of Music

Middletown, CT 06459
860-685-2650
Fax: 860-685-2651
E-mail: music@wesleyan.edu
www.wesleyan.edu/music/home.html

Western Connecticut State University
Department of Music

181 White St.
Danbury, CT 06810
203-837-8350
Fax: 203-837-8630
www.wcsu.edu

BA in Music, Music Education, Performance, Jazz
Studies, Music Education

Yale School of Music
Office of Admissions

P.O. Box 208246
New Haven, CT 06520-8246
Thomas Masse
203-432-4155
Fax: 203-432-7448
E-mail: gradmusic.admissions@yale.edu
www.yale.edu/music

DELAWARE

Population: 843,524 (2005 Estimate)
Capital City: Dover
Bird: Blue Hen Chicken
Motto: Liberty and Independence
Flower: Peach Blossom
Tree: American Holly
Residents Called: Delawareans
Origin of Name: Named after an early Virginia governor, Lord De La Warr
Area: 2,489 square miles (49th largest)
Statehood: December 7, 1787 (1st state)
Largest Cities: Wilmington, Dover, Newark, Milford, Seaford, Middletown, Elsmere, Smyrna, New Castle, Georgetown
College Band Programs: Delaware State College, University of Delaware

DELAWARE

Delaware State College
Department of Music

1200 North Dupont Hwy.
Dover, DE 19901
302-739-4937
Fax: 302-739-4957
www.dsc.edu

University of Delaware
Department of Music

100 Orchard Rd.
Amstel Avenue and Orchard Rd.
Newark, DE 19716-2560
Mary Dunnack
302-831-8426
Fax: 302-831-3589
E-mail: mdunnack@udel.edu
www.music.udel.edu

BMAS, BAAS

Undergraduate and Graduate degree programs,
instrumental/vocal. Bachelor of Music in Applied
Music, Music Education, & Theory/Composition.
Bachelor of Arts in Music also with Music Management Concentration and a 5 1/2 year plan for
continuing on to an MBA in music management.

Population: 550,521 (2005 Estimate)
Capital City: Washington
Bird: Wood Thrush
Motto: Justitia Omnibus - Justice to all
Flower: American Beauty Rose
Origin of Name: The district is named after Christopher Columbus.
Area: 68 square miles
Music Colleges and Universities: American University, Benjamin T. Rome School of Music, Catholic University of America, George Washington University, Georgetown University, Howard University, Levine School of Music, Mount Vernon College, Trinity College, University of the District of Columbia
Marching Bands: Georgetown University

American University
Dept of Performing Arts

4400 Massachusetts Ave. N.W
Washington, DC 20016-8053
Daniel E. Abraham
202-885-3420
Fax: 202-885-1092
E-mail: dabrowski@american.edu
www.american.edu

Benjamin T. Rome School of Music
Department of Music

111 Ward Hall, The Catholic University of America
620 Michigan Ave. NE
Washington, DC 20064
202-319-5414
Fax: 202-319-6280
E-mail: cua-music@cua.edu
www.cua.edu

George Washington University
Department of Music

801 22nd St. NW
Academic Center B-144
Washington, DC 20052
Admissons Office
202-994-6245
Fax: 202-994-9038
E-mail: gwmusic@gwu.edu
www.gwu.edu/~music/index.html

Bachelor of Arts

Georgetown University
Department of Art, Music and Theater

Davis Performing Arts Center
Box 571063
Washington, DC 20057-1063

202-687-3838
Fax: 202-687-5757
E-mail: hiltona@georgetown.edu
www.georgetown.edu

Howard University
Department of Music

2400 Sixth St. NW
Washington, DC 20059
202-806-6100
Fax: 202-806-9673
www.howard.edu

Levine School of Music
Admissions Office

2801 Upton St. NW
Washington, DC 20008
Admissions Office
202-686-8000
Fax: 202-686-9773
E-mail: info@levineschool.org
www.levineschool.org

Mount Vernon College
Dept of Performing Arts

2100 Foxhall Rd. NW
Washington, DC 20007
800-682-4636
Fax: 202-625-4688
www.mvc.gwu.edu

University of the District of Columbia
Music Program

4200 Connecticut Ave. NW
MB 4601
Washington, DC 20008
202-274-6110
Fax: 202-274-6341
www.udc.edu

BA in Music, AA in Music

Population: 17,789,864 (2005 Estimate)
Capital City: Tallahassee
Bird: Mockingbird
Motto: In God We Trust
Flower: Orange Blossom
Tree: Sabal Palmetto
Residents Called: Floridians
Origin of Name: Named on Easter 1513 by Ponce de Leon for Pascua Florida, meaning "Flowery Easter."
Area: 65,758 square miles (22nd largest state)
Statehood: March 3, 1845 (27th state)
Largest Cities: Jacksonville, Miami, Tampa, Saint Petersburg, Hialeah, Orlando, Fort Lauderdale, Tallahassee, Hollywood, Pembroke, Pines
College Band Programs: Bethune-Cookman College, Florida State University, Jacksonville State University, University of Central Florida, University of Miami, University of South Florida

Barry University
School of Arts and Sciences

11300 NE 2nd Ave.
Miami Shores, FL 33161-6695
Department of Fine Arts
305-899-3100
E-mail: admissions@mail.barry.edu
www.barry.edu

Bethune-Cookman College
Department of Music

640 Dr. Mary Mcleod Bethune Blvd.
Daytona Beach, FL 32114
386-481-2000
www.cookman.edu

Brenau University
Department of Music

500 Washington St. SE
Gainesville, FL 30501
Andre Birch
770-718-5325
Fax: 770-534-6777
E-mail: abirch@brenau.edu
www.brenau.edu/sfah/music

Brevard Community College
Department of Music

1519 Clearlake Rd.
Cocoa, FL 32922
321-632-1111
www.brevardcc.edu

Broward Community College
Department of Music

3501 SW Davie
Fort Lauderdale, FL 33314-1694
Loretta Scherperel
954-475-6840
Fax: 954-475-6605
E-mail: lscherpe@broward.cc.fl.us
www.broward.cc.fl.us

Chipola Junior College
Department of Music

3094 Indian Cir.
Marianna, FL 32446
850-526-2761
www.chipola.cc.fl.us

Edison Community College at Lee County
Department of Music

8099 College Pkwy. SW
Fort Myers, FL 33919
239-489-9300
Fax: 941-489-9482
E-mail: inquiry@edison.edu
www.edison.edu

Edward Waters College
Department of Fine Arts

1658 Kings Rd.
Jacksonville, FL 32209
904-470-8132
Fax: 904-470-8030
E-mail: sshingles@ewc.edu
www.ewc.edu

Bachelor of Arts in Vocal Performance, in Instrumental Performance in Sacred Music

Florida A&M University
Department of Fine Arts

Foster Tanner Music Building
Tallahassee, FL 32307
850-599-3334
Fax: 850-561-2176
www.famu.edu

Florida Atlantic University
Department of Music

777 Glades Rd.
Boca Raton, FL 33431
561-297-3000
www.fau.edu

Florida College
Department of Music

119 North Glen Arven Ave.
Temple Terrace, FL 33617
Doug Barlar
813-899-6745
E-mail: barlard@floridacollege.edu
www.flcoll.edu

Florida International University
Wertheim Performing Arts Center

School of Music PAC 14
11100 S.W. 17th St.
Miami, FL 33199
Music Department
305-348-3726
Fax: 305-348-2896
www.fiu.edu

Florida Keys Community College
Department of Music

5901 College Rd.
Key West, FL 33040
Cheryl Malsheimer
305-296-9081
Fax: 305-292-5155
E-mail: malsheim. c@firn.edu
www.firn.edu/cc/fkcc

Florida Southern College
Department of Music

111 Lake Hollingsworth Dr.
Lakeland, FL 33801-5698
Music Department
836-680-4229
Fax: 836-680-4395
www.flsouthern.edu

Florida State University
School of Music

Tallahassee, FL 32306-1180
Benjamin Ebener
850-644-6102
Fax: 850-644-2033
E-mail: musicadmissions@fsu.edu
www.music.fsu.edu

Full Sail Real World Education

3300 University Blvd.
Winter Park, FL 32792
Mary Beth Plank
800-226-7625
E-mail: admissions@fullsail.com
www.fullsail.com

Recording Arts / Show Production & Touring/
Entertainment Business

Since 1979, Full Sail Real World Education, a college outside Orlando, FL, has been an innovative educational leader for those pursuing a career in the entertainment industry. With nearly 20,000 alumni, graduate credits include work on Oscar and GRAMMY-winning projects, best selling video games, and the #1 grossing U.S. concert tour five out of the last five years. Full Sail's 91-acre campus proudly welcomes students from all 50 states and 35 countries worldwide. Currently, Full Sail offers Bachelor of Science Degrees in the following disciplines: Computer Animation, Digital Arts & Design, Entertainment Business, Film and Game Design & Development, as well as Associate of Science Degrees in Recording Arts and Show Production & Touring. Students experience a "real world" education, with a professional class structure of 8-12 hours per day, and a 24-hour round the clock schedule which earned Full Sail the Most Innovative Program Award by the Florida Association of Postsecondary Schools and Colleges. Full Sail has also been named one of the top three entertainment media colleges by *Shift Magazine* alongside the Massachusetts Institute of Technology (No. 1) and New York University (No. 2); Electronic Gaming Monthly named Full Sail one of the top five Game Design Schools in the world; and *Rolling Stone Magazine* recently named Full Sail one of the Best

Music Programs in the country, in addition to one of the "Best Music Business Departments" in the *Schools That Rock: The Rolling Stone College Guide.*

Gulf Coast Community College
Department of Music

5230 West US 98
Panama City, FL 32401
Rosemarie O'Bourke
850-872-3887
Fax: 850-873-3520
E-mail: robourke@gulfcoast.edu
www.gc.cc.fl.us

Harid Conservatory
School of Music

2285 Potomac Rd.
Boca Raton, FL 33431-2677
561-997-2677
Fax: 561-997-8920
E-mail: info@harid.edu
www.harid.edu

Hillsborough Community College
Department of Music

P.O. Box 5096
Tampa, FL 33675
James Burge
813-253-7684
Fax: 813-253-7610
E-mail: jburge@hcc.cc.fl.us
www.hcc.cc.fl.us

Jacksonville University
Department of Music

2800 University Blvd. North
Jacksonville, FL 32211
Laura Burrows
904-745-7370
Fax: 904-745-7375

E-mail: lburrow1@ju.edu
www.ju.edu

BM, BS Music Business, BFA Music Theatre, BME (Music Education), BA Music

Programs leading to degrees in music at Jacksonville University are designed to meet a variety of student needs. All programs include a dominant music component employing classroom, individualized and studio instruction combined with JU's liberal arts emphasis. Music majors are prepared for future endeavors in performance, education, composition, arrangement, or business. By virtue of their liberal arts preparation, music graduates find themselves well-equipped for careers in a wide variety of other fields and for advanced study at the graduate level.

Jeff Berlin Players School of Music
Department of Music

923 McMullen Booth Rd.
Clearwater, FL 33759
Vicky Berlin
800-724-4242
E-mail: vfberlin@playerschool.com
www.playerschool.com

Lake City Community College
Department of Music

149 SE College Place
Lake City, FL 32025
386-754-4287
E-mail: admissions@lakecityycc.edu
www.lakecity.cc.fl.us

Lynn University
Conservatory of Music

3601 North Military Trail
Boca Raton, FL 33431
Lisa Leonard
561-237-9012
Fax: 562-237-9002
E-mail: Lleonard@lynn.edu

www.lynn.edu/music

Bachelor of Arts in Music

Miami-Dade Community College at Kendall
Department of Music

11011 SW 104th St.
Room 8221
Miami, FL 33176
305-237-2282
Fax: 307-237-2411
www.mdcc.edu/kendall

Associates of Arts in Music Education

Oskaloosa Walton Community College
Department of Music

100 College Blvd. East
Building J
Niceville, FL 32578
Mary Baker
850-729-5382
Fax: 850-729-5286
E-mail: bakerm@owc.edu
www.owcc.cc.fl.us

Palm Beach Atlantic College
School of Music and Fine Arts

901 South Flagler Dr.
P.O. Box 24708
West Palm Beach, FL 33401
Lloyd Mims
561-803-2000
E-mail: admit@pba.edu
www.pba.edu

Palm Beach Community College
Department of Music

4200 South Congress Aveue
Lake Worth, FL 33461

561-868-3350
E-mail: enrollmt@pbcc.edu
www.pbcc.cc.fl.us

Pensacola Junior College
Department of Music and Theatre

1000 College Blvd.
Pensacola, FL 32504
Donald Snowden
850-484-1800
www.pjc.cc.fl.us

Rollins College
Department of Music

1000 Holt Ave. #2731
Winter Park, FL 32789
407-646-2233
www.rollins.edu

Santa Fe Community College
Department of Music

3000 NW 83rd St.
Room R112
Gainesville, FL 32606
352-395-7322
Fax: 352-395-4118
www.sfcc.edu

South Florida Community College
Department of Music

600 West College Dr.
Avon Park, FL 33825
Catherine Burge
863-453-6661
www.sfcc.cc.fl.us

St. Leo University
School of Arts and Sciences

33701 State Rd. 52
P.O. Box 665 Mc 2127
Saint Leo, FL 33574-6665

June Hammond
800-334-5532
Fax: 352-588-8300
E-mail: june.hammond@saintleo.edu
www.saintleo.edu

St. Petersburg College
Department of Music

P.O. Box 13489
St. Petersburg, FL 33733
Jonathan Stelle
727-341-4360
E-mail: steelej@spcollege.edu
www.spcollege.edu/spg/music

Stetson University
School of Music

421 North Woodland Blvd.
Unit 8378
Deland, FL 32723
Rachel Boldman
386-822-8975
Fax: 386-822-8948
E-mail: music@stetson.edu
www.stetson.edu

Bachelor of Music, Music Education,
Bachelor of Arts

University of Central Florida
Department of Music

4000 Central Florida Blvd.
Orlando, FL 32816
Eugene Montague
407-823-1145
E-mail: emontagu@mail.ucf.edu
www.ucf.edu

University of Florida
School of Music

101 Fine Arts Building A
P.O. Box 115800
Gainesville, FL 32611-5800
Lucinda Lavelli

352-392-0207
Fax: 352-392-3802
www.arts.ufl.edu/music

University of Miami
Frost School of Music

P.O. Box 248165
Coral Gables, FL 33124-7610
Catherine Tanner
305-284-2241
Fax: 305-284-6475
E-mail: ctanner@miami.edu
www.music.miami.edu

BM,BS,BA,MM,MS,PhD,DMA

Since 1926 the Frost School of Music has grown in numbers, prestige and selectivity, balancing conservatory-style training with contemporary approaches and innovative programs producing artists and leaders in the music industry.

University of North Florida
Department of Music

4567 St. John's Bluff Rd.
Jacksonville, FL 32224-2645
904-620-2960
www.unf.edu

B.M., Bachelor of Arts, and Bachelor of Arts.

Located in its brand new $22 million facility, the UNF Music Department is developing into one of the important music programs in the region. Long known for its top jazz program, the music area offers a complete program for undergraduates interested in the music major. An energetic, talented faculty of artist-teachers and strong ties with the Jacksonville Symphony Orchestra help to make this an exciting place to study.

University of South Florida
School of Music

4202 East Fowler Ave.
FAH 110
Tampa, FL 33620-7350
813-974-2311
Fax: 813-974-8721

E-mail: music@arts.usf.edu
www.usf.edu

University of Tampa
Department of Music

401 West Kennedy Blvd.
Tampa, FL 33606
Jeffery Traster
813-253-3333
Fax: 813-254-4955
E-mail: admissions@ut.edu
www.utampa.edu

University of West Florida
Department of Music

11000 University Pkwy.
Pensacola, FL 32514
Kyle Marrero
850-474-2147
Fax: 850-474-3247
E-mail: kmarrero@uwf.edu
www.uwf.edu

Bachelor of Arts in Music Performance (Instrumental, Piano, Strings & Voice), Bachelor of Arts in Music Performance

Valencia
Community College
Music Program

P.O. Box 3028
Orlando, FL 32802
Larry Graham
407-582-2332
www.valenciacc.edu

Warner Southern College
Department of Music

13895 Hwy. 27
Lake Worth, FL 33859
Steven Darr
813-638-7231
E-mail: darrs@warner.edu
www.warner.edu

GEORGIA

Population: 9,072,576 (2005 Estimate)
Capital City: Atlanta
Bird: Brown Thrasher
Motto: Wisdom, justice, and moderation
Flower: Cherokee Rose
Tree: Live Oak
Residents Called: Georgians
Origin of Name: Named for King George II of England.
Area: 59,441 square miles (24th largest state)
Statehood: January 2, 1788 (4th state)
Largest Cities: Atlanta, Augusta, Columbus, Savannah, Athens, Macon, Roswell, Albany, Marietta, Warner Robins
College Band Programs: Clark Atlanta University, Georgia Southern University, Georgia Institute of Tech, University of Georgia

Agnes Scott College
Department of Music

141 East College Ave.
Decatur, GA 30030
LeeAnn Afton
404-471-6285
Fax: 404-471-6414
E-mail: lafton@agnesscott.edu
www.agnesscott.edu

Andrew College
Department of Music

413 College St.
Cuthbert, GA 39840
Josie Moore
800-664-9250
Fax: 229-732-5991
E-mail: josiemoore@andrewcollege.edu
www.andrewcollege.edu

Associates of Music

Armstrong Atlantic State University
Department of Art, Music and Theater

11935 Abercorn St.
Savannah, GA 31419-1909
Kim West
912-927-5277
Fax: 912-921-5462
E-mail: adm-info@mail.armstrong.edu
www.armstrong.edu

Augusta State University
Department of Fine Arts

2500 Walton Way
Augusta, GA 30904-2200
706-737-1632
www.aug.edu/finearts

B.M. in Performance, Music Education

Berry College
Department of Fine Arts

P.O. Box 0309
Mt. Berry, GA 30149-0309
Stan Pethel
706-232-5374
Fax: 706-238-7847
E-mail: spethel@berry.edu
www.berry.edu

Brenau University
Department of Music

500 Washington St. SE
Gainesville, GA 30501
Michelle Roueche
770-534-6234
Fax: 770-534-6777
E-mail: mroueche@brenau.edu
www.brenau.edu/sfah/music

BM in Vocal Performance, BM in Piano Performance, BM in Choral Music Education, BAM

Founded in 1878, Brenau University's music program provides music instruction of the highest caliber within the setting of an intimate, friendly college.

Brewton-Parker College
Division of Music

Hwy 280 at 201 David-Eliza Fountain Cir.
P.O. Box 197
Mount Vernon, GA 30445
Glenn Eernisse
912-583-3131
Fax: 912-583-2997
E-mail: geeerniss@bpc.edu
www.bpc.edu

Clark Atlanta University
Department of Music

Park St. Music and Art Complex
793 Park St. SW
Atlanta, GA 30314

Sharon J. Willis
404-880-8211
Fax: 404-880-6267
E-mail: swillis@cau.edu
www.cau.edu

Clayton College and State University
Department of Music

2000 Clayton State Blvd.
Morrow, GA 30260
William Graves
678-466-4000
Fax: 678-466-4769
www.clayton.edu

Columbus State University
Schwab School of Music

900 Broadway
Columbus, GA 31901
Diane Andrae
706-649-7225
Fax: 706-649-7369
E-mail: schwobmusic@colstate.edu
www.colstate.edu

B.M. in Performance, Music Education, Piano
Pedagogy, Bachelor of Arts in Music

Covenant College
Department of Music

1409 Scenic Hwy. Lookout Mountain
Lookout Mountain, GA 30750-9901
Ken Anderson
706-419-1455
Fax: 706-419-2165
E-mail: anderson@covenant.edu
www.covenant.edu

Darton College
Department of Music

2400 Gillionville Rd.
Albany, GA 31707-3098
Jeff Kluball

229-317-6856
Fax: 229-317-6650
E-mail: kluballj@darton.edu
www.darton.edu

Emory University at Oxford
Division of Humanities

100 Hamill St.
Oxford, GA 30054
Maria Archetto
770-784-8888
E-mail: marchetto@learnlink.emory.edu
www.emory.edu

Fort Valley State University
Department of Music

1005 State University Dr.
Fort Valley, GA 31030-4313
Bobby Dickery
478-825-6387
Fax: 478-825-6132
E-mail: dickeyb@fvsu.edu
www.fvsu.edu

Bachelor of Arts in Music

Georgia College and State University
Department of Music and Theatre

Campus Box 66
Milledgeville, GA 31061
Richard Mercier
478-445-4226
E-mail: richard.mercier@gcsu.edu
www.gcsu.edu

Georgia Institute of Technology
Department of Music

Couch Building
Atlanta, GA 30332-0456
404-894-3193

Fax: 404-894-9952
E-mail: music@coa.gatech.edu
www.gatech.edu

Georgia Perimeter College
Department of Fine Arts

555 North Indian Creek Dr.
Building CF-2230
Clarkston, GA 30021
David Koffman
678-891-3577
E-mail: dkoffman@gpc.edu
www.gpc.edu

Georgia Southern University
Department of Music

P.O. Box 8052
Statesboro, GA 30460
912-681-5396
Fax: 912-871-1295
E-mail: music@georgiasouthern.edu
www2.gasou.edu/music

Georgia Southwestern College
Department of Fine Arts

800 Wheatley St.
Americus, GA 31709
229-391-2204
Fax: 912-932-9270
www.gsw.edu

Bachelor of Arts in Music

Georgia State University
School of Music

P.O. Box 4097
Atlanta, GA 30302-4097
David Smart
404-651-3213
Fax: 404-651-1583
E-mail: music@gsu.edu
www.gsu.edu

Gordon College
Music Program

419 College Dr.
Barnesville, GA 30204
800-282-6504
Fax: 770-358-5140
E-mail: admissions@gdn.edu
www.gdn.edu/music

Kennesaw State University
Department of Music

1000 Chastain Rd.
Kennesaw, GA 30144
770-423-6151
Fax: 770-423-6368
E-mail: musicadm@kennesaw.edu
www.kennesaw.edu

LaGrange College
Department of Music

601 Broad St.
Lagrange, GA 30240
706-880-8005
www.lagrange.edu

Mercer University
Townsend School of Music

1400 Coleman Ave.
Macon, GA 31207
Gina Nelson
478-301-2748
E-mail: nelson_gc@mercer.edu
www.mercer.edu

B.M., B.M.E., Bachelor of Arts, M.M.

For over 173 years, Mercer University has provided a heritage and tradition of excellence in education. This same intensity of purpose and caring of intention is found in Townsend School of Music where the nurturing of solid musicianship is cultivated within a rich university environment. Musical knowledge and skills are fostered in an atmosphere that endeavors to create inquiring minds that are able to relate the musical art to a larger body of knowledge in humanity.

This integration of skills and knowledge instills self-reliance and flexibility that allows the music graduate to pursue a career in a changing and demanding profession. Mercer is an institutional member of NASM.

Middle Georgia College
Department of Music

1100 Second St. SE
Cochran, GA 30104
478-934-3103
Fax: 478-934-3403
www.mgc.peachnet.edu

Morehouse College
Department of Music

830 Westview Dr.
Atlanta, GA 30341
Uzee Brown
404-215-2601
Fax: 404-215-3479
E-mail: ubrown@morehouse.edu
www.morehouse.edu

Morris Brown College
Department of Music

643 Martin Luther King Jr. Dr. NW
Atlanta, GA 30314
404-739-1000
www.morrisbrown.edu

North Georgia College and State University
Department of Fine Arts

Fine Arts Department
Dahlonega, GA 30597
Estelle Gilstrap
706-864-1423
Fax: 706-864-1429
E-mail: egilstrap@ngcsu.edu
www.ngcsu.edu

Bachelor of Arts in Music

Oglethorpe University
Division of Music

4484 Peachtree Rd. NE
Atlanta, GA 30319
800-428-4484
www.oglethorpe.edu

Paine College
Department of Music

1235 15th St.
Augusta, GA 30901
706-821-8200
Fax: 706-821-8293
E-mail: info@mail.paine.edu
www.paine.edu

Piedmont College
Department of Music

165 Central Ave.
Demorest, GA 30535
706-778-3000
Fax: 706-776-2811
E-mail: whinson@piedmont.edu
www.piedmont.edu

Bachelor of Arts in Music Performance, Bachelor of Arts in Church Music, Master of Arts in Teaching, Master of Arts in Music Education, Minor in Music

Reinhardt College
Music Program

7300 Reinhardt College
Waleska, GA 30183
770-720-5562
Fax: 770-720-5636
E-mail: poc@reinhardt.edu
www.reinhardt.edu

Savannah State College
Department of Music and Fine Arts

Office of Admissions
Hodge Hall, P.O. Box 20209
Savannah, GA 31404
912-356-2181
E-mail: admissions@savstate.edu
www.savstate.edu/class/finearts

Shorter College
Department of Music

315 Shorter Ave.
Rome, GA 30165
Alan Wingard
800-868-6980
www.shorter.edu/academ/soa/index.htm

Bachelor of Music

Spelman College
Department of Music

350 Spelman Lane, SW
Atlanta, GA 30314
Kevin Johnson
404-270-5476
E-mail: www.spelman.edu
www.spelman.edu

Bachelor of Arts

A comprehensive and active music performance program (choral, jazz, strings, winds, voice, piano and other instruments) and a broad curriculum including music technology & ethnomusicology. The department is fully accredited by the National Association of Schools of Music.

Thomas University
Department of Music

1501 Millpond Rd.
Thomasville, GA 31792
800-538-9784
Fax: 229-226-1653
www.thomas.edu

Toccoa Falls College
School of Music

325 Chapel Dr.
Toccoa, GA 30598
888-785-5624
www.tfc.edu

Truett-McConnel College
Department of Music and Fine Arts

100 Alumni Dr.
Cleveland, GA 30528
Greg Woodward
706-865-2134 x117
E-mail: gwoodward@truett.edu
www.truett.cc.ga.us

B.A. in Music

University of Georgia
Department of Music

Athens, GA 30602
404-542-3737
E-mail: visctr@uga.edu

University of West Georgia
Department of Music

1601 Maple St.
Carrollton, GA 30170
Kevin Hibbard
678-839-6516
Fax: 678-839-6259
E-mail: musicdpt@westga.edu
www.westga.edu

BM Performance, Music Education, Performance with Emphasis in Jazz Studies, Piano Performance with Emphasis in Piano Pedagogy, BMusic with Elective Studies in Business, Music Minor

The department enriches the cultural life of the West Georgia region and has an excellent reputation for preparing musicians who seek careers in teaching, in performance, and in the music industry. The department's distinguished artist/teacher faculty has extensive credentials and professional experience in performance, music education, production, and other specialized areas of work in music. Undergraduate and graduate students receive individualized instruction in a full range of music course offerings including private study in voice, piano, organ, guitar, and all woodwind, brass, and percussion instruments. In addition to undergraduate and graduate degree programs in Music, students find enrichment through concerts, recitals, workshops, and master classes by visiting performers, composers, scholars, and teachers, and by the department's faculty. Students of all majors participate in a wide range of ensembles for university credit. The university ensembles include the Concert Choir, Chamber Singers, Opera Workshop, Marching Band, Wind Symphony, Jazz Ensemble & combos, Basketball Band, Percussion Ensemble, Jazz Percussion Group, Keyboard Ensemble, Collegium Musicum, and a variety of woodwind and brass ensembles. The department also serves the CORE curriculum, offering courses such as Music Appreciation (Core Area C), Survey of Jazz, Rock, and Popular Music (Core Area C), and Survey of World Music (Core area B.2.). These courses are designed to enrich the artistic and cultural understandings of students throughout the university.

Valdosta State University
Department of Music

1500 North Patterson St.
Valdosta, GA 31698
James Shrader
229-333-5804
Fax: 229-259-5578
www.valdosta.edu

Bachelor of Music with a major in music education, Bachelor of Music with a major in music performance, Bachelor of Arts with a major in music, Master of Music education, Master of Music performance

Wesleyan College
Department of Music

4760 Forsyth Rd.
Macon, GA 31210
Nadine Whitney
478-757-5259
Fax: 478-757-5268
E-mail: nwhitney@wesleyancollege.edu
www.wesleyancollege.edu

West Georgia College
Department of Music

1601 Maple St.
Carrollton, GA 30118
678-839-6516
Fax: 678-839-6259
E-mail: musicdpt@westga.edu
www.westga.edu

Bachelor of Music

Young Harris College
Department of Music

1 College Street
PO Box 116
Young Harris, GA 30582
800-241-3754
www.yhc.edu

HAWAII

Population: 1,275,194 (2005 Estimate)

Capital City: Honolulu

Bird: Nene

Motto: Ua mau ke ea o ka aina I ka pono – The life of the land is perpetuated in righteousness

Flower: Hibiscus or Pua Aloalo

Tree: Candlenut or Kukui

Residents Called: Hawaiians

Origin of Name: It could be based on native Hawaiian word for homeland, "Owhyhee."

Area: 10,932 square miles (43rd largest state)

Statehood: August 21, 1959 (50th state)

Largest Cities: Honolulu, Hilo, Kailua, Kaneohe, Waipahu, Pearl City, Waimalu, Mililani, Kahului, Kihe

College Band Programs: Hawaii Pacific University, University of Hawaii-Manoa

Chaminade University
of Honolulu
Department of Music

3140 Waialae Ave.
Honolulu, HI 96816-1578
808-735-4711
www.chaminade.edu

Hawaii Pacific College
Department of Music

1164 Bishop St.
Honolulu, HI 96813
866-CALL-HPU
www.hpu.edu

Honolulu
Community College
Department of Music

874 Dillingham Blvd.
Honolulu, HI 96817
Lorna Mouont
808-845-9415
Fax: 808-845-9416
E-mail: lmount@hcc.hawaii.edu
www.hcc.hawaii.edu

University of Hawaii at Hilo
Department of
Performing Arts

200 West Kawili St.
Hilo, HI 96720
Lee Richard
808-974-7351
Fax: 808-974-7736
E-mail: leericha@hawaii.edu
www.uhh.hawaii.edu

University of Hawaii
at Manoa
Department of Music

2411 Dole St.
Honolulu, HI 96822
Teresa Hong
808-956-7756
Fax: 808-956-9657
E-mail: teresah@hawaii.edu
www.hawaii.edu/uhmmusic

Along with the full range of traditional western
ensembles (bands, choirs, orchestra, opera,
jazz, chamber, contemporary), the University of
Hawaii is also noted for its studies in ethnomusicology, particularly in the music of Asia and the
Pacific Islands.

Windward
Community College
Music Program

45-720 Keaahala Rd.
Kaneohe, HI 96744
808-235-7400
www.wcc.hawaii.edu

IDAHO

Population: 1,429,096 (2005 Estimate)
Capital City: Boise
Bird: Mountain Bluebird
Motto: Esto perpetua - Let it be perpetual (It is forever)
Flower: Syringa
Tree: Western White Pine
Residents Called: Idahoans
Origin of Name: Idaho is a coined or invented word, and is not a derivation of an Indian phrase "E Dah Hoe (How)" supposedly meaning "gem of the mountains."
Area: 83,574 square miles (14th largest state)
Statehood: July 3, 1890 (43rd state)
Largest Cities: Boise, Nampa, Pocatello, Idaho Falls, Meridian, Coeur d'Alene, Twin Falls, Lewiston, Caldwell, Moscow
College Band Programs: College of Southern Idaho, North Idaho College

Albertson College
Department of Music

Box 36
2112 Cleveland Blvd.
Caldwell, ID 83605-4432
208-459-5275
Fax: 208-459-5885
www.albertson.edu

Boise State University
Department of Music

1910 University Dr.
Boise, ID 83725-1560
800-824-7017
www.boisestate.edu/music

The Department of Music at Boise State University has a rich tradition of musical excellence. In support of this excellent heritage, the Idaho State Board of Education has designated BSU as a primary emphasis area in the performing arts. The department has 23 full-time faculty/staff and 19 associate faculty noted for teaching and performing. BSU faculty and students have won state, regional, national and international music awards and competitions. One of the primary strengths of the department is equal opportunity in all areas of musical preparation, as evidenced by the degrees offered. College of Southern Idaho Department of Music 315 Falls Ave. P.O. Box 1238 Twin Falls, ID 83303 Micheal Green 208-733-9554 Fax: 208-736-3015 E-mail: mgreen@csi.edu www.csi.edu The Music Department offers a full range of courses to meet the needs of music students. Private instruction is available in voice and all wind, keyboard, and percussion instruments as well as violin and guitar. Students have the opportunity to perform on both solo recitals and in numerous college- and community-based ensembles. Among the performing groups available are the Chamber Choir, Madrigal Ensemble, Magic Valley Chorale, Wind Ensemble, Symphonic Band, Pep Band, Jazz Band, Jazz Combos, and Magic Valley Symphony.

Brigham Young University Idaho
Department of Music

SNO 215
Rexburg, ID 83460-1210
Gordon Westenskow
208-496-1036
Fax: 208-496-1220
E-mail: admissions@byui.edu
www.byui.edu

Idaho State University
Department of Music

P.O. Box 8099
Pocatello, ID 83209
208-282-3636
Fax: 208-282-4884
E-mail: music@isu.edu
www.isu.edu/music

Bachelor of Music, Music Education, Bachelor of Arts in Music, Master of Education in Music Education

Lewis and Clark State College
Music Program

500 8th Ave.
Lewiston, ID 83501
Bill Perconti
208-792-2334
Fax: 208-792-2324
www.lcsc.edu

Minors only in music.

North Idaho College
Department of Music

1000 West Garden Ave.
Coeur D Alene, ID 83814
208-769-3276
www.nic.edu

Northwest Nazarene College
Department of Music

623 Holly St.
Nampa, ID 83666-5897
877-NNU-4-YOU
Fax: 208-467-8645
www.nnu.edu

University of Idaho
Lionel Hampton
School of Music

P.O. Box 444015
Moscow, ID 83844-4015
Susan Hess
208-885-6231
Fax: 208-885-7254
E-mail: music@uidaho.edu
www.uidaho.edu/ls/music

Performance, Education, Composition, Business, Applied

The Lionel Hampton School of Music, so designated in 1987 in honor of the eminent American jazz musician, is an accredited institutional member of the National Association of Schools of Music.

American Conservatory
of Music

252 Wildwood Rd.
Hammond, ID 46324
219-931-6000
www.americanconservatory.edu

ILLINOIS

Population: 12,763,371 (2005 Estimate)
Capital City: Springfield
Bird: Cardinal
Motto: State Sovereignty, National Union
Flower: Purple Violet
Tree: White Oak
Residents Called: Illinoisans
Origin of Name: Algonquin Indian for "warriors."
Area: 57,918 square miles (25th largest state)
Statehood: December 3, 1818 (21st state)
Largest Cities: Chicago, Rockford, Aurora, Naperville, Peoria, Springfield, Joliet, Elgin, Waukegan, Cicero
College Band Programs: Eastern Illinois University, Northern Illinois University, Northwestern University, Southern Illinois University- Carbondale, Southern Illinois University-Edwardsville, University of Chicago, University of Illinois

Augustana College
Department of Music

639 38th St.
Rock Island, IL 61201-2296
Jon Hurty
309-794-7233
E-mail: muj-hurty@augustana.edu
www.augustana.edu

Several high quality ensembles are available for majors and non-majors. Students in this school learn by performing, listening, analyzing, and creating music. Emphasis is on the understanding of musical styles and techniques of all eras, including contemporary music. Musical studies balance the aesthetic and the practical, with ample opportunity for exploration and self-reliance

Aurora University
Department of Music

347 South Gladstone Ave.
Aurora, IL 60506-4892
Kelly Anderson
800-742-5281
E-mail: kanderso@aurora.edu
www.aurora.edu

Minor in Music

Black Hawk College
Department of Music

6600 34th Ave.
Moline, IL 61265-5899
Jeanne Tamisiea
309-796-5470
www.bhc.edu

Blackburn College
Department of Performing Arts

700 College Ave.
Carlinville, IL 62626
Elizabeth Zobel
217-854-3231 x4329
Fax: 217-854-3713
E-mail: performingarts@blackburn.edu
www.blackburn.edu

BA in Performing Arts with Concentration in Music or Theater

Blackburn College, founded in 1837 and affiliated with the Presbyterian Church (USA), provides a coeducational student body with a rigorous, distinctive, and affordable liberal arts education that prepares graduates to be responsible, productive citizens. The Blackburn community values critical and independent thinking, leadership development, respect for all individuals, and lifelong learning. The College fosters a sense of service, community, and moral responsibility through its unique student-managed work program, its collegial concept of shared governance, and its faculty/staff mentor relationship with students.

Bradley University
Department of Music

1501 West Bradley Ave.
Peoria, IL 61625
David Vroman
309-677-2595
Fax: 309-677-3871
E-mail: dvroman@bradley.edu
www.bradley.edu/cfa/music

Bachelor of Music (performance, music education, music composition, Bachelor of Science (music business), Bachelor of Arts (music business), Music Minor

Bradley University is committed to nurturing the multifaceted development of students to enable them to become leaders, innovators, and productive members of society. Our graduates are prepared for life and professions in a changing world and they are able to cross academic, geographic, and cultural boundaries. A Bradley education is characterized by small classes, active learning, mentoring by highly qualified faculty, challenging academic programs, opportunities for study abroad, and numerous co-curricular activities. The Department of Music at Bradley University consists of a growing student body comprised of undergraduates who share Bradley,s educational mission. These students, along with faculty and staff, have provided advancement in the classroom and the concert hall that has resulted in local, national, and international recognition. Graduates who earn a degree in music at Bradley find success in their chosen professional path.

Carl Sandburg College
Music Program

2400 Tom L. Wilson Blvd.
Galesburg, IL 61401
Tom Pahel
309-344-2518
Fax: 309-344-1395
www.sandburg.edu

Chicago College of Perform-ing Arts/Roosevelt University
The Music Conservatory

430 South Michigan Ave.
Chicago, IL 60605
Amy White
312-341-3789
Fax: 312-341-6358
E-mail: music@roosevelt.edu

Bachelor of Music in Music Performance (including Orchestral Studies), Music Education, Jazz Studies, and Composition. Master of Music in Music Performance, Orchestral Studies, Musicology, Music Theory, and Composition. Post-Masters Diploma Programs in Music Performance, including Orchestral Studies and Opera

The Music Conservatory at Roosevelt University's Chicago College of Performing Arts provides professional training and education within the context of a vibrant university in a world-class city. It is a place where musical genres from classical to jazz are valued, where the energies of one discipline spill over to enliven other artistic endeavors, where preparing to be a teacher is as important as preparing to be a performer or scholar, and where students come to enhance their unique talents and polish them to perfection. The Music Conservatory is well situated on the top floors of the historic landmark Auditorium Building, designed by world-famous architects Dankmar Adler and Louis Sullivan. The building includes the 3,800-seat Auditorium Theatre, renowned for its beauty and exquisite acoustics. Located on the corner of Michigan Avenue and Congress Parkway, this edifice is now an integral part of the educational corridor of more than 50,000 students enrolled in various institutions in the famous downtown Loop. Across the street are the Pritzker Music Pavilion of Millennium Park, the magnificent Buckingham Fountain, and the sparkling beauty of Lake Michigan. The state-of-the-art residence hall, the University Center of Chicago, is located just one block away on the corner of State Street and Congress Parkway. Within walking distance are many of the city,s major cultural institutions, including Symphony Center, home of the Chicago Symphony Orchestra; the Lyric Opera; the Jazz Showcase; the Goodman, Chicago, Oriental, and Cadillac theaters; the Art Institute; the Field Museum of Natural History; and the Magnificent Miles of shops and galleries. This ideal location provides opportunities for learning from some of the most accomplished musicians in the world, from principals in the Chicago Symphony to Grammy-nominated jazz artists.

Chicago School of Violin Making
Department of Music

3636 Oakton St.
Skokie, IL 60076
847-673-9545
Fax: 847-673-9546
E-mail: info@csvm.org
www.csvm.org

Chicago State University
Department of Music

9501 South King Dr.
Harold Washington Hall, Room 331
Chicago, IL 60628
773-995-2155
Fax: 773-995-3767
E-mail: music@csu.edu
www.csu.edu

Bachelor of Music, Music Education

College of DuPage
Department of Music

425 Fawell Blvd.
Glen Ellyn, IL 60137-6599
Lee Kesselman
630-942-2552
www.cod.edu

A.A. in Music, A.F.A. in Music

College of Lake County
Music Program

19351 West Washington St.
Grayslake, IL 60030-1198
Michael Flack
847-543-2566
Fax: 847-543-3040
E-mail: mflack@clcillinois.edu
www.clc.cc.il.us

Columbia College Chicago
Department of Music

600 South Michigan Ave.
Chicago, IL 60605
Murphy Monroe
312-344-7133
Fax: 312-344-8024
E-mail: mmonroe@colum.edu
www.colum.edu

Bachelor of Music Composition

Concordia University
Department of Music

7400 Augusta St.
River Forrest, IL 60305-1499
Steven Wente
708-771-8300
E-mail: www.cuchicago.edu
www.curf.edu

DePaul University
School of Music
School of Music

804 West Belden St.
Chicago, IL 60614
Ross Beacraft
773-325-7444
Fax: 773-325-7429
E-mail: rbeacraf@ depaul.edu
www. depaul.edu

Bachelors and Masters in Music and a Performers Certificate

In the heart of Chicago's Lincoln Park neighborhood, The DePaul program offers degrees in Music Performance Music Education, Jazz Studies, Composition, Performing Arts Management and Sound Recording Technology.There is a strong emphasis ensemble participation and all undergraduates must audition regardless of their intended major.

Dominican University
Music Discipline

7900 W. Division St.
River Forest, IL 60305
800-828-8475
Fax: 708-524-5990
E-mail: domadmis@dom.edu
www.dom.edu

Eastern Illinois University
Department of Music

600 Lincoln Ave.
Charleston, IL 61920
217-581-3010
E-mail: music@elu.edu
www.eiu.edu

Master of Arts in Music Education

Elgin Community College
Music Program

1700 Spartan Dr.
Elgin, IL 60123
847-697-1000
E-mail: jheilmann@elgin.edu
www.elgin.edu

Elmhurst College
Department of Music

190 Prospect Aveue
Elmhurst, IL 60126-3296
Kevin Olson
630-617-3524
Fax: 630-617-3738
E-mail: kevino@elmhurst.edu
www.elmhurst.edu

B.M. in Music Education, Jazz Studies, B.M. or
B.S. in Music Business, Bachelor of Arts in Music,
Minors in Music

Eureka College
Department of Music

300 East College Ave.
Eureka, IL 61530
Joseph Henry
309-467-6397
Fax: 309-467-6386
E-mail: Jdhenry@eureka.edu
www.eureka.edu

Greenville College
Department of Music

315 East College Ave.
Greenville, IL 62246-0159
800-345-4440
www.greenville.edu

Harold Washington College
Department of Humanities and Music

30 East Lake St.
Chicago, IL 60601
Matt Shevitz
312-553-5600
E-mail: mshevitz@ccc.edu
www.hwashington.ccc.edu

A.F.A. in Music Performance, A.F.A. in Music
Education, Basic Certificate in Music Technology,
Basic Certificate in Music Business

Harold Washington College is a two-year com-munity college located in the heart of downtown
Chicago. Our newly renovated facilities, including
our new recording studio, make us one of the
most progressive colleges in Chicago. In addition,
our faculty have all earned their masters and/or
doctorate degrees from such institutions as Indiana University, Northwestern University, McGill
University, and Duke University and are active
as performers and guest lecturers throughout
the country. Such prominent faculty members,
excellent facilities, and affordable tuition, make
Harold Washington College a great place for
anyone interested in music to study.

Illinois College
Department of Music

1101 West College Ave.
Jacksonville, IL 62650
217-245-3030
www.ic.edu

Illinois State University
School of Music

P.O. Box 5660
Normal, IL 61790-5660
Janet Tulley
309-438-7631
Fax: 309-438-5833
E-mail: music@ilstu.edu
www.music.ilstu.edu

Illinois Valley Community College
Department of Music

815 N. Orlando Smith Ave.
Oglesby, IL 61348
815-224-2720
Fax: 815-224-3033
www.ivcc.edu

Illinois Wesleyan University
School of Music

P.O. Box 2900
Bloomington, IL 61702-2900
Laura Dolan
309-556-3061
Fax: 309-556-3121
E-mail: ldolan@iwu.edu

B.M. in Performance, B.M. in Composition, B.M. in Educattion, and Bachelor of Arts degree in Music

For well over a century, the School of Music at Illinois Wesleyan University has enjoyed a tradition of excellence. A prestigious faculty, admirable facilities, and a substantial scholarship program ensure that the study, performance, and creation of music will shape the lives of current and future Illinois Wesleyan students. The School of Music provides students with the comprehensive knowledge and skills required for careers as performing musicians, educators, composers, and scholars. Selective admission policies guarantee an inspiring environment in which students learn from their peers as well as from the faculty. Limited enrollments in music courses allow for individual attention, which enhances faculty-student interaction. With regard to the study of an instrument, students receive private lessons primarily from a full-time faculty of artists/ teachers. Because IWU is an undergraduate institution with a decided emphasis on the arts, students at all levels are able to experience a wide range of performance opportunities seldom available at schools of comparable size. Indeed, Illinois Wesleyan University is one of the few schools in the country where young musicians con combine the breadth of an outstanding liberal arts education with the rigorous professional training of a fully-accredited school of music (the School of Music was accredited by the National Association of School of Music in 1930).

John A Logan College
Music Program

700 Logan College Rd.
Carterville, IL 62918
618-985-3741
Fax: 618-985-4433
www.jal.cc.il.us

John Wood Community College
Department of Music

1301 South 48th St.
Quincy, IL 62305
Gary Declue
217-641-4999
E-mail: DeClue@jwcc.edu
www.jwcc.edu

Joliet Junior College
Department of Fine Arts at Music

1215 Houbolt Rd.
Joliet, IL 60431-8938
Sue Malmberg
815-280-2287
Fax: 815-280-6739
E-mail: smalmber@jjc.edu
www.jjc.cc.il.us

Judson College
Department of Music

1151 North Stat St.
Elgin, IL 60123-1498
847-695-2500
www.judson-il.edu

Judson College has a separate fine arts building, an excellent recital hall with a new Steinway grand piano, music classrooms, practice rooms, faculty teaching studios, and a beautiful chapel with a Steinway concert grand and a large pipe organ. Majors offered include music education, music performance (piano, voice, and orchestral instruments) and music ministry. Music minors and music concentrations are also offered in those areas. Many music graduates hold significant music positions in churches, schools, and the music profession in general. Judson also offers symphonic band, orchestra, jazz ensemble, hand bell choir and chamber singers, all of which perform regularly. The choir tours extensively in the U.S.A. and abroad, including Europe and Brazil in the last four years, and the symphonic band, chamber singers, and hand bell choir also tour. Our 80-acre campus is located in Elgin, Ill. Housing is available. Students find part-time, off-campus employment easily accessible because of its location. Judson is located 30 minutes from O'Hare Airport and one hour from downtown Chicago, the Lyric Opera, the Chicago Symphony Orchestra, the Ravinia Festival, and other performing arts organizations.

Kishwaukee College
Music Program

21193 Malta Rd.
Malta, IL 60150
815-825-2086
Fax: 815-825-2072
E-mail: www.kishwaukeecollege.edu
www.kish.cc.il.us

Knox College
Department of Music

2 East South St.
Galesburg, IL 61401-4999
309-341-7000
E-mail: admissions@knox.edu
www.knox.edu

Lake Forest College
Department of Music

555 North Sheridan Rd.
Lake Forest, IL 60045
Don Meyer
847-735-5171
E-mail: meyer@lakeforest.edu
www.lfc.edu

Lewis and Clark Community College
Department of Music

5800 Godfrey Rd.
Godfrey, IL 62035-2466
800-642-1794
Fax: 618-467-3208
www.lc.cc.il.us

Lewis University
Department of Music

1 University Pkwy.
Romeoville, IL 60446
815-836-5619
www.lewisu.edu

Lincoln Christian College
Department of Music

100 Campus View Dr.
Lincoln, IL 62656
217-732-3168
Fax: 217-732-4078
E-mail: coladmis@lccs.edu
www.lccs.edu

Lincoln College
Music Program

300 Keokuk St.
Lincoln, IL 62656
217-732-3155
www.llcc.cc.il.us

Lincoln Land Community College
Music Program

5250 Shepherd Rd.
Box 19256
Springfield, IL 62794-9256
800-727-4161

Loyola University Chicago
Division of Arts and Sciences

1020 West Sheridan Rd.
Room 713
Chicago, IL 60626
773-508-8327
Fax: 773-508-8748
E-mail: music-info@luc.edu
www.luc.edu

MacMurray College
Department of Music

447 East College Ave.
Jacksonville, IL 62650
217-479-7091
E-mail: music.dept@mac.edu
www.mac.edu

Manmouth College
Department of Music

700 East Broadway
Manmouth, IL 61462
309-457-2311
Fax: 309-457-2310
E-mail: info@monm.edu
www.monm.edu

McKendree College
Department of Music

701 College Rd.
Lebanon, IL 62254
Adrianne Honnold
618-537-6554
Fax: 618-537-6259
E-mail: alhonnold@mckendree.edu
www.mckendree.edu

Music Performance, Music Performance-Jazz
Emphasis, Music Education, Music Business,
Music History, Church Music, Music Minor, Music
Minor-Elementary Education

McKendree College is ranked among the top 12
percent of "Comprehensive Colleges Bachelor's"
in the nation by *U.S.News & World Report's
America's Best Colleges 2006*. McKendree
College also is the only private college in Illinois
to be named one of America's 100 Best College
Buys®. Engaged students, great teaching, a
vibrant community and successful outcomes also
have earned McKendree College the designation
"College of Distinction." The McKendree College
Music Department offers eight programs of study,
including six Music majors and two Music minors. Scholarships are available to Music majors,
minors, and Marching Bearcat Band members,
including Color Guard and Dance Team. The

Music Education degree was designed by music
educators for music educators. McKendree offers
plenty of performance opportunities such as the
Marching Bearcat Band, Percussion Ensemble,
and Cantori. Students receive individual attention
from our highly experienced and talented faculty
and staff in the brand new Hettenhausen Center
for the Arts, a state-of-the-art rehearsal and
performance venue.

Milliken University
School of Music

1184 West Main St.
Decatur, IL 62522
Nancy Freeman
217-424-6300
E-mail: admission@mail.milikin.edu
www.millikin.edu

Bachelor of Arts Music, B.M. Music Business,
Commercial Music, Music Performance

Moody Bible Institute
Department of Sacred Music

820 North La Salle Blvd.
Chicago, IL 60610
312-329-4080
www.moody.edu

Moraine Valley Community College
Department of Fine Arts

9000 West College Pkwy.
Palos Hills, IL 60465
Nick Thomas
708-974-5755
E-mail: thomasn@morainevalley.edu
www.morainevalley.edu

Morton College
Department of Music

3801 South Central Ave.
Cicero, IL 60804

708-656-8000
www.morton.edu

National-Louis University
Department of Music

Evanston, IL 60201
888-658-8632
www.nl.edu

North Central College
Department of Music

30 North Braiard St.
Naperville, IL 60540
Melisa Barber
630-637-5100
Fax: 630-637-5819
E-mail: mkbarber@noctrl.edu
www.noctrl.edu

B.M. (Performance), B.M. (Music in Worship),
B.M.E. (K-12), B.A., M.M. (Vocal Performance)

A park-like setting in the City of Chicago, with
performance opportunities both on- and off-campus. Students receive personal attention from
teachers who are both high quality educators as
well as performers.

North Park University
School of Music

3225 West Foster Ave.
Chicago, IL 60631
Joe Lill
773-244-5630
Fax: 773-244-5230
E-mail: jlill@northpark.edu
www.northpark.edu

Northeastern Illinois University
Department of Music

5500 North St. Louis Ave.
Chicago, IL 60625
R. Shayne Cofer

773-442-5900
Fax: 773-442-5910
E-mail: music@neiu.edu

Minor in Music Education

Northern Illinois University
School of Music

550 Lucinda Ave.
DeKalb, IL 60115
Lynn Slater
815-753-1546
Fax: 815-753-1759
E-mail: lslater@niu.edu
www.niu.edu/music

Bachelor of Arts, B.M., M.M., Performer's Cert.

Northwestern University
School of Music

711 Elgin Rd.
Evanston, IL 60208
Cory Wikan
847-491-3141
Fax: 847-467-7440
E-mail: wikan@northwestern.edu
www.music.northwestern.edu

Located on the shores of Lake Michigan in
Evanston, Illinois, the Northwestern University School of music offers a unique musical
education based on tradition, innovation and
excellence. The university's 240-acre campus lies
just 12 miles north of downtown Chicago and its
rich cultural opportunities provide faculty and
students with a vibrant educational setting that
blends the best of the urban with the suburban. Established in 1895 as an integral and
inseparable part of Northwestern University, the
school combines the privileges and resources of
an excellent private research university with a
nationally ranked music program of conservatory
intensity. As one of the oldest degree-granting
music schools in the United States, it has been
shaped by those dedicated to honoring tradition
while pursuing innovation, reflecting an ever-evolving music aesthetic. Its distinguished faculty
of musician-scholars, the small and highly quali-

fied student body and the extraordinary breadth of academic programs have brought distinction to the school for more than 100 years, building a foundation for developing the informed musicians, productive scholars and inspired teachers of the 21st century.

Olivet Nazarene University
Department of Music

One University Ave.
Bourbonnais, IL 60914-2345
Tiffany Snyder
815-939-5110
Fax: 815-939-5112
E-mail: tsnyder@olivet.edu
www.olivet.edu/departments/finearts

B.S. with a Concentration in Church Music, B.S. with a Concentration in Music Education Vocal Instrumental, B.S. with a Concentration in Music Performance, B.S. with a Concentration in Music Composition/Theory, B.A. with a General Concentration in Music, Minor in Music

Parkland College
Department of Music

2400 West Bradley Ave.
Champaign, IL 61821
800-346-8089
E-mail: skumler@parkland.edu
www.parkland.edu

Quincy University
Music Program

1800 College Ave.
Quincy, IL 62301
Sara Alstat
618-437-5321 x1817
E-mail: alstats@rlc.edu
www.quincy.edu

Rend Lake College
Department of Liberal Arts

468 North Ken Gray Pkwy.
Ina, IL 62846

618-437-5321
Fax: 618-437-5677
E-mail: wilkerson@rlc.cc.il.us
www.rlc.cc.il.us

Rock Valley College
Department of Music

3301 North Mulford Rd.
Rockford, IL 61114
815-921-3340
Fax: 815-921-3369
www.rvc.cc.il.us

Roosevelt University
Music Conservatory

430 South Michigan Ave.
Chicago, IL 60605
Amy White
312-341-3789
Fax: 312-341-6358
E-mail: music@roosevelt.edu

Bachelor of Music in Music Performance (including Orchestral Studies), Music Education, Jazz Studies, and Composition. Master of Music in Music Performance, Orchestral Studies, Musicology, Music Theory, and Composition. Post-masters Diploma Programs in Music Performance, including Orchestral Studies and Opera

Rosary College
Dominican University
Department of Music

7900 West Division St.
River Forest, IL 60305
Kevin Nutley
708-524-6918
www.domin.dom.edu

Saulk Valley
Community College
Department of Fine Arts

173 Illinois Route 2
Dixon, IL 61021

815-288-5511
Fax: 815-288-1880
E-mail: skyhawk@svcc.edu
www.svcc.edu

Sherwood Conservatory of Music

1312 South Michigan Ave.
Chicago, IL 60605
312-427-6267
Fax: 312-427-6677
E-mail: info@sherwoodmusic.org
www.sherwoodmusic.org

South Suburban College
Department of Music

15800 South State St.
South Holland, IL 60473
Al Jackson
708-596-2000
www.ssc.cc.il.us

Southern Illinois University at Carbondale
School of Music

1000 South Normal Ave.
Altgeld Hall
Carbondale, IL 62901-4302
Jeanine Wagner
618-536-8742
Fax: 618-453-5808
E-mail: jwagner@siu.edu
www.siu.edu/~music

Bachelor of Music- Performance, Education, Composition and Theory Specializations; Bachelor of Arts, Music Business-- Music Theater, Open Studies Specializations

Located in beautiful Southern Illinois, SIUC School of Music has completed our move back into Altgeld Hall, our historic home that recently underwent an $11 million renovation. We now have a state of the art facility for the study of music. The School of Music is a major contributor of the cultural community of Southern Illinois.

Approximately 150 concerts and recitals are given on-campus every year in performance facilities ranging from 1,200 seats to 150 seats. Students perform as soloists with major ensembles and are given the opportunity to experience conducting and teaching first hand. Faculty members share their national and international backgrounds with graduates and undergraduates alike, often performing alongside their students. Alumni of SIUC School of Music enjoy success in education, performance and music industry venues worldwide.

Southwestern Illinois College
Department of Music

2500 Carlyle Ave.
Belleville, IL 62221
Jerry Bolen
618-235-2700
Fax: 618-235-1578
E-mail: bolen@apci.net
www.southwestern.cc.il.us

Springfield College at Illinois
Department of Music

1500 North 5th
Springfield, IL 62702
Terri Hinrichs
217-525-1420 x287
E-mail: thinrichs@sci.edu
www.sci.edu

St. Xavier University
Department of Music

3700 West 103rd St.
Chicago, IL 60655
Lara Regan
773-298-3050
Fax: 773-298-3076
E-mail: admissions@sxu.edu
www.sxu.edu

Trinity Christian College
Department of Music

6601 West College Dr.
Palos Heights, IL 60463
708-239-4879
www.trnty.edu

Trinity International University
Department of Music

2065 Half Day Rd.
Deerfield, IL 60015
800-822-3225
Fax: 847-317-8097
E-mail: tcadmissions@tiu.edu
www.tiu.edu

Triton College
Department of Music

2000 North 5th Ave.
River Grove, IL 60171
708-456-0300
www.triton.cc.il.us

University of Chicago
Department of Music

1010 East 59th St.
Chicago, IL 60637
773-702-8484
Fax: 773-753-0558
E-mail: musicdept@uchicago.edu

University of Illinois
Department of Music

901 West Garden St.
Urbana, IL 61801
217-333-0302
www.uiuc.edu

University of Illinois at Chicago
Department of Performing Arts

1040 West Harrison St. MC 255
Chicago, IL 60607
312-996-2977
Fax: 312-996-0954
www.uic.edu/depts/adpa

This is a smaller program with a low teacher-to-student ratio in an urban setting. A traditional program in theory, history and ear-training or performance track is offered. Private teachers feature outstanding Chicago artist-performers. Ensembles include concert band, jazz ensembles, three choirs, chamber music.

University of Illinois at Urbana
School of Music

1114 West Nevada
Urbana, IL 61801
217-244-7899
Fax: 217-244-4585
E-mail: musicadmissions@uiuc.edu

University of St. Francis
Department of Music

500 Wilcox St. Joliet
Joliet, IL 60435
800-735-7500
www.stfrancis.edu

B.A. in Music

VanderCook College of Music
Department of Music

3140 South Federal St.
Chicago, IL 60616
Amy Lenting
312-335-6288
Fax: 312-255-5211
E-mail: alenting@vandercook.edu
www.vandercook.edu

Western Illinois University
Department of Music

1 University Cir.
Macomb, IL 61455-1390
Yvonne Oliver
309-298-1087
Fax: 309-298-1968
E-mail: YL-Oliver@wiu.edu
www.wiu.edu/music

Wheaton College
Conservatory of Music

501 College Ave.
Wheaton, IL 60187
Debbie Rogers
800-325-8718
Fax: 630-752-5341
E-mail: music@wheaton.edu
www.wheaton.edu/Conservatory

Bachelor of Music Education

William Rainey Harper College
Department of Music

1200 West Algonquin Rd.
Palatine, IL 60067
Gregory Clemons
847-925-6569
E-mail: gclemons@harpercollege.edu
www.harpercollege.edu

Population: 6,271,973 (2005 Estimate)
Capital City: Indianapolis
Bird: Cardinal
Motto: The Crossroads of America
Flower: Peony
Tree: Tulip tree
Residents Called: Hoosiers
Origin of Name: "Land of the Indians"
Area: 36,420 square miles (38th state)
Statehood: December 11,1816 (19th state)
Largest Cities: Indianapolis, Fort Wayne, Evansville, South Bend, Gary, Hammond, Bloomington, Muncie, Anderson, Terre Haute
College Band Programs: Ball State University, Indiana University, Purdue University, University of Notre Dame

INDIANA

Ancilla College
Division of Humanities

P.O. Box 1
Donaldson, IN 46513
Charles LaFrane
574-936-8898 x337
E-mail: charles.lafrance@ancilla.edu
www.ancilla.edu

Since its beginning in 1917, music has played a significant role in the life of Anderson University. That tradition continues today. The music department at A.U. is thriving with vibrant students, accomplished faculty, high caliber performances, challenging classes, and satisfying musical experiences. The music department offers four degree programs: music performance, music education, music business and church music. The music performance degree program prepares students with the basic knowledge and skills needed to pursue a career in instrumental or vocal performance. The music education degree program prepares students for a career in teaching instrumental and choral music in elementary and secondary schools. The music business degree program prepares students for a career in one of the many facets of the music industry. The church music degree program prepares students to lead music ministries and assist the church in worship through music. Audition information: all students who want to major in music at Anderson University must complete an audition before registering for music classes. For audition dates, requirements and forms, please contact the music department office at (800) 428-6414, ext. 4450. The department of music at Anderson University is an accredited institutional member of the National Association of Schools of Music.

Anderson University
School of Music

1100 East 5th St.
Anderson, IN 46012
Shands Stolzfus
800-964-2627
E-mail: admissions@ambs.edu
www.anderson.edu

Associated Mennonite Biblical Seminary
Department of Church and Ministry

3003 Benham Ave.
Elkhart, IN 46517-1999
Regina
219-295-3726
Fax: 219-295-0092
E-mail: rslough@ambs.edu
www.ambs.edu

Ball State University
School of Music

Muncie, IN 47306
John Scheib
765-285-5402
Fax: 765-285-5401
E-mail: music@bsu.edu
www.bsu.edu/cfa

Bethel College
Department of Fine Arts

1001 West McKinley Ave.
Mishawaka, IN 46545
Randy Beachy
574-257-3393
Fax: 574-257-2646
E-mail: admissions@bethelcollege.edu
www.bethelcollege.edu

Music Ed, Performance, Church Music

A solid Christian atmosphere, an excellent resident faculty, and a growing campus make Bethel College an exciting setting for the study of music. With 65 major fields of study, six master's degree programs, full accreditation by North Central Association and NCATE, Bethel College is an excellent choice for your college education. If you are interested in pursuing a career in music, Bethel offers Majors in Music Education (instrumental, vocal and combined concentrations), Music Performance and Church Music. With almost 2,000 students, Bethel is large enough to offer many performance opportunities, yet small enough to provide students with personalized attention and experiences.

Butler University
Jordan College of Fine Arts

4600 Sunset Blvd.
Indianapolis, IN 46208
Kathy Lang
317-940-9656
Fax: 317-940-9658
E-mail: dlang@butler.edu
www.butler.edu

De Pauw University
School of Music

P.O. Box 37
Greencastle, IN 46135-0037
765-658-4380
Fax: 765-658-4042
www.depauw.edu

Earlham College
Department of Music

801 National Rd. West
Richmond, IN 47374-4095
Connie Haselby
765-983-1410
E-mail: haselco@earlham.edu
www.earlham.edu

Goshen College
Department of Music

1700 South Main St.
Goshen, IN 46526
Lynn Jackson
574-535-7535
Fax: 574-535-7609
E-mail: admission@goshen.edu
www.goshen.edu

Grace College
Department of Music

200 Seminary Dr.
Winona Lake, IN 46590
Kim Kraft
800-54GRACE x6351
E-mail: music@grace.edu
www.grace.edu

Hanover College
Department of Music

P.O. Box 108
Hanover, IN 47243
Kimm Hollis
812-866-7342
E-mail: hollis@hanover.edu
www.hanover.edu

Central to this program is a faculty of 150 teachers and scholars and a select student body. The quality of the School of Music faculty has four times led the deans and faculty members of the country's music schools to rank IU number one in the nation. More than 1,600 students from throughout the United States and from 35 foreign countries attend the School of Music during the school year. The facilities of the School of Music include six buildings housing more than 100 offices and studios, 200 practice rooms, choral and instrumental rehearsal rooms, three recital halls, and a music library with more than 380,000 books, scores, microfilms, and periodicals and nearly 160,000 recordings. The School of Music is highlighted by the Musical Arts Center, a complex featuring an acoustically-refined auditorium and a stage with technical capabilities unequaled by any other U.S. university facility.

Huntington College
Department of Music

2303 College Ave.
Huntington, IN 46750
260-356-6000
www.huntington.edu/music

Indiana University at Bloomington
School of Music

1201 East Third St.
Merrill Hall 003
Bloomington, IN 47405-2200
812-855-1583
www.music.indiana.edu

Indiana University at Purdue
School of Music

IT Building, Room 352
525 North Blackford
Indianapolis, IN 46202
317-274-4000
E-mail: nmthomps@iupui.edu
www.iupui.edu

Indiana University at South Bend
Department of Music

Ernestine M. Raclin School of the Arts
Northside Hall 101
South Bend, IN 46634
574-520-4134
www.iusb.edu

Indiana University at Southeast
Department of Music

4201 Grant Line Rd.
New Albany, IN 47150
812-941-2655
Fax: 812-941-2660
E-mail: semusic@ius.edu
www.ius.edu/music

Bachelor of Arts in Music

Indiana Wesleyan University
Division of Music

4201 South Washington St.
Marion, IN 46953

Melody Cabe
765-677-2710
Fax: 765-677-4900
E-mail: melody.cabe@indwes.edu
www.indwes.edu

Manchester College
Department of Music

604 East College Ave.
North Manchester, IN 46962
Debora DeWitt
219-982-5292
E-mail: dedewiit@manchester.edu
www.manchester.edu

Marian College
Department of Performance Arts

3200 Cold Spring Rd.
Indianapolis, IN 46222
317-955-6108
www.marian.edu

Major in Music Performance, B.A. (Vocal or Instrumental), Major in Music Education, B.A. (Choral or Instrumental), Minor in Music Associate in Arts Degree in Music

Oakland City University
Department of Music

138 North Lucretia St.
Oakland City, IN 47660-1038
800-737-5125
www.oak.edu

St. Joseph's College
Department of Music

US Hwy. 231
P.O. Box 231
Rensselaer, IN 47978
800-447-8782
E-mail: admissions@saintjoe.edu
www.saintjoe.edu

INDIANA

St. Mary of the Woods College
Department of Music

St. Mary of the Woods, IN 47876
812-535-5151
E-mail: smwc@smwc.edu
www.smwc.edu

St. Mary's College
Department of Music

313 Moreau Center for the Arts
Notre Dame, IN 46556-5001
Nancy Menk
574-284-4632
Fax: 574-284-4884
E-mail: nmenk@saintmarys.edu
www.saintmarys.edu/~music

Programs: B.M. in Vocal or Piano Performance, B.M. in Music Education, B.A. in Music, Minor in Music

St. Mary's College, the nation's premier Catholic women's college, was founded over 150 years ago by the Sisters of the Holy Cross. Saint Mary's is a four-year institution offering five bachelor's degrees and more than 30 major areas of study. Saint Mary's legacy of leadership and vision has made it a recognized force in higher education. *"U.S. News & World Report"* ranks Saint Mary,s College first among the nation's 110 "Best Midwest Comprehensive Colleges" offering bachelor,s degrees. Saint Mary's has earned a number one ranking eleven of the last twelve years, and has ranked among the top ten in its category of more than 100 institutions since the survey began in 1985. Since its founding, the college has remained steadfast to its mission to maintain exceptional standards in promoting academic achievement, religious and ethical values, social responsibility and personal development. A co-exchange program with the nearby University of Notre Dame provides students with additional academic, social, and cultural opportunities. The department od music has an energetic faculty of artists that works closely together, providing studies leading to the B.M. in Vocal or Piano Performance and Music Education, and the B.A. There are extensive on-campus performance activities

for the music major as well as the general student. Housed in the Moreau Center for the Arts, the department's facilities include computer and piano labs, excellent practice facilities, the Little Theatre recital hall and the 1,300-seat O'Laughlin Auditorium. The Moreau Center also serves as home to performances of the South Bend Chamber Singers and the chambe ensemble Claricello. Saint Mary's College is an accredited institutional member of the National Association of Schools of Music. For more information, please visit our web page at http://www.saintmarys.edu/~music.

Taylor University at Upland
Department of Music

236 West Reade Ave.
Upland, IN 46989
Steve Mortland
800-882-3456
Fax: 765-998-4810
E-mail: stmortlan@taylor.edu
www.tayloru.edu

Performance, Education, Composition

Taylor University is a Christ Centered educational institution committed to advancing lifelong learning. the music department is accredited by NASM and has 10 performing ensembles including Wind Ensemble, Symphony Orchestra, Jazz Ensemble, Concert Chorale, Chamber Choir, Women's Chorus and a full production opera and musical theatre program. Scholarships are available and audtions must be completed by March 1 each year for scholarship consideration.

The University of Indianapolis
1400 East Hanna Ave.

Indianapolis, IN 46227
317-788-3255
Fax: 317-788-6105
E-mail: music.uindy.edu
www.uindy.edu

Bachelor of Music in Music Education, Bachelor of Music in Music Performance, Bachelor of Science or Bachelor of Arts in Music Bachelor of Science in Music, Minor in Music , Minor in Music Technology and Recording, Minor in Music Teaching.

University of Evansville
Department of Music

1800 Lincoln Ave.
Evansville, IN 47722
Eva Kay
812-488-2754
Fax: 812-488-2101
E-mail: music@evansville.edu

Music Therapy, Music Education, Music Performance, Music Management, Bachelor of Arts in Music

The University of Evansville is a fully accredited, independent, liberal arts and sciences university. The Department of Music is fully accredited by the National Association of Schools of Music. The department has 120 music majors, 18 full-time faculty members and 12 part-time faculty members. The ensembles include five bands, four choirs, an orchestra and many chamber ensembles. The Department of Music has high standards of excellence in the study and performance of music. Job placement within each degree program is highly successful.

University of Indianapolis
Department of Music

1400 E. Hanna Ave.
Indianapolis, IN 46227
Gavyn Ryan
317-788-3216
E-mail: gryan@uindy.edu

University of Notre Dame
Department of Music

105 Crowley Hall of Music
Notre Dame, IN 46556
Office of Admissions
574-631-6211
Fax: 574-631-4539
E-mail: music@nd.edu
www.nd.edu/~music

3 degree programs offered

Students may study music in a variety of ways, according to their interests and professional goals. All music majors study a core curriculum designed to provide a firm musical foundation in Music History and Theory, Performance, or Music and Culture.

Valparaiso University
Department of Music

VU Center for the Arts
Valparaiso, IN 46383
Katharine Wehling
219-464-5454
Fax: 219-464-5244
www.valpo.edu/music

Valparaiso's department of music, fully accredited by the National Association of Schools of Music, offers liberal and professional degree programs in music, balancing practical training and experiences in music with academic foundations in music and general studies. It occupies the VU Center for the Arts, dedicated in 1995, which functions as a working laboratory for performance, production, presentation, and management of arts events, as well as for academic study. Its dedicated faculty of artist-teachers are committed to helping students develop as musicians and as people. Valparaiso University is a private university associated with the Lutheran church, with 3,500 students drawn from across the U.S. and many foreign countries. Approximately 150 students major in music, and hundreds more take part in music ensembles, studio lessons, and elective studies.

Vincennes University
Department of Music

1002 North 1st St.
Vinvennes, IN 47591
Scott Mercer
812-888-5460
Fax: 812-888-5531
E-mail: smercer@vinu.edu
www.vinu.edu

Wabash College
Department of Music

P.O. Box 352
Crawfordsville, IN 47933
765-361-6100
www.wabash.edu/depart/music

The fine arts have played a large part in the lives of Wabash College students, faculty, and community members since 1841, and they continue to be central to the liberal arts curriculum and to the college community. The Fine Arts Center is home to the department of music, as well as the theater, art and speech departments. The building includes a concert hall, a lecture hall suitable for recitals and multi-media presentations, practice rooms, classrooms, faculty studios, and electronic music studios, a suite of three studios that support a variety of educational and research activities. A wide variety of musical instruments are available for student use, including a Boesendorfer concert piano, grand pianos for practicing, a Dowd harpsichord, a pipe organ (in the college chapel), and wind, brass, string and percussion instruments. The Wabash Music Department has a number of ensembles, including a glee club, orchestra, brass ensemble, brass quintet, jazz big band, jazz improvisation combo, string quartet, and the Wamidan World Music Ensemble. The music department offers a variety of courses in music history, theory, analysis, composition, electronic music, world music and special topics courses in American music, music and technology, and instrument design.

Population: 2,966,334 (2005 Estimate)
Capital City: Des Moines
Bird: Eastern Goldfinch
Motto: Our liberties we prize and our rights we will maintain
Flower: Wild Prairie Rose
Tree: Oak
Residents Called: Iowans
Origin of Name: The word "Iowa" comes from the American Indian tribe of the same name.
Area: 56,276 square miles (26th largest state)
Statehood: December 28, 1846 (29th state)
Largest Cities: Des Moines, Cedar Rapids, Davenport, Sioux City, Waterloo, Iowa City, Council Bluffs, Dubuque, Ames, Cedar Falls
College Band Programs: Iowa State University, University of Iowa

Ashford University
Department of Music

400 North Bluff Blvd.
Clinton, IA 52732
866-711-1700
www.ashford.edu

Minor in Music

Briar Cliff College
Department of Music

3303 Rebecca St.
Sioux City, IA 51104
800-662-3303
E-mail: admissions@briarcliff.edu
www.briarcliff.edu

Buena Vista University
Department of Music

610 West Fourth St.
Storm Lake, IA 50588
Jerry Bertrand
712-749-2176
Fax: 712-749-2037
E-mail: Betrand@bvu.edu
www.bvu.edu

Buena Vista University
Department of Music

Storm Lake, IA 50588
Jerry Bertrand
712-749-2176
E-mail: bertrand@bvu.edu
www.bvu.edu

Central College
Department of Music

812 University
Pella, IA 50219
877-462-3687
E-mail: admission@central.edu
www.central.edu

Clarke College
Department of Music

1500 Clarke Dr.
Dubuque, IA 52001
James Sullivan
563-588-6359
E-mail: James.sullivan@clarke.edu
www.clarke.edu

Coe College
Department of Music

1220 First Ave. NE
Cedar Rapids, IA 52402
Sharon Kay Stang
800-CALL-COE
www.coe.edu

B.M.

Cornell College
Music Department

600 First St. West
Mount Vernon, IA 52314
Donald Chamberlain
319-895-4356
E-mail: music@cornellcollege.edu
www.cornellcollege.edu

Bachelor of Arts with a major in music

Dort College
Department of Music

498 4th Ave. NE
Sioux Center, IA 51250-1606
712-722-6000
E-mail: admissions@dordt.edu
www.dordt.edu

Drake University
Department of Music

2507 University Ave.
Des Moines, IA 50311
Clarence Padilla

800-44-Drake
E-mail: Clarence.Padilla@drake.edu
www.drake.edu

Graceland University
Department of Music

One University Ave.
Lamoni, IA 50140
Brian Shantz
614-784-5276
Fax: 641-784-5487
E-mail: hart@graceland.edu
www.graceland.edu

Grandview College
Department of Music

1200 Grandview Ave.
Des Moines, IA 50316
Admissions Office
515-263-2810
E-mail: admissions@gvc.edu
www.gvc.edu

Bachelor's Degrees in Music and Music Education

A four-year liberal arts college located in Des
Moines, Iowa, Grand View hosts 1,750 students
in 35 different academic programs. The College
is committed to a rich academic and residential
life and to preparing students for careers through
hands-on learning experiences.

Grinnell College
Department of Music

Grinnell, IA 50112
John Rommereim
641-269-3068
Fax: 641-269-4420
E-mail: romm@grinnell.edu
www.grinnell.edu/music

Indian Hills
Community College
Department of Music

525 Grandview Ave.

Ottumwa, IA 52501
Don Darland
800-726-2585 x5153
www.ihcc.cc.ia.us

Iowa State University
Department of Music

Iowa State University
Ames, IA 50011-2180
Tammy Krock
515-294-3831
Fax: 515-294-6409
E-mail: takrock@iastate.edu
www.music.iastate.edu

Iowa Wesleyan College
Department of Music

601 North Main St.
Mount Pleasant, IA 52641
David Johnson
319-385-6351
E-mail: djohnson5@iwc.edu
www.iwc.edu

BA Music Ed., BA Music

Iowa Wesleyan College is a Methodist affiliated
4-year private college in southeast Iowa offering 8
choral and instrumental performing ensembles
with undergraduate degrees in music education
and music.

Kirkwood
Community College
Department of Arts
and Humanities

6301 Kirkwood Blvd. SW
Cedar Rapids, IA 52404
319-398-4913
E-mail: jreiff@kirkwood.edu
www.kirkwood.cc.ia.us

Loras College
Department of Music

1450 Alta Vista

Dubuque, IA 52001
800-245-6727
Fax: 563-588-7119
E-mail: admissions@loras.edu
www.loras.edu

Luther College
Department of Music

700 College Dr.
Decorah, IA 52101-1045
800-458-8437
Fax: 563-387-2158
E-mail: www@luther.edu
www.luther.edu

Morningside College
Department of Music

1501 Morningside Ave.
Sioux City, IA 51106
800-831-0806 x5210
Fax: 712-274-5280
E-mail: bouma@morningside.edu

Bachelor or Music, Bachelor of Music Education

Mount Mercy College
Department of Music

1330 Elmhurst Dr. NE
Cedar Rapids, IA 52402
Daniel Kleinknecht
800-248-4504
E-mail: admission@mtmercy.edu
www.mtmercy.edu

Mount St. Clare College
Department of Music

400 North Bluff Blvd.
Clinton, IA 52732
Robert Engelson
800-242-4153

North Iowa Area Community College
Department of Music

500 College Dr.
Mason City, IA 50401
641-423-1264
www.niacc.cc.ia.us

Northwestern College
Department of Music

101 7th St. SW
Orange City, IA 51041
Mark Bloemendaal
800-747-4757
Fax: 712-707-7164
E-mail: admissions@nwciowa.edu
www.nwciowa.edu

Simpson College
Department of Music

701 North C St.
Indianola, IA 50125
Maria DiPalma
800-362-2454
Fax: 515-961-1498
E-mail: dipalma@simpson.edu
www.simpson.edu

Southwestern Community College
School for Music Vocation

1501 West Townline St.
Creston, IA 50801
Phil Mattson
641-782-7081
www.swcciowa.edu

St. Ambrose University
Department of Music

518 West Locust St.
Davenport, IA 52803
Joan Trapp
563-333-6148
E-mail: TrappJoanM@sau.edu
www.sau.edu/music

University of Dubuque
Department of Music

2000 University Ave.
Dubuque, IA 52001
Music Department
800-722-5583
Fax: 563-589-3690
E-mail: admssns@dbq.edu
www.dbq.edu

University of Iowa
School of Music

1006 Voxman Music Bldg
Iowa City, IA 52242
Pauline Wieland
319-335-1603
E-mail: music-admissions@uiowa.edu
www.uiowa.edu/~music

University of Northern Iowa
School of Music

131 Russell Hall
Cedar Falls, IA 50614
Alan Schmitz
319-273-2024
Fax: 319-273-7320
E-mail: Alan.Schmitz@uni.edu
www.uni.edu/music/web

BA, BM (Perf., Mus. Ed., Comp.)

State supported institution offering Bachelors and Masters degrees in Music. Member of NASM.

Upper Iowa University
Division of Liberal Arts

605 Washington St.
Fayette, IA 52142
800-553-4150
www.uiu.edu

Vennard College
Department of Music

P.O. Box 29
University Park, IA 52595
800-686-8391
E-mail: admiss@vennard.edu
www.vennard.edu

Waldorf College
Department of Music

106 South 6th St.
Forrest City, IA 50436
641-585-8177
E-mail: music@waldorf.edu
www.waldorf.edu

Wartburg College
Department of Music

100 Wartburg Blvd.
Waverly, IA 50677
Karen Black
319-352-8275
E-mail: www.wartburg.edu
www.wartburg.edu

Western Iowa Tech Community College
Department of Music

4647 Stone Ave.
Sioux City, IA 51106
Ralph Swain
712-274-8733 x1274
E-mail: swainr@witcc.edu
www.witcc.com

William Penn College
Department of Fine Arts

201 Trueblood Ave.
Oskaloosa, IA 52577
800-779-7366
www.wmpenn.edu

Population: 2,744,687 (2005 Estimate)
Capital City: Topeka
Bird: Western Meadowlark
Motto: Ad astra per aspera – To the stars through difficulties
Flower: Sunflower
Tree: Cottonwood
Residents Called: Kansans
Origin of Name: From the Sioux Indian for "south wind people."
Area: 82,282 square miles (15th largest state)
Statehood: January 29, 1861 (34th state)
Largest Cities: Wichita, Overland Park, Kansas City, Topeka, Olathe, Lawrence, Shawnee, Salina, Manhattan, Hutchinson
College Band Programs: Kansas State University, University of Kansas

Allen County Community College
Department of Music

1801 North Cottonwood St.
Iola, KS 66749
620-365-5116
www.allen.cc.ks.us

Baker University
Department of Music

P.O. Box 65
Baldwin City, KS 66006-0065
785-594-6451
www.bakeru.edu

Barclay College
Department of Music

607 North Kingman
Haviland, KS 67059
800-862-0226
Fax: 620-862-5242
www.barclaycollege.edu

Benedictine College
Department of Music

1020 North 2nd St.
Atchison, KS 66002
Ruth E. Krusemark
913-367-5340
www.benedictine.edu

The music department at Benedictine College is a comprehensive music program accredited by the National Association of Schools of Music within the context of the Benedictine College Mission: liberal arts, Benedictine, residential, and Catholic.

Bethany College
Department of Music

421 North 1st St.
Lindsborg, KS 67456-1897
785-227-3311

Fax: 785-227-2004
www.bethanylb.edu

Bethel College
Department of Music

300 East 27th St.
North Newton, KS 67117
Allen Bartel
800-522-1887
Fax: 316-284-5286
E-mail: kschlab@bethelks.edu
www.bethelks.edu/academics/music

Butler County Community College
Department of Music

901 S. Haverhill Rd.
El Dorado, KS 67042
Larry Patton
316-322-3328 x3328
E-mail: lpatton@butlercc.edu
www.buccc.cc.ks.us

Central Christian College
Department of Music

1200 South Main St.
P.O. Box 1403
Mc Pherson, KS 67460
800-835-0078
Fax: 620-241-6032
www.centralchristian.edu

Cloud County Community
Department of Music

2221 Camous Dr.
P.O. Box 1002
Concordia, KS 66901
Everett Miller
785-243-1435 x286
www.cloud.edu

Emporia State University
Department of Music

1200 Commercial Rd.
P.O. Box 4029
Emporia, KS 66801
620-341-5431
Fax: 620-341-5601
www.emporia.edu

Nationally accredited music program within a Liberal Arts University. Opportunities for advanced studies in all instruments, composition, music theory, music history, and music education. Facilities include the newly renovated Beach Music Hall and the new Shepherd Music Center, constructed in 2000. The facility houses a state-of-the-art music computer laboratory, electronic composition studio, recital hall, and keyboard laboratory. Degree programs prepare students for active careers in music and for graduate and doctoral music studies. The bachelor of music education degree offers a K-12 State of Kansas certification to teach vocal and instrumental music. The Music Department currently has 100 percent placement rate of its music education graduates.

Fort Hays State University
Department of Music

600 Park St.
Hays, KS 67601
Tricia Cline
785-628-4091
Fax: 785-628-4085
E-mail: tcline@fhsu.edu
www.fhsu.edu/music

Fort Scott
Community College
Department of Music

2108 South Horton St.
Fort Scott, KS 66701
Gregory Turner
620-223-2700 x561
E-mail: gregt@fortscott.edu
www.ftscott.cc.ks.us

Garden City
Community College
Department of Music

801 Campus Dr.
Garden City, KS 67846-6333
Priscilla Hallberg
620-276-9637
E-mail: priscilla.hallberg@gcccks.edu
www.gcccks.edu

Hesston College
Department of Music

P.O. Box 3000
Hesston, KS 67062
Jake Rittenhouse
620-327-8143
E-mail: jaker@hesston.edu
www.hesston.edu

Hutchinson Community
Junior College
Department of Fine Arts

1300 North Plum St.
Hutchinson, KS 67501
Neal E. Allsup
620-665-3468
Fax: 620-665-3310
E-mail: allsupn@hutchcc.edu
www.hutchcc.edu

Independence
Community College
Music Program

1057 West College Ave.
Independence, KS 67301
Paula Davis
620-332-5428
Fax: 620-331-6821
E-mail: pdavis@indycc.edu
www.indycc.edu

Johnson County Community College
Department of Music

12345 College Blvd.
P.O. Box 31
Overland Park, KS 66210-1299
Mike Garrett
913-469-8500 x 3689
E-mail: mgarre11@jccc.edu
www.jccc.net

Kansas City Kansas Community College
Department of Music

7550 State Ave.
Kansas City, KS 66112
913-334-1100
www.kckcc.cc.ks.us

Kansas State University
Department of Music

109 McCain Auditorium
Manhattan, KS 66506-4702
Paul Hunt
785-532-3800
E-mail: phunt@ksu.edu
www.ksu.edu/music

Kansas State performing groups include five band/wind ensembles, three jazz bands, one orchestra, chamber music groups, one musical theater group, four choruses, and one opera.

Kansas Wesleyan University
Department of Music

100 East Claflin Ave.
Salina, KS 67401-6196
Williamr McMosley
785-827-5541 x5213
Fax: 785-827-0927
E-mail: mcmosley@kwu.edu
www.kwu.edu

Labette Community College
Department of Music

200 South 14th St.
Parsons, KS 67357
Robert Walker
620-421-6700 x1021
E-mail: robertw@labette.cc.ks.us
www.labette.cc.ks.us

McPherson College
Department of Music

1600 East Euclid
McPherson, KS 67460
Steven Gustafson
620-242-0524
E-mail: gustafs@mcpherson.edu
www.mcpherson.edu

Neosho County Community College
Department of Music

800 West 14th St.
Chanute, KS 66720
Al Guinn
316-431-2820
Fax: 316-431-0082
E-mail: afguinn@neosho.cc.ks.us
www.neosho.cc.ks.us

Newman University
Department of Fine Arts

3100 McCormick St.
Wichita, KS 67213-2097
John Laevitt
316-942-4291 x2196
E-mail: leavittj@newmanu.edu
www.newmanu.edu

Ottawa University
Department of Music

1001 South Cedar St.
Ottawa, KS 66067-3399

800-755-5200
Fax: 785-229-1008
E-mail: admiss@ottawa.edu
www.ottawa.edu

Pittsburgh State University
Department of Music

1701 South Broadway
Pittsburgh, KS 66762
Craig Fuchs
620-235-4467
E-mail: cfuchs@pittstate.edu
www.pittstate.edu

Seward County Community College
Department of Music

P.O. Box 1137
Liberal, KS 67905
Darin Workman
800-373-9951
www.sccc.cc.ks.us

Sterling College
Department of Music

P.O. Box 98
Sterling, KS 67579
Melody Hanberry
620-278-4382
E-mail: mhanberry@sterling.edu
www.stercolks.edu

Tabor College
Department of Music

400 S. Jefferson St.
Hillsboro, KS 67063
Deanne Duerksen
620-947-3121 x1045
E-mail: deanned@tabor.edu
www.tabor.edu

University of Kansas
School of Fine Arts

Lawrence, KS 66045
David Bushouse
785-864-3436
Fax: 785-864-5866
E-mail: music@ku.edu
www.music.ukans.edu

University of Saint Mary
Department of Music

4100 South 4th St.
Leavenworth, KS 66048
913-682-5151
E-mail: admissions@stmary.edu
www.stmary.edu

Washburn University
Department of Music

1700 SW College Ave.
Topeka, KS 66621
Kirt Saville
785-670-1512
Fax: 785-670-1042
E-mail: Kirt.saville@washburn.edu
www.washburn.edu/cas/music

Bachelor of Music in Education and Performance, Bacelor of Arts

The Department of Music is a unit of the College of arts and Sciences in the Divsion of Creative and Performing Arts. The music department prepares individuals for careers and further study in the field of music, while promoting a lifetime of continuous learning and appreciation for music.

Wichita State University
School of Music

1845 North Fairmount
Wichita, KS 67260-011
316-978-3555
Fax: 316-978-3625
E-mail: musicinfo@wichita.edu
www.wichita.edu

Population: 4,173,405 (2005 Estimate)
Capital City: Frankfort
Bird: Cardinal
Motto: United We Stand, Divided We Fall
Flower: Goldenrod
Tree: Tulip Tree
Residents Called: Kentuckians
Origin of Name: Based on the Iroquois Indian word, "Ken-tah-ten," meaning "land of tomorrow."
Arca: 40,411 square miles (37th largest state)
Statehood: June 1, 1792 (15th state)
Largest Cities: Lexington, Fayette, Louisville, Owensboro, Bowling Green, Covington, Hopkinsville, Frankfort, Henderson, Richmond, Jeffersontown
College Band Programs: Campbellsville University, Eastern Kentucky University, Kentucky State University, Northwestern State University of Louisiana, University of Kentucky, University of Louisville

Asbury College
Department of Music

1 Macklem Dr.
Wilmore, KY 40390
Lynn Cooper
859-858-3511
www.asbury.edu

Ashland Community College
Department of Music

1400 College Dr.
Louisville, KY 41101
Karen George
606-326-2022
E-mail: karen.george@kctcs.edu
www.ashlandcc.org

Bellarmine University
Department of Music

2001 Newburg Rd.
North Music Building 207
Louisville, KY 40205
Richard Burchard
502-452-8497
E-mail: rburchard@bellarmine.edu
www.bellarmine.edu

Berea College
Department of Music

CPO 2194
Berea, KY 40403
Jeanette Davidson
859-985-3466
E-mail: jeanette_davidson@berea.edu
www.berea.edu

Boyce College
2825 Lexington Rd.

Louisville, KY 40280
800-626-5525
E-mail: admissions@sbts.edu

www.boycecollege.com

Degree of science in Biblical Studies: Music
Ministry Major

Brescia University
Department of Music

717 Frederica St.
Owensboro, KY 42301
270-685-3131
E-mail: admissions@brescia.edu
www.brescia.edu

Campbellsville University
School of Music

1 University Dr.
Campbellsville, KY 42718-2799
270-789-5237
Fax: 270-789-5524
E-mail: music@campbellsville.edu
www.campbellsville.edu/music

Centre College
School of Music

600 West Walnut St.
Danville, KY 40422
Gretchen Hines-Ward
859-238-5424
Fax: 859-238-5448
E-mail: gretchen@centre.edu
www.centre.edu

Cumberland College
Department of Music

6191 College Station Dr.
Williamsburg, KY 40769
606-539-4332
E-mail: crobinso@cumberland.edu
www.cumberlandcollege.edu

Eastern Kentucky University
Department of Music

521 Lancaster Ave.
Richmond, KY 40475
Rob James
859-622-3266
Fax: 859-622-1333
E-mail: rob.james@eku.edu
www.music.eku.edu

Georgetown College
Department of Music

400 East College St.
Georgetown, KY 40324-1696
502-863-8100
www.georgetowncollege.edu

Bachelor of Arts, Bachelor of Music in Church
Music, Bachelor of Music Education; Music
Minor, Music Minor in Church Music

Kentucky Christian University
School of Music

100 Academic Pkwy.
Grayson, KY 41143
Mark Deakins
606-474-3290
E-mail: mdeakins@kcu.edu
www.kcu.edu

Degrees in Music Business, Music Education,
Music Performance,

Kentucky State University
Division of Fine Arts

400 East Main St.
Frankfort, KY 40601
Timothy Chambers
502-597-5815
Fax: 502-597-5999
E-mail: tchambers@gwmail.kysu.edu
www.kysu.edu

Kentucky Wesleyan College
Department of Music

3000 Frederica St.
Owensboro, KY 42302

Diane Earle
270-852-3617
E-mail: dearle@kwc.edu
www.kwc.edu

Bachelor of Music, Music Education and Arts in
Music Industry

Lees College
Department of Music

Jackson, KY 41339
Kathy Smoot
606-666-8142
Fax: 606-666-8910
www.lees.hazcc.kctcs.net

Lindsey Wilson College
Department of Music

210 Lindsey Wilson St.
Columbia, KY 42728-9974
800-264-0138
Fax: 270-384-8200
E-mail: info@lindsey.edu
www.lindsey.edu

Morehead State University
Department of Music

150 University Morehead
Morehead, KY 40351
606-783-2221
www.morehead-st.ede

Morehead State University
Department of Music

Baird Music Hall 106
Morehead, KY 40351-1689
606-783-2473
Fax: 606-783-5447
E-mail: music@moreheadstate.edu
www.moreheadstate.edu

Murray State University
Department of Music

504 Fine Arts Building
Murrey, KY 42071
Pamela Wurgler
270-809-4288
Fax: 270-762-3965
E-mail: pamela.wurgler@murraystate.edu
www.murraystate.edu

Northern Kentucky University
Department of Music

Fine Arts Center 253
Highland Heights, KY 41099
Vance Wolverton
859-572-6399
Fax: 859-572-6076
E-mail: wolvertonv1@nku.edu
www.nku.edu

Bachelor of Music in Performance, Music Education

Southern Baptist Theological Seminary
Department of Music

2825 Lexington Rd.
Louisville, KY 40280
Esther Crookshank
859-897-4507
Fax: 859-897-4115
E-mail: ecrookshank@sbts.edu
www.sbts.edu

St. Catharine College
Department of Music

2735 Bardstown Rd.
St. Catharine, KY 40061
Terry Ward
859-336-5082
E-mail: tward@sccky.edu
www.sccky.edu

Transylvania University
Music Program

300 North Broadway
Lexington, KY 40508

859-281-3546
Fax: 859-233-8797
E-mail: admissions@transy.edu
www.transy.edu

AB in Music (majors in applied music, music education, music technology)

The Music Program, as part of a liberal arts education, provides study for majors and minors in music and for general university students. The music minor is very popular and nearly 20% of Transy students participate in a music ensemble.

Union College
Department of Music

310 College St.
Barbourville, KY 40906
800-489-8646
www.unionky.edu

University of Kentucky
School of Music

105 Fine Arts Building
Lexington, KY 40506-0022
Dwight Newton
859-257-4900
Fax: 859-257-9576
E-mail: music@uky.edu
www.uky.edu/finearts/music

BM in Music Education, BM in Performance, BA in Music, MA in Musicology, MA in Music Theory, MM in Composition, MM in Conducting, MM in Performance, MM in Sacred Music, MM in Music Education, Rank I in Music Education, Graduate Certificate in Orff Schulwerk, Cert. in Music Theory Pedagogy, PhD in Musicology, PhD in Music Education, PhD in Music Theory, DMA in Composition, DMA in Conducting, DMA in Performance

The UK School of Music has achieved awards and national recognition for high-caliber education in opera, choral and instrumental music performance, as well as for music education, composition, theory and music history. Our faculty has gained national and international prominence in their respective fields.

University of Kentucky at Louisville
Jefferson
Community College

109 East Broadway
Belknap Campus
Louisville, KY 40292
502-852-6907
Fax: 502-852-0520
E-mail: gomusic@louisville.edu
www.louisville.edu

University of Kentucky Lexington
School of Music

105 Fine Arts Building
Lexington, KY 40506-0022
Ben Arnold
859-257-4900
E-mail: ben.arnold@uky.edu
www.uky.edu/FineArts/Music

University of Louisville
School of Music

School of Music Admissions
Louisville, KY 40292
Amanda Boyd
502-852-1623
Fax: 502-852-0520
E-mail:
gomusic@louisville.edu
www.louisville.edu

Bachelor of Music Degree

West Kentucky Community & Technical Collage
Department of Music

4810 Alben Barkley Dr.
P.O. Box 7380
Paducah, KY 42002-7380
Norman Wurgler
270-534-3219
E-mail: Norman.Wurgler@kctcs.edu

Western Kentucky University
Department of Music

1906 College Heights Blvd. #41029
Bowling Green, KY 41029
Mitzi Groom
270-745-3751
Fax: 270-745-6855
E-mail: mitzi.groom@wku.edu
www.wku.edu/music

BM (edu. or perf.); BA (liberal arts)

WKU's Department of Music emphasizes music education and the preparation of professional musicians and teachers of music. A personal touch from the faculty-taught classes contributes to the musical community of learners to produce excellent ensembles, choral/band directors and award-winning soloists.

Population: 4,523,628 (2005 Estimate)
Capital City: Baton Rouge
Bird: Eastern Brown Pelican
Motto: Union, justice, and confidence
Flower: Magnolia
Tree: Bald Cypress
Residents Called: Louisianians
Origin of Name: Named in honor of France's King Louis XIV.
Area: 51,843 square mile (31st largest state)
Statehood: April 30, 1812 (18th state)
Largest Cities: New Orleans, Baton Rouge, Shreveport, LaFayette, Lake Charles, Kenner, Bossier City, Monroe, Alexandria, New Iberia
College Band Programs: Grambling State University, Louisiana State University, Northwestern State University, Southern University

Centenary College of Louisiana
Hurley School of Music

2911 Centenary Blvd.
Shreveport, LA 71104
Anita Crafts
318-869-5235
Fax: 318-869-5248
E-mail: music@centenary.edu
www.centenary.edu

BM Performance, BM Sacred Music, BM Theory and Composition; BM Education; BA in Music

Centenary College is a selective liberal arts college, affiliated with the United Methodist Church. The Hurley School of Music is accredited by the National Association of Schools of Music.

Grambling State University
Department of Music

403 Main St.
Grambling, LA 71245
Larry Pannell
318-274-2682
Fax: 318-274-3723
E-mail: Pannell@gram.edu
www.gram.edu

B.A. in Music , B.S. in Music

Louisiana College
Department of Music

LC Box 604
Pineville, LA 71359
Cleamon R. Downs
318-487-7336
Fax: 318-487-7337
E-mail: downs@lacollage.edu
www.lacollege.edu

Louisiana State University
School of Music

Dalrymple & Infirmary

Baton Rouge, LA 70803-2504
Carol Larsen
225-578-3261
Fax: 225-578-2562
E-mail: clarse1@lsu.edu
www.music.lsu.edu

BA, BM, BME, MM, DMA, PhD

Nationally-prominent school of music with outstanding programs in bands, choirs, composition, orchestra, music education, opera, and theoretical/musicological studies.

Louisiana Technical University
Department of Music

School of the Performing Arts
P.O. Box 8608
Ruston, LA 71272
Jon A. Barker
318-257-4200
Fax: 318-257-4571
E-mail: jbarker@latech.edu
http://performingarts.latech.edu

B.A., B.M. in Music Performance, B.A. in Music Education, M.E in Music Education.

The department of Music in the School of the Performing Arts is accredited by NASM and boasts a fine faculty, curriculum, facilities, and performance schedule. The vocal, strings, guitar, piano, and theory programs are housed in the Howard Center for the Performing Arts. The instrumental area of the department of music is housed in the band building, and includes two rehearsal halls, instrumental faculty studios, and offices for the Director of Bands. Louisiana Tech is a fully accredited comprehensive institution within the University of Louisiana system, with graduate and undergraduate curricula. The school of the performing arts is recognized by the regents as an area of excellence and is a vital part of the College of Liberal Arts working closely with other units within the college. A new Steinway grand piano graces the recital hall. Other venues include the 1,300-seat Howard Center and the 120-seat Stone Theatre.

Loyola University at New Orleans
College of Music and Fine Arts

6363 St. Charles Ave.
New Orleans, LA 70115
Georgia McBride
504-865-3039
Fax: 504-865-2852
E-mail: gbmcbrid@loyno.edu
www.loyno.edu

BM, BME, BMT, BS, BA

In the Jesuit tradition of providing a well-rounded education, Loyola's College of Music and Fine Arts provides students with an opportunity to pursue both a strong foundation in the liberal arts and professional training in the performing and fine arts. In this fashion, students can study subjects such as history and philosophy along with graphic design, music therapy, music performance, music industry studies, sculpture, and stagecraft. The College of Music and Fine Arts prides itself on the relationship between its faculty and students and its comprehensive array of opportunities for performances, exhibits, and ensembles which afford students the opportunity to present their work on a consistent basis. The low ratio of students to faculty enables a strong emphasis on individual student attention and individual instruction.

McNeese State University
Department of Music

4205 Ryan St.
Lake Charles, LA 70609
Michele K. Martin
318-475-5028
Fax: 318-475-5922
E-mail: mmartin@mail.mcneese.edu
www.mcneese.edu

New Orleans Baptist Theology Seminary
Division of Church Music Ministries

3939 Gentilly Blvd.
New Orleans, LA 70126
800-662-8701
www.nobts.edu

Bachelor of Arts in Music

Nicholls State University
Division of Music

P.O. Box 2017-NSU
Thibodaux, LA 70310
Carol Britt
985-448-4600
Fax: 985-448-4674
E-mail: SFAM@nicholls.edu
www.nicholls.edu/perform

Northeast Louisiana University
Division of Music

700 University Ave.
Monroe, LA 71209
318-342-1569
Fax: 318-342-1599
E-mail: music@ulm.edu
www.ulm.edu

Bachelor of Music Education, Music

Northwestern State University
Department of Music

School of Creative and Performing Arts
Natchitoches, LA 71497
Tony Smith
318-357-5897
Fax: 318-357-5906
E-mail: smitht@nsula.edu
www.nsuok.edu

Southeastern Louisiana University
Department of Music

SLU P.O. Box 10815
Hammond, LA 70402-0815

David Evenson
985-549-2184
Fax: 985-549-2892
E-mail: devenson@selu.edu
www.selu.edu/music

B.M. in performance; B.M.E.; M.M. in performance, M.M. in theory

The Music Department and Dramatic Arts boasts a lengthy heritage of excellence in the training of educators and professional musicians. Central to its mission are a faculty of sixteen full-time and nineteen part-time teachers and scholars, and a diverse student body from throughout the United States, and several foreign countries including Honduras, Bulgaria, Russia, Romania, and the Republic of Moldova. Southeastern's faculty is respected performers, composers, and educators, who take a deep and lasting interest in their students. Faculty are leaders in their fields, holding offices in state and national professional organizations and receiving national and university awards in teaching, research, and creative activity. They can be heard performing nationally and internationally in live concerts and on compact discs. Graduates have distinguished themselves as performers and educators in public school, colleges, and universities. The Music Department and Dramatic Arts is faculty accredited by the NASM.

Southern University at Baton Rouge
Office of Admissions

P.O. Box 9820
Baton Rouge, LA 70813
225-771-2360
Fax: 225-771-9252
E-mail: admit@subr.edu
www.subr.edu

St. Joseph Seminary College
Music Program

75376 River Rd.
St. Benedict, LA 70457
985-892-1800
E-mail: info@stjosephabbey.org
www.seminary.saintjosephabbey.com

Tulane University
Department of Music

102 Dixon Hall
New Orleans, LA 70118-5683
504-865-5267
Fax: 504-865-5270
E-mail: music@tulane.edu
www2.tulane.edu/main.cfm

University of Louisiana at Lafayette
School of Music

601 East St. Mary
Lafayette, LA 70503
Leroy Broussard
337-482-6012
Fax: 337-482-5017
E-mail: sbeasley@louisiana.edu
www.arts.louisiana.edu

B.M., B.M.E., M.M.

The school of music's programs have been accredited by the NASM since 1952. The enrollment is approximately 200 undergraduate and graduate students. The faculty consists of twenty full-time faculty, twelve adjunct faculty, two laboratory assistants and twelve graduate assistants. Recognized as a center for musical performance, composition, and research, the school of music is housed in 56,000 square foot Angelle Hall and hosts approximately 100 concerts, recitals, competitions, or other performances each year. All classrooms are equipped with modern audio, video and Ethernet capability. Facilities include 40 practice rooms and 3 large ensemble rehearsal rooms. Concert facilities include Angelle Hall Auditorium, a 900-seat hall, and the Choral-Recital Hall, a 125 seat hall used for lectures as well as recitals., Special facilities include the MIDI Lab, the Griffin Recording Studio and the Griffin Music Resource Center. These facilities are equipped with state of the art electronic and computer technology.

University of New Orleans
Department of Music

University of New Orleans
New Orleans, LA 70148
Office of Admissions
504-280-6381
Fax: 504-280-6098
E-mail: unomusic@uno.edu
www.uno.edu

The Music Department at the University of New Orleans is a reflection of its community, one of the most musically significant, historically important, and culturally diverse cities of the world. By promoting the highest levels of musicianship, scholarship and creativity, the mission of the department is to train the musicians capable of furthering the music legacy of the city and of assuming significant positions in society through offering a B.A. with the emphasis in performance, jazz performance, theory/composition, and history and an M.M. in performance, jazz studies, composition and conducting. The creative activity of the department serves the cultural needs of the community through numerous performances by faculty and students. The Music Department's service activity includes the support of community music making it a commitment to the development of regional, national, and international partnerships. In addition, the Music Department serves the needs of non-majors through instruction and performance opportunities designed to nurture lifelong appreciation and support of music.

Xavier University of Louisiana
Department of Music

1 Drexel Dr.
New Orleans, LA 70125
504-486-7411
www.xula.edu

Population: 1,321,505 (2005 Estimate)
Capital City: Augusta
Bird: Chickadee
Motto: Dirigo – I direct
Flower: White pine cone and tassel
Tree: White pine
Residents Called: Mainers
Origin of Name: Assumed to be a reference to the state region being a mainland, different from its many surrounding Islands.
Area: 35,387 square miles (39th largest state)
Statehood: March 15, 1820 (23rd state)
Largest Cities: Portland, Lewiston, Bangor, South Portland, Auburn, Brunswick, Biddeford, Sanford, Augusta, Scarborough
College Band Programs: University of Maine

Bates College
Department of Music

75 Russell St.
Lewiston, ME 04240
William Matthews
207-786-6139
Fax: 207-786-8335
E-mail: wmatthew@abacus.bates.edu
www.bates.edu

Bowdoin College
Department of Music

9200 College Station
Brunswick, ME 04011-8492
Linda Marquis
207-725-3321
Fax: 207-725-3748
E-mail: lmarquis@bowdoin.edu
www.bowdoin.edu

Colby College
Department of Music

5670 Mayflower Hill Dr.
Waterville, ME 04901
Vivian Lemieux
207-872-3236
Fax: 207-872-3141
www.colby.edu/music

College of the Atlantic
Department of Music

105 Eden St.
Bar Harbour, ME 04609
John Cooper
207-288-5015
Fax: 207-288-4126
E-mail: cooper@coa.edu
www.coa.edu

Delta College
Department of Music

1961 Delta Rd.
Office S-247
University Center, ME 48710
989-686-9101
E-mail: humaniti@alpha.delta.edu
www.delta.edu

University of Maine
Department of Performing Arts

25 Pleasant St.
Fort Kent, ME 04743
207-834-7506
www.umfk.maine.edu

University of Maine at Augusta
Department of Music

46 University Dr.
Augusta, ME 04330
June MacLeod
207-621-3286
www.uma.maine.edu

Bachelor of arts in music, bachelor of music education and bachelor of music performance

As a fully accredited member of the National Association of Schools of Music, the department also offers a complete range of music courses and performing experiences to all of the over 9,400 students on campus. The major vocal ensembles balance the major instrumental performing groups. A large number of chamber music ensembles is maintained as well. The school offers students a state-of-the-art facility for study and performance. There are teaching, rehearsal and performing studios for music, a "high tech" classroom, and a fully digital recording studio. Performances take place in a newly built 280-seat Minsky Recital Hall as well as in the Maine Center for the Arts, located on the University of Maine campus.

University of Maine Orono
Division of Music

5788 Class of 1944 Hall
Orono, ME 04459
207-581-4700
E-mail: music@maine.edu
www.umaine.edu

University of Southern Maine
Department of Music

37 College Ave.
Gorham, ME 04038
Bill Street
207-780-5265
E-mail: billstreetsax@netzero.net
www.usm.maine.edu/~mus

Population: 5,600,388 (2005 Estimate)
Capital City: Annapolis
Bird: Baltimore Oriole
Motto: Fatti Maschii Parole Femine – Strong deeds, gentle words
Flower: Black-eyed Susan
Tree: White Oak
Residents Called: Marylanders
Origin of Name: Named to honor Henrietta Maria, wife of England's King Charles I.
Area: 12,407 square miles (42nd largest state)
Statehood: April 28, 1788 (7th state)
Largest Cities: Baltimore, Frederick, Gaithersburg, Bowie, Rockville, Hagerstown, Annapolis, College Park, Salisbury, Cumberland
College Band Programs: John Hopkins University, Morgan State University, Towson University, University of Maryland

Baltimore School for the Arts
Department of Music

712 Cathedral St.
Baltimore, MD 21201
Chris Ford
410-396-1185
www.bsfa.org

Chesapeake College
Department of Music

P.O. Box 8
1000 College Cir.
Wye Mills, MD 21679-0008
410-822-5400
Fax: 410-827-5875
www.chesapeake.edu

College of Notre Dame of Maryland
Department of Music

4701 N. Charles St.
Baltimore, MD 21210
Ernest Ragogini
410-435-0100
E-mail: eragogini@ndm.edu
www.ndm.edu

Columbia Union College
Department of Music

7600 Flower Ave.
Takoma Park, MD 20812-7796
James Bingham
301-891-4032
E-mail: jbingham@cuc.edu
www.cuc.edu

Community College of Baltimore City
Department of Music
Essex Campus

7201 Rossville Blvd.
Baltimore, MD 21237
410-780-6110
Fax: 410-780-6117
E-mail: essexadmissions@ccbcmd.edu
www.ccbcmd.edu

Coppin State College
Department of Music

2500 West North Ave.
Baltimore, MD 21216
800-635-3674
www.coppin.edu

Frederick Community College
Department of Humanities

7932 Opossumtown Pike
Frederick, MD 21702
Jan Holly
301-846-2566
E-mail: jholly@frederick.edu
www.frederick.edu

Frostburg State University
Department of Music

101 Braddock Rd.
Frostburg, MD 21532
Karen Soderberg Sarnaker
301-687-4110
Fax: 301-687-4784
E-mail: ksoderberg@frostburg.edu
www.frostburg.edu

Garrett Community College
Department of Art

687 Mooser Rd.
Mc Henry, MD 21541
Ann Wellham
301-387-3059
E-mail: awellham@garrettcollege.edu
www.garrettcollege.edu

Goucher College
Department of Music

1021 Dulaney Valley Rd.
Baltimore, MD 21204
Lisa Weiss
410-337-6148
E-mail: lisa.weiss@goucher.edu
www.goucher.edu

Hartford Community College
Department of Music

401 Thomas Run Rd.
Bel Air, MD 21015
Paul Labe
410-836-4291
E-mail: Plabe@harford.edu
www.harford.edu

Hood College
Department of Music

401 Rosemont Ave.
Frederick, MD 21701
301-663-3131
www.hood.edu

McDanial College
Department of Music

Levine Hall
Westminster, MD 21157
Caldwell
410-857-2552
Fax: 410-857-2729
E-mail: gcaldwel@mcdaniel.edu
www.wmdc.edu

Montgomery College
Department of Music

51 Mannakee St.
Rockville, MD 20850
Molly Donnelly
301-279-5209
Fax: 301-251-7553

E-mail: mdonnell@mc.cc.md.us
www.montgomerycollege.edu

Morgan State University
Department of Fine Arts

1700 East Cold Spring Lane
Baltimore, MD 21251
443-885-3333
E-mail: info@morgan.edu
www.morgan.edu

Mount St. Mary's College
Department of Visual Performing Arts

16 Flynn Hall
Emmetsburg, MD 21727
Kurt Blaugher
301-447-5308
Fax: 301-447-7401
E-mail: blaugher@msmary.edu
www.msmary.edu

Prince Georges Community College
Department of Music

301 Largo Rd.
Upper Marlboro, MD 20774
Barbara Johnson
301-322-0966
www.pg.cc.md.us

Salisbury University
Department of Music

1101 Camden Ave.
Fulton Hall, Room 200
Salisbury, MD 21801
Karen Noble
410-543-6385
E-mail: kmnoble@salisbury.edu
www.salisbury.edu

Bachelor of Arts in Music

St. Mary's College of Maryland
Department of Music

18952 East Fisher Rd.
St. Mary's City, MD 20686
Gwen Degentesh
240-895-4498
E-mail: gtdegentesh@smcm.edu
www.smcm.edu

The Peabody Institute of Johns Hopkins University
Peabody Public Information Office

1 E. Mount Vernon Place
Baltimore, MD 21202
David Lane
410-659-8110
Fax: 410-659-8102
E-mail: admissions@peabody.jhu.edu
www.peabody.jhu.edu

Minors in Music only

Towson University
Department of Music

8000 York Rd.
Towson, MD 21252
Mary Ann Criss
410-704-2836
E-mail: mcriss@towson.edu
www.towson.edu/music

University of Maryland
School of Music

2110 Clarice Smith Performing Arts Center
College Park, MD 20742
Ashley Fleming
301-405-8435
Fax: 301-314-7966
E-mail: musicadmissions@umd.edu
www.music.umd.edu

B.A., B.M., B.M.E., M.A., M.M., D.M.A, and D.P

Located in the culturally vibrant corridor between Washington D.C. and Baltimore, the University of Maryland School of Music offers all the opportunities of a conservatory with the advantages of a world-class research university.

University of Maryland Baltimore County
Department of Music

1000 Hilltop Cir.
Baltimore, MD 21250
Linda Dusman
410-455-2026
E-mail: dusman@umbc.edu
www.umbc.edu

University of Maryland Eastern Shore
Department of Fine Arts

Backbone Rd.
Princess Anne, MD 21853
Ernest Satchell
410-651-2200
www.umes.edu

Washington Bible College
Department of Music

6511 Princess Garden Pkwy.
Lanham, MD 20706
301-552-1400
www.bible.edu

Washington College
Gibson Department of Music

300 Washington Ave.
Chesterton, MD 21620
410-778-2800
www.washcoll.edu

Washington Conservatory
of Music

One Westmoreland Cir.
Bethesda, MD 20816
301-320-2770
Fax: 301-320-2794
E-mail: info@washingtonconsdervatory.org
www.washingtonconservatory.com

Population: 6,398,743 (2005 Estimate)
Capital City: Boston
Bird: Chickadee
Motto: Ense petit placidam sub libertate quietem – By the sword we seek peace, but peace only under liberty.
Flower: Mayflower
Tree: American Elm
Residents Called: Bay Staters
Origin of Name: Named after local Indian tribe whose name means "a large hill place."
Area: 10,555 square miles (44th largest state)
Statehood: February 6, 1788 (6th state)
Largest Cities: Boston, Worcester, Springfield, Lowell, Cambridge, Brockton, New Bedford, Fall River, Lynn, Quincy
College Band Programs: Boston College, Boston University, Harvard University, Massachusetts Institute of Technology (MIT) Marching Band, Worcester Polytechnic Institute's Pep Band, University of Massachusetts-Amherst, Williams College

American International College
Division of Humanities and Fine Arts

1000 State St.
Springfield, MA 01109
800-242-3142
E-mail: inquiry@aic.edu
www.aic.edu

Amherst College
Department of Music

224 Arms Music Center
Amherst, MA 01002
Chris Kim
413-542-2195
E-mail: chkim@amherst.edu
www.amherst.edu

Anna Maria College
Music Program

50 Sunset Lane
Paxton, MA 01612
Roger Greene
508-849-3452
E-mail: rgreene@annamaria.edu
www.annamaria.edu

Assumption College
Department of Art and Music

500 Salisbury St.
Worcester, MA 01609
Michelle Graveline
508-767-7000
www.assumption.edu

Berklee College of Music

1140 Boylston St.
Boston, MA 02215
800-BERKLEE

E-mail: admissions@berklee.edu
www.berklee.edu

For over 60 years, Berklee College of Music has become the world's largest independent school of music. Today, it is widely recognized as the leading college for the study of contemporary music. Berklee's environment is designed to give its 3,500 students and 450 faculty members real-world learning experiences and the proper tools to help further their craft. It all adds up to the most complete music learning experience anywhere. With Boston as a backdrop, Berklee's state-of-the-art facilities provide students with opportunities to develop their skills and talent in every area from composition to performance to production. As have so many successful graduates before him or her, each student will also learn how to make informed business and career decisions. Berklee's faculty reads like a "Who's Who" of the contemporary music world, including saxophonist Joe Lovano, and Walter Beasley; vocalist of Manhattan Transfer, Cheryl Bentyne; pianist JoAnne Brackeen; drummer Kenwood Dennard; guitarist Mick Goodrick; saxophonist Bill Pierce; and vibist Dave Samuels.

Berkshire Community College
Department of Music

1350 West St.
Pittsfield, MA 01201
413-499-4660
Fax: 413-496-9511
E-mail: admissions@berkshirecc.edu
www.berkshirecc.edu

Boston College
Department of Music

Lyons 407
Chestnut Hill, MA 02467-3805
Pattie Longbottom
617-552-8720
E-mail: patricia.longbottom@bc.edu
www.bc.edu

Boston Conservatory
Music Conservatory

Boston, MA 02215
Kristy Errera
617-912-9153
Fax: 617-247-3159
E-mail: admissions@bostonconservatory.edu
www.bostonconservatory.edu

Boston University
School for the Arts,
Music Division

855 Commonwealth Ave.
Boston, MA 02215
Jake Youmell
617-353-3341
E-mail: cfamusic@bu.edu
www.bu.edu/cfa

The Boston University School of Music offers a conservatory-style education with the advantages of being in a large university setting. Undergraduate degrees can be obtained in performance, music education, history and literature, theory and composition.

Brandeis University
Department of Music

P.O. Box 549110
MS 051
Waltham, MA 02254-9110
Mark Kagan
781-736-3312
E-mail: kagan@brandeis.edu
www.brandeis.edu

Bridgewater State College
Department of Music

Maxwell Library Room 312
Bridgewater, MA 02325
508-531-1377
Fax: 508-531-1772
E-mail: ssachdev@bridgew.edu
www.bridgew.edu

Cape Cod Community College
Department of Music

2240 Lyanough Rd.
West Barnstable, MA 02668
877-846-3672
E-mail: info@capecod.edu
www.capecod.mass.edu

Clark University
Department of Visual
and Performing Arts

950 Main St.
Worcester, MA 01610
508-793-7711
E-mail: academicaffairs@clarku.edu
www.clarku.edu/clarkarts

College of the Holy Cross
Department of Music

1 College St.
Worcester, MA 01610
508-793-2011
www.holycross.edu

Eastern Nazarene College
Department of Music

23 East Elm Ave.
Quincy, MA 02170
617-745-3000
www.enc.edu

Emerson College
Department of Music

10 Boylston Place 5th Floor
Boston, MA 02116-4626
Jason Allen
617-824-8780
E-mail: auditions@emerson.edu
www.emerson.edu

Emmanuel College
Department of Music

400 The Fenway
Boston, MA 02115
617-735-9945
www.emmanuel.edu

Endicott College
North Shore Conservatory of Music

376 Hale St.
Beverly, MA 01915
Music Department
978-927-0585
www.endicott.edu

Minor in Music

Gordon College
Division of Fine Arts

255 Grapevine Rd.
Wenham, MA 01984
Oliver Goodrich
978-867-4273
Fax: 978-867-4655
E-mail: music@gordon.edu
www.gordon.edu

The Music Department, a part of the Division of Fine Arts, offers degree programs (B.M., B.A.) in which students may specialize in performance, music education, theory, church music or liberal arts. The department, which has over 30 full-time and part-time instructors and 95 music majors, is fully accredited by the National Association of Schools of Music. The Interstate Certification Compact also certifies the music education program. Performance groups include the college choir, symphony orchestra, wind ensemble, chamber singers, women's choir, hand bell choir, jazz ensemble and many other small chamber organizations. Membership in these ensembles is open by audition to all students regardless of major.

Hampshire College
Department of Music

Emily Dickinson Hall
Amherst, MA 01002
Susan Tracy
413-559-5361
E-mail: admissions@hamphire.edu
www.hampshire.edu

Harvard University
Department of Music

Music Building
North Yard
Cambridge, MA 02138
617-495-2791
Fax: 617-496-8081
E-mail: musicdpt@fas.harvard.edu
www.fas.harvard.edu/~musicdpt

Holyoke Community College
Department of Music

303 Homestead Ave.
Holyoke, MA 01040
Elissa Brill
413-552-2291
www.hcc.mass.edu

Longy School of Music

1 Follen St.
Cambridge, MA 02138
Heather McCowen Viles
617-876-0956
Fax: 617-354-8841
E-mail: music@longy.edu
www.longy.edu/main.htm

Massachusetts College of Liberal Arts
Department of Fine and Performance Arts

375 Church St.
North Adams, MA 01247
www.mcla.mass.edu

Massachusetts Institute of Technology
Department of Music

77 Massachusetts Ave.
Room E51-255
Cambridge, MA 02139
617-253-3450
Fax: 617-258-9344
www.mit.edu

Mount Holyoke College
Department of Music

Room 208 Pratt
South Hadley, MA 01075
Michele Scanlon
413-538-2306
Fax: 413-538-2547
E-mail: mgscanlo@mtholyoke.edu
www.mytholyok.edu

New England Conservatory
Office of Admissions

290 Huntington Ave.
Boston, MA 02115
Thomas Novak
617-585-1101
E-mail: admission@newenglandconservatory.edu
www.newenglandconservatory.edu.

North Bennet Street School
Admissions

39 North Bennet St.
Boston, MA 02113
617-227-0155
Fax: 617-227-0155
E-mail: admissions@nbss.org
www.nbss.org

Northeastern University
Department of Music

351 Ryder Hall
Boston, MA 02115
617-373-2440
Fax: 617-373-4129
E-mail: l.janikian@neu.edu,
www.music.neu.edu

B.S. in Music Industry, B.S. in Music Technology, B.A. in Music History and Analysis. The nations pre-eminent Coop institution.

Northern Essex Community College
Department of Music

100 Elliott St.
Haverhill, MA 01830
978-556-3000
www.necc.mass.edu

Our Lady of the Elms College
Division of Humanities and Fine Arts

291 Springfield St.
Chicopee, MA 01013
Cristina Canales
413-265-2425
E-mail: canalasm@elms.edu
www.elms.edu

Salem State College
Department of Music

Central Campus Room 265
Salem, MA 01970
Philip Swanson
978-542-6504
E-mail: philip.swanson@salemstate.edu
www.salemstate.edu/music

Simmons College
Dept of Art and Music

300 The Fenway
Boston, MA 02215
Marcia Lomedico
617-521-2268
Fax: 617-521-3199
E-mail: marcia.lomedico@simmons.edu

www.simmons.edu

Smith College
Department of Music

Northampton, MA 01063
413-585-3150
www.smith.edu/music

Springfield College
Department of Art

263 Alden St.
Springfield, MA 01109
Ron Maggio
413-748-3753
www.spfldcol.edu

Tufts University
Department of Music

48 Professors Row
Medford, MA 02155
Lucille Jones
617-627-3564
E-mail: musicadmin@tufts.edu
www.tufts.edu/as/music

University of Massachusetts at Amherst
Department of Music

FAC/151 Presidents Dr.
Amherst, MA 01003
Christopher Thornley
413-545-6048
Fax: 413-545-2092
E-mail: cthornley@music.umass.edu
www.umass.edu/music-dance

University of Massachusetts at Boston
Wheatley Department of Music

100 Morrissey Blvd.
Boston, MA 02125-3393

617-287-6330
E-mail: undergrad.education@umb.edu
www.umb.edu

University of Massachusetts at Lowell
Department of Music

35 Wilder St. Suite 3
Lowell, MA 01854
John Shirley
978-934-3886
Fax: 978-934-3034
E-mail: John_Shirley@uml.edu
www.uml.edu/dept/music/home.htm

Wellesley College
Department of Music

106 Central St.
Wellesley, MA 02481
Emily Kennedy
781-283-2077
E-mail: ekennedy@wellesley.edu
www.wellesley.edu/Music/home.html

Westfield State College
Department of Music

577 Western Ave.
Westfield, MA 01086
Andrew Bonacci
413-572-5356
Fax: 413-572-5287
www.wsc.mass.edu

Wheaton College
Department of Music

Watson M214
Norton, MA 02766
Elizabeth Ann Sears
508-286-3592
E-mail: asears@wheatoncollege.edu
www.wheatoncollege.edu

Wheelock College
Department of Music

200 Riverway
Boston, MA 02215
617-879-2206
E-mail: undergrad@wheelock.edu
www.wheelock.edu

Williams College
Department of Music

54 Chapin Hall Dr.
Williamstown, MA 01267
413-597-2127
Fax: 413-597-3100
E-mail: admissions@williams.edu
www.williams.edu/depts.html

BA Music

Williams College has an extremely dynamic and varied music program. The Music Department's mission is to educate its students in the art of musical performance, composition, and active listening as well as the skills associated with thinking and writing about music. The curriculum includes a wide variety of courses appropriate to both the major and the general student. In addition to classroom courses students are invited to participate in many ensembles including the Berkshire Symphony Orchestra, Williams Choirs, Kusika, Jazz Ensemble, Symphonic Winds and many others. Individual vocal and instrumental lessons are also available.

Worcester State College
Department of Visual and Performance Arts

486 Chandler St.
Office L132
Worcester, MA 01602
Michael Hachey
508-929-8828
E-mail: mhachey@worcester.edu
www.worcester.edu

Population: 10,120,860 (2005 Estimate)
Capital City: Lansing
Bird: Robin
Motto: Si Quaeris Peninsulam Amoenam, Circumspice – If you seek a pleasant peninsula, look about you.
Flower: Apple Blossom
Tree: White pine
Residents Called: Michiganians
Origin of Name: Based on Chippewa Indian word, "meicigama" meaning, "great water" and refers to the Great Lakes.
Area: 96,810 square miles (11th largest state)
Statehood: January 26, 1837 (26th state)
Largest Cities: Detroit, Grand Rapids, Warren, Flint, Sterling Heights, Lansing, Ann Arbor, Livonia, Dearborn, Westland
College Band Programs: Central Michigan University, Eastern Michigan University, Michigan State University, Northern Michigan University, University of Michigan, Western Michigan University

Adrian College
Department of Music

110 South Madison St.
Adrian, MI 49221
517-264-3868
E-mail:
www.adrian.edu

B.M., B.M.E., B.A.

Albion College
Department of Music

611 East Porter St.
Goodrich Chapel
Albion, MI 49224
Maureen Balke
517-629-0471
E-mail: mbalke@albion.edu
www.albion.edu/music

Alma College
Department of Music

614 West Superior St.
Alma, MI 48801-1599
Kelly Masley
989-463-7167
E-mail: masley@alma.edu
www.alma.edu

Degree of Arts in Music, Music Education,
Performance

Andrews University
Department of Music

207 Hamel Hall
US 31/33 N.
Berrien Springs, MI 49014
Peter J. Cooper
269-471-6341
Fax: 269-471-6339
E-mail: pcooper@andrews.edu
www.andrews.edu/MUSIC

Bachelor of Arts in Music

Aquinas College
Department of Music

1607 Robinson Rd. SE
Grand Rapids, MI 49506
Kathy Zimmerman
616-632-2413
Fax: 616-732-4487
E-mail: zimmerkat@aquinas.edu
www.aquinas.edu

Calvin College
Department of Music

3201 Burton St. SE
Grand Rapids, MI 49546
Bert Polman
616-957-6253
Fax: 616-526-6777
E mail: admissions@calvin.edu
www.calvin.edu

Central Michigan University
School of Music

Music Building 162
Mt. Pleasant, MI 48859
Randi L'Hommedieu
989-774-4000
E-mail: randi.l'hommedieu@cmich.edu
www.mus.cmich.edu

Cornerstone University
Department of Music

1001 East Beltline Ave. NE
Grand Rapids, MI 49525
616-222-1545
E-mail: music@cornerstone.edu
www.cornerstone.edu

Bachelor of Music

Delta College
Department of Music

1961 Delta Rd.

S-214
University Center, MI 48710
Rich Mcgaw
989-686-9455
Fax: 989-686-9485
E-mail: ramcgaw@delta.edu
www.delta.edu

Eastern Michigan University
Department of Music

Alexander Music Building Room N101
Ypsilanti, MI 48197
David Woike
734-487-4380
Fax: 734-487-6939
E-mail: david.woike@emich.edu
www.emich.edu

Why choose EMU? Full-time professors, rather than graduate assistants, teach most major classes at EMU. Course offerings provide a wide variety of class choices. Students find the educational environment at Eastern "stimulating." EMU faculty members are recognized for their dedicated teaching and outstanding performance skills. Students find faculty at EMU to be approachable, fair, caring, and fun to be around. EMU also has fine ensembles. The orchestra, winds symphony, symphonic band and Barnhill Concert Band perform regularly, often visiting area schools and participating (by invitation) in the Midwestern Music Conference. They are known for the difficulty of their repertoire and their exemplary performing skills. The bands often break up into performing chamber groups, work in clinic situations with area high school groups, and through the band fraternity and sorority, participate in meaningful charity events. The nearly 200-member marching band stirs up excitement on EMU football Saturdays, and on several occasions, has performed at televised professional football games. And, the band is the featured attraction at our annual Bandorama in historic Pease Auditorium. EMU's Pep Band generates excitement during the basketball season. EMU's jazz ensemble and percussion ensemble play to standing-room-only crowds. In early 2001, the EMU Symphony Orchestra spent a weekend "on retreat" in Detroit, working with DSO musicians, and attending their Saturday

night orchestra concert. They have collaborated in opera, ballet and other dance productions, and performed with professional entertainers like Marvin Hamlisch. Every fall, the orchestra and band team up to present a children's concert that is so popular with local school children that EMU's 1,400-seat Pease Auditorium is filled to capacity in two consecutive performances. EMU also has excellent performing ensembles, including University Choir (which plans to return for a third time next year to sing in New York's Carnegie Hall), Chamber Choir (which has toured the southeast and western United States, Mexico, and Europe), Women's Chorus and Collegium Musicum (a vocal-instrumental ensemble specializing in 18th- and 20th-century music).

Grand Rapids Community College
Department of Performance Arts

100 Music Center
Grand Rapids, MI 49503
616-234-3940
Fax: 616-234-3973
E-mail: performingarts@grcc.edu
www.grcc.cc.mi.us

Grand Valley State University
Department of Music

1300 PAC
Allendale, MI 49401-9403
616-895-3484
www.gvsu.edu

Great Lakes Christian College
Department of Music

6211 West Willow Hwy.
Lansing, MI 48917
Ryan Apple
517-321-0242
Fax: 517-321-5902
E-mail: rapple@glcc.edu
www.glcc.edu

Henry Ford Community College
Department of Performance Arts and Music

5101 Evergreen Rd.
Dearborn, MI 48128
Kevin Dewey
313-845-6474
E-mail: kdewey@hfcc.edu
www.henryford.cc.mi.us

Hillsdale College
Department of Music

33 East College St.
Hillsdale, MI 49242-1205
517-607-2327
www.hillsdale.edu

Hope College
Department of Music

127 East 12th St.
Holland, MI 49423
Margaret Kennedy-Dygas
616-395-7650
Fax: 616-395-7182
E-mail: kennedym@hope.edu
www.hope.edu

B.A./B.M. in Performance, Instrumental Music Education and Vocal Music Education

Interlochen Center for the Arts
Admissions

P.O. Box 199
Traverse City, MI 49643-0199
231-276-7472
Fax: 231-276-7464
E-mail: admissions@intrlochen.org
www.interlochen.org

Jackson Community College
Department of Music

2111 Emmons Rd.
Jackson, MI 49201
Keith Drayton
517-796-8573
E-mail: keith_drayton@ccmi.edu
www.jccmi.edu

Kalamazoo College
Department of Music

1200 Academy St.
Kalamazoo, MI 49006
JoEllen Silberman
269-337-7070
Fax: 269-337-7251
E-mail: admission@kzoo.edu
www.kzoo.edu/music

B.A. Music

Kellogg Community College
Department of Music

450 North Ave.
Battle Creek, MI 49017
616-965-3931
www.kellogg.cc.mi.us

Lake Michigan College
Department of Music

2755 E. Napier Ave.
F203 Mendel Center
Benton Harbor, MI 49017
Dan Hendrickson
269-927-8100 x6588
E-mail: hendrick@lakemichigancollege.edu
www.lmc.cc.mi.us

Lansing Community College
Music Program

P.O. Box 40010
Lansing, MI 48901
Michael Nealon
517-483-1507
E-mail: nealonm@lcc.edu
www.lcc.edu

MICHIGAN

Macomb Community College Center Campus
Department of Music

44575 Garfield Rd.
Clinton Township, MI 48038
John Krnacick
810-286-2045
Fax: 810-286-2272
www.macomb.cc.mi.us

Madonna University
Department of Music.

36600 Schoolcraft Rd.
Livonia, MI 48150
Linette Popoff-Parks
734-432-5709
E-mail: lpopoff-parks@madonna.edu
www.munet.edu

Marygrove College
Department of Music

8425 W. McNichols Rd.
Detroit, MI 48221
Ellen Duncan
313-927-1252
E-mail: eduncan@marygrove.edu
www.marygrove.edu

Bachcelor of Music, Music Minor

Michigan State University
School of Music

Music Building
East Lansing, MI 48824
John Martin
517-355-2140
Fax: 517-432-8209
E-mail: Debbie.Killan@mcc.edu
www.music.msu.edu

Mott Community College
Department of Music

100 Visual Arts & Design Center

Flint, MI 48503
Debbie Killian
810-762-0459
E-mail: Debbie.
www.mcc.edu

Northern Michigan University
Department of Music

1401 Presque Isle Ave.
Marquette, MI 49855
Donald R. Grant
906-227-2563
Fax: 906-227-2163
E-mail: dgrant@nmu.edu
www.nmu.edu/music
BA, BS, BME

Northwestern Michigan College
Music Program

1701 East Front
Traverse City, MI 49684
231-995-1325
Fax: 231-995-1696
www.nmc.edu

Oakland Community College
Department of Music

2480 Opdyke Toad
Bloomfield Hills, MI 48304
248-341-2000
www.oaklandcc.edu

Oakland University
Department of Music, Theatre, and Dance

211 Varner Hall
Rochester, MI 48309-4401
248-370-2030
www.otus.oakland.edu

From an excellent location accessible to all area

cultural events, OU offers music in a dynamic growing environment rich with performance opportunities and a world-class faculty.

Olivet College
Department of Arts and Communication

Music Program
Conservatory 235
Olivet, MI 49076
Kirk Hendershott-Kraetzer
269-749-7621
E-mail: khendershott@olivetcollege.edu
www.olivetcollege.edu

Rochester College
Department of Music

800 West Avon Rd.
Rochester Hills, MI 48307
248-218-2000
www.rc.edu

Saginaw Valley State University
Department of M2usic

7400 Bay Rd.
May City, MI 48710
989-964-4000
www.svsu.edu

Schoolcraft College
Department of Music

18600 Haggerty Rd.
Livonia, MI 48152
313-462-4400
www.schoolcraft.cc.mi.us

Spring Arbor University
Department of Music

106 East Main St.
Spring Arbor, MI 49283-9799
Lindsay Goodrich

517-750-6493
Fax: 517-750-3410
E-mail: lgoodrich@arbor.edu
www.arbor.edu

B.A. in Music Performance, B.A. In Music Education, B.A. In Worship Arts Performance, B.A. in Worship Arts Leadership, A.A. in Piano Pedagogy

Performance opportunities include Concert Choir, Chamber Singers, University-Community Band, Jazz Band, String Ensemble and Contemporary-Christian Ensembles (known as "Wellspring"). Smaller ensembles include Percussion Ensemble, Horn Ensemble, Flute Choir and Guitar Ensemble. Many other performance opportunities on campus including Chapel Band and Gospel Choir.

University of Michigan at Ann Arbor
School of Music

1100 Baits Dr.
2290 Moore Bldg.
Ann Arbor, MI 48109
Francea Goodridge
734-763-7558
Fax: 734-763-5097
E-mail: francieg@umich.edu
www.music.umich.edu

Founded in 1880 when the University of Michigan engaged Calvin B. Cady as its first faculty member in music, the school of music is one of the oldest and largest music schools in the United States. It has consistently ranked among the top half-dozen music schools and conservatories for as long as such polls have been conducted. Earl V. Moore, one of music's greatest educators, headed the school from 1923-1960, developing programs that are still widely emulated throughout the U.S. In 1964, the school of music moved to its new building on north campus; the building was subsequently named for Dean Emeritus Moore. With over 1,000 students from all 50 states and almost two dozen countries, the school is located in a park-like setting on the university's north campus, in the city of Ann Arbor, a classic college town in the tradition of Cambridge and Berkeley, where intellectual, artistic and recreational activities abound. The school of music provides performance training comparable to Juilliard or Curtis and academic training in music comparable to Princeton and Yale. The school contains rehearsal facilities, two concert halls, 45 performance-teaching studios, 18 classrooms, 135 practice rooms and other special facilities.

University of Michigan at Dearborn
Department of Humanities

4901 Evergreen Rd.
Dearborn, MI 48128
Kathryn Anderson-Levitt
313-593-5490
www.umd.umich.edu

University of Michigan at Flint
Department of Music

French Hall 126
Flint, MI 48502
Kirk Aamot
810-762-3375
E-mail: kaamot@umich.edu
www.flint.umich.edu/departments/mus

Wayne State University
Department of Music

1321 Old Main
Detroit, MI 48202
Norah Dunccan
313-577-1795
Fax: 313-577-5420
E-mail: music@wayne.edu
www.music.wayne.edu

B.M., M.M., B.A., and Graduate Certificate in Orchestral Studies

Part of the college of fine, performing and communication arts, the Wayne State University Department of Music has 16 full-time and over 60 adjunct faculty. Located in the heart of Detroit's University Cultural Center, it enrolls over 325 music majors. Since 1918, the department has been recognized for its artistic and academic

excellence. The department is fully accredited by the NASM, and 22 members of the part-time faculty are members of the Detroit Symphony Orchestra. Aspiring musicians have the opportunity to study with professional musicians of regional, national and international acclaim at one of the largest urban research universities in the United States. Our renovated facilities in Old Main feature a new recording studio and a digital synth-lab; expanded rehearsal and office space; updated library/computer labs; and the new 160-seat Music Recital Hall.

Western Michigan University
School of Music

1903 West Michigan Ave.
Kalamazoo, MI 49008
Margaret Hamilton
269-387-4672
Fax: 269-387-1113
E-mail: margaret.hamilton@wmich.edu
www.wmich.edu/music

William Tyndale College
Department of Music

35700 East 12th Mile Rd.
Farmington Hills, MI 48331
Kimberly Swan
248-553-7200
Fax: 248-553-5963
E-mail: kswan@williamtyndale.edu
www.williamtyndale.com

Population: 5,132,799 (2005 Estimate)
Capital City: Saint Paul
Bird: Common Loon
Motto: L'Etoile du nord – The star of the north
Flower: Pink and white lady's-slipper
Tree: Red Pine
Residents Called: Minnesotans
Origin of Name: It is based on the Dakota Sioux Indian word for "sky-tinted water," referring to the Minnesota River or the state's many lakes.
Area: 86,943 square miles (12th largest state)
Statehood: May 11, 1858 (32nd state)
Largest Cities: Minneapolis, Saint Paul, Duluth, Rochester, Bloomington, Brooklyn Park, Plymouth, Eagan, Coon Rapids, Burnsville
College Band Programs: University of Minnesota

Anoka Ramsey Community College at Coon Rapids
Department of Music

11200 Mississippi Blvd. NW
Coon Rapids, MN 55433-3470
Mary Raeker-Rebek
763-433-1317
E-mail: Mary.Raeker-Rebek@anokaramsey.edu
www.an.cc.mn.us

Augsburg College
Department of Music

2211 Riverside Ave.
Minneapolis, MN 55454
Keith McCoy
612-330-1577
Fax: 612-330-1590
E-mail: mccoyk@augsburg.edu
www.augsburg.edu/music

Bemidji State University
Department of Music

1500 Birchmont Dr. NE
Bemidji, MN 56601-2699
Cindy Ladany
218-755-2915
Fax: 218-755-4369
E-mail: cladany@bemidjistate.edu
www.bemidjistate.edu

Bethel College
Department of Music

3900 Bethel Dr.
St. Paul, MN 55112
Jay Fedje
651-638-6380
Fax: 651-638-6001
E-mail: music@bethel.edu
www.bethel.edu

B.Mus.Ed., B.Mus., B.A. in Sacred Music, B.A. in Music, M.A. in Ethnomusicology, Certificate in Applied Ethnomusicology

Carleton College
Department of Music

1 North College St.
Northfield, MN 55057
Music Department Chair
507-646-4347
Fax: 507-646-5561
E-mail: music@carleton.edu
www.carleton.edu

College of St. Benedict
Benedicta Arts Center

37 S. College Ave.
St. Joseph, MN 56374
Edward Turley
320-363-5011
Fax: 612-363-6097
E-mail: eturley@csbju.edu
www.csbsju.edu

College of St. Catherine
Department of Music

2004 Randolph
Saint Paul, MN 55105
Patricia Connors
651-690-6690
Fax: 651-690-8819
E-mail: pcconnors@stkate.edu
www.stkate.edu

BA in Music and Music Education

The College of St. Catherine is a Catholic liberal arts college for women. The Department of Music offers major programs in music and music education. Students who pursue a music major follow one of three courses of study, all leading to the Bachelor of Arts degree. The most basic course of study is the liberal arts major in music. Courses required for the liberal arts music major provide an opportunity for the student to develop performance skills and to gain an understanding of music in theory and culture. Students wishing to pursue a more rigorous course of study in music must be accepted into either the performance and pedagogy concentration or the music education program, which leads to state certification for a K-12 music teaching license. These two courses of study are open only to vocalists, pianists or harpists and require an audition.

College of St. Scholastica
Department of Music

1200 Kenwood Ave.
Duluth, MN 55811
Admissions Office
218-723-6046
E-mail: admissiions@css.edu
www.css.edu

Concordia College
Department of Music

901 8th St. South
Moorehead, MN 56562
800-699-9897
E-mail: admissions@cord.edu
www.cord.edu

Concordia College at Moorhead
Department of Music

901 8th St. South
Moorehead, MN 56562
Omar Correa
218-299-3004
Fax: 218-299-3058
E-mail: correa@cord.edu
www.cord.edu/music

B.A. (Music and Music Education)

The department of music at Concordia College at Moorhead is widely recognized for excellence in music making. Its fully accredited, rigorous B.A. and B.M. programs (in Music, Music Education, Performance and Theory) contribute broadly to a student-centered, liberal arts academic environment, and generate an exceptional quality of music performance rare at the undergraduate level. The department's premier touring ensembles (The Concordia Choir, Band and Orchestra) enjoy national and international acclaim, and perpetuate their respective legacies through a growing list of Concordia Recordings. Artist faculties, who are much in demand on the stage, are first and foremost gifted teachers and dedicated mentors. The department's 200-plus music majors and 45 faculty are housed in the beautiful, expanded and newly renovated Hivdsten Hall of Music. Like all departments at Concordia the Department of Music seeks to nurture the development of the whole person and to imbue in each student the benefits of comprehensive learning and of a global vision, and to provide opportunities not only for professional preparation, but also for personal, social and spiritual development through faith-based education and lives of service.

Crossroads College
Department of Music

920 Mayowood Rd. SW
Rochester, MN 55902-2382
Brian Dunbar
800-456-7651
Fax: 507-288-9046
E-mail: bdunbar@crossroadscollege.edu
www.crossroadscollege.edu

B.A. Music, B.S. Music, B.A. Music Ministry, B.S. Music Ministry

Christian College with emphasis on music in ministry.

Crown College
Department of Music

8700 College View Dr.
Saint Bonifacius, MN 55375
David Donelson
952-446-4231
Fax: 952-446-4149
E-mail: donelsod@crown.edu
www.crown.edu

Bachelor of Music Education

Fergus Falls Community College
Department of Music

1414 College Way
Fergus Falls, MN 56537
218-736-1500
Fax: 218-736-1510
www.minnesota.edu/campuses/fergus_falls/

Gustavus Adolphus College
Department of Music

800 West College Ave.
St. Peter, MN 56082
Alan Meier
507-933-7676
Fax: 507-933-7474
E-mail: ameier@gustavus.edu
www.gustavus.edu

Hamline University
College of Liberal Arts

1536 Hewitt Ave.
Saint Paul, MN 55104-1284
800-753-9753
www.hamline.edu

Hibbing Community College
Department of Music

1515 East 25th St.
Hibbing, MN 55746
800-224-4HCC
E-mail: admissions@hibbing.edu
www.hcc.mnscu.edu

Itasca Community College
Department of Music

Grand Rapids, MN 55744
Robert Perterson
218-327-4477
Fax: 218-327-4350
www.itasca.mnscu.edu

Macalester College
Department of Music

1600 Grand Ave.
St. Paul, MN 55105
Marjorie Merryman
615-696-6804
E-mail: merryman@macalester.edu
www.macalester.edu

Mankato State University
Department of Music

122 Taylor Center
Mankato, MN 56001
507-389-2118
Fax: 507-389-2922
E-mail: music@mnsu.edu
www.mnsu.edu

Martin Luther College
Department of Music

1995 Luther Court
New Ulm, MN 56073
507-354-8221
Fax: 507-354-8225
www.mlc-wels.edu

McNalley Smith College
Department of Music

19 Exchange St. East
St. Paul, MN 55101
612-291-0177
E-mail: info@mcnallysmith.edu
www.mcnallysmith.edu
B.M. in Perfofrmance

Minneapolis Community and Technology College
Department of Music

1501 Hennepin Ave.
Minneapolis, MN 55403
Judith Mehaffey

612-659-6118
E-mail: Judith.Mehaffey@minneapolis.edu
www.minneapolis.edu

Minnesota Bible College
Department of Music

920 Mayowood Rd. SW
Rochester, MN 55902
507-288-4563
E-mail: admissions@mnbc.edu
www.homeschoolfriendlycolleges.com

Minnesota State College Southeast Technical
Department of Music

1501 State St.
Fine Arts Building, Room 207
Marshall, MN 56258
D'Ann Newman
507-537-7234
Fax: 507-537-7014
E-mail: newman@southwestmsu.edu
www.southwestmsu.edu

The music instrument repair programs at
MSC-ST are designed to offer both educators and
performers viable career alternatives within the
field of music.

Minnesota State University at Mankato
Department of Music

310 Maywood Ave.
Mankato, MN 56001
John Lindberg
507-389-2118
Fax: 507-389-2292
E-mail: music@mnsu.edu
www.mnsu.edu

BA, BM in Piano, BM in Organ, BM in Voice, BM
in Instruments, BS Music Industry, BS Music
Education, MM in Music Education, MM in
Performance, MM in Choral Conducting, MM in
Wind Band Conducting

State university, serving south central Minnesota.
Excellent placement rates for graduates, particu-
larly in music education and music industry.
Member, NASM.

Minnesota State University at Moorhead
Department of Music

1104 7th Ave. South
Moorhead, MN 56563
Gina Monson
800-593-7246
Fax: 216-477-4374
E-mail: dragon@mnstate.edu
www.mnstate.edu

Normandale Community College
Department of Music

9700 France Ave. South
Bloomington, MN 55431
Admissions
952-487-8209
www.normandale.edu

North Carolina University
Department of Music

910 Elliot Ave. South
Minneapolis, MN 55404-4778
612-343-4700
Fax: 612-343-4138
E-mail: finearts@northcentral.edu
www.northcentral.edu

North Central Bible College
Department of Music

910 Elliot Ave. South
Minneapolis, MN 55404
612-343-4400
www.northcentral.edu

Northland Community and Technology College

Department of Music

1101 Hwy. 1 East
Thief River Falls, MN 56701
800-959-6282
Fax: 218-681-0774
www.northland.cc.mn.us

Northwestern College
Department of Music

3003 Snelling Ave. North
St. Paul, MN 55113
888-878-5514
E-mail: music@nwc.edu
www.nwc.edu

Red Wing Technical College
Minnesota Southeast Technical

1250 Homer Rd.
Winona, MN 55987
Music Department
800-372-8164
www.southeastmn.edu

Riverland Community College
Department of Music

1900 8th Ave. NW
Austin, MN 55912
Scott Blankenbaker
507-433-0547
E-mail: Sblanken@riverland.edu
www.riverland.edu

A.A.

Riverland community College is a two-year comprehensive community college offering 3,000 students outstanding opportunities in transfer and career education. Students may choose to work toward an A.A. degree while studying music. An A.F.A. degree has been developed specifically for music majors with a target date of Fall 2004 for implementation. Riverland offers a friendly, collegial atmosphere with a department small enough to feel personal, but large enough to provide many exciting educational opportunities. Private and class instruction, performing ensembles, theory, and survey courses are offered in a rapidly growing, active department. Riverland's choirs have appeared at Lincoln Center, Carnegie Hall, and other venues throughout North America.

Southwest State University
Department of Music

1501 State St.
Marshall, MN 56258
D'Ann Newman
507-537-7234
Fax: 507-537-7014
E-mail: newman@southwestmsu.edu
www.southwest.msus.edu

B.A. in Music

St. Cloud State University
Department of Music

238 Performing Arts
Saint Cloud, MN 56301
320-255-3223
Fax: 320-255-2902
E-mail: music@stcloudstate.edu
www.stcloudstate.edu

B.A. in Music

St. John's University
Department of Music

P.O. Box 2000
Collegeville, MN 56321
Edward Turley
E-mail: eturley@csbsju.edu
www.csbsju.edu/music

St. Mary's University of Minnesota
School of the Arts and Music

150 St. Yon's Hall
P.O. Box 1447

Winona, MN 55987
Patrick O'Shea
507-457-1598
E-mail: poshea@smumm.edu
www.smumn.edu/music

B.A. Music Performance, Music Education, Music Industry (two tracks: music business and sound recording and technology), and B.A. in music (general studies degree)

The St. Mary's Music Department offers a challenging and enriching curriculum for music majors and minors, as well as many musical opportunities for non-majors. Music majors prepare themselves for careers in music education (both instrumental and vocal with classroom music), music industry (music technology on/or music business) or graduate school. Most SMU music education students complete the Master's of Instruction degree in their fifth year, thus obtaining both a B.A. in music and M of I degree for their professional teaching licensure. The music faculties are both active professionals and nurturing mentors for students. Students and faculty present an ambitious calendar of recitals and concerts throughout the year. Major ensembles at SMU include: concert band, wind ensemble, concert choir, chamber singers, jazz ensemble, jazz combos, academy chamber orchestra, batuacata percussion ensemble, and many instrumental chamber ensembles. Studies in music allow students to enhance their spiritual and personal lives, and develop the basis for life-long appreciation of music and the arts in a Catholic, liberal arts university setting.

St. Olaf College
Department of Music

1520 St. Olaf Ave.
Northfield, MN 55057
Mary Hakes
507-646-3297
Fax: 507-646-3527
E-mail: music@stolaf.edu
www.stolaf.edu/depts/music

Bachelor of Music, Bachelor of Arts in Music

The music department at St. Olaf College offers an educational experience that unites the artistic standards of a professional program with the intellectual strength and academic breath of the liberal arts in an academically-rigorous environment of free, creative and critical inquiry. St. Olaf is a residential campus of about 3000 full-time undergraduate students, nationally-ranked in music, science and study-abroad programs.

University of Minesota Minneapolis
School of Music

2106 South 4th St.
100 Ferguson Hall
Minneapolis, MN 55404-0437
Lynwood Jones
612-624-5740
Fax: 612-624-8001
E-mail: mus-adm@umn.edu
www.music.umm.edu

BA, BM, MA, MM, DMA, PhD

University of Minnesota at Crookston
Department of Music and Theatre

2900 University Ave.
Crookston, MN 56716
George French
218-281-8277
Fax: 218-637-6600
E-mail: gfrench@umn.edu
www.crk.umn.edu

University of Minnesota at Duluth
Department of Music

1201 Ordean Court
Humanities 231
Duluth, MN 55812
Jeanne Doty
218-726-8208
Fax: 218-726-8210

E-mail: mu@d.umn.edu
www.d.umn.edu/music

University of Minnesota at Morris
Department of Music

73 Humanities/Fine Arts
Morris, MN 56267
Richard 'Jean' Richards
320-589-6235
E-mail: richarrj@morris.umn.edu
www.mrs.umn.edu/academic/music

University of Minnesota at Twin Cities
Ferguson Hall

200E Ferguson Hall
Minneapolis, MN 55445
Noel Zahler
612-626-1882
E-mail: nbz@umn.edu
www.music.umn.edu

University of St. Thomas
Department of Music

2115 Summit Ave.
Saint Paul, MN 55105
Matthew George
652-962-5850
Fax: 652-962-5976
E-mail: mjgeorge@stthomas.edu
www.stthomas.edu

BM (Performance & Music Ed) BA (Music, Litugi-
cal & Music Business)

Winona State University
Department of Music

Performing Arts Center
175 West Mark
Winona, MN 55987
Julie Levinski
507-457-5000
Fax: 507-457-5620

E-mail: jlevinski@winona.edu
www.winona.msus.edu/music

B.S. Music Education; B.A. Music-Performance;
B.S.Music-Liberal Arts; B.S. Music Business;
Music Minors--B.S. (Teaching) and B.A.

Winona State University is located in the pictur-
esque Mississippi River Valley of southeastern
Minnesota with easy access to the twin Cities,
Madison,Milwaukee and Chicago. The Winona
State University Departmentof Music offers
students a variety of programs that balance
academic quality and performance, supported
by the resources of a major regional university.
The department features a dedicated teaching
faculty of active performing artists, small classes,
personal instruction, and a wide variety of
performing opportunities in both large and small
ensembles.

Worthington Community College
Department of Music

P.O. Box 107
Worthington, MN 56187
Galen Benton
507-372-2107
Fax: 507-372-5801
www.mnwest.mnscu.edu

Population: 2,921,088 (2005 Estimate)
Capital City: Jackson
Bird: Mockingbird
Motto: Virtute Et Armis – By valor and arms
Flower: Magnolia
Tree: Magnolia
Residents Called: Mississippians
Origin of Name: Possibly based on Chippewa Indian words "mici zibi," loosely meaning great river.
Area: 48,434 square miles (32nd largest state)
Statehood: December 10, 1817 (20th state)
Largest Cities: Jackson, Gulfport, Biloxi, Hattiesburg, Greenville, Meridian, Tupelo, Southaven, Vicksburg, Pascagoula
College Band Programs: Mississippi College, Mississippi State University, University of Mississippi, University of Southern Mississippi

Alcorn State University
Department of Fine Arts

1000 ASU Dr. #29
Alcorn State, MS 39096-7500
Larry Konecky
601-877-6261
Fax: 601-877-6262
E-mail: lkonecky@alcorn.edu
www.alcorn.edu

Belhaven College
Department of Music

1500 Peachtree St.
Jackson, MS 39202
800-960-5940
E-mail: music@belhaven.edu
www.belhaven.edu

Blue Mountain College
Department of Music

201 W. Main
Blue Mountain, MS 38610
Jerri Lamar Kantack
662-685-4771
E-mail: jkantack@bmc.edu
www.bmc.edu

Copiah-Lincoln Community College
Department of Music

P.O. Box 649
Wesson, MS 39191-0649
Brad Johnson
601-643-8431
Fax: 601-643-8212
E-mail: brad.johnson@colin.cc.ms.us
www.colin.edu

Delta State University
Department of Music

P.O. Box 3256
Cleveland, MS 38733
662-846-4615
E-mail: csteele@deltastate.edu
www.deltastate.edu

Hinds Community College
Department of Music

P.O. Box 1100
Raymond, MS 39154
Berry Rhines
601-857-3271
Fax: 601-857-3458
E-mail: bsrhines@hinds.cc.ms.us
www.hindscc.edu

Itawamba Community College
Department of Music

602 West Hill St.
Fulton, MS 38843-1099
Karen Davis
662-862-8306
E-mail: kdavis@iccms.edu
www.iccms.edu

Itawamba Community College is a fully accredited member of the Southern Association of Colleges and Schools. The music curriculum offers freshman and sophomore level music courses that transfer to four-year institutions. Performing organizations and opportunities include marching band; concert bands; choir; woodwind; brass, percussion, vocal, jazz, and pop-rock ensembles; student recital; music theater; and music technology.

Jackson State University
Department of Music

Jackson, MS 39217
Jimmy James Jr.
601-979-2141
Fax: 610-968-2568
E-mail: jjames@ccaix.jsums.edu
www.jsums.edu

Jones County Junior College
Department of Music

900 South Court St.
Ellisville, MS 39437
Susan Smith
601-477-4094
Fax: 601-477-4017
E-mail: susan.smith@jcjc.edu
www.jcjc.cc.ms.us

A.A. (major in music education or music)

The Jones County Junior college music department features courses designed to meet the requirements of university degree programs for major in music performance or music education. The Jones Band and Choir are among the best known in the southeastern United States. The band has performed at the Macy's Thanksgiving Day Parade, the Orange Bowl Parade, the Tournament of Roses Parade and the Marshall Field's Jungle Elf Parade in Chicago. The Choir has performed in Dallas, Atlanta, Minneapolis, New York and London, England.

Meridian Community College
Department of Music

910 Hwy. 19
N Meridian, MS 39307
Robert Hermetz
601-483-8241
Fax: 601-482-3936
www.mcc.cc.ms.us

Millsaps College
Department of Music

1701 North State St.
Jackson, MS 39210
Tim Coker
601-974-1000
E-mail: cokertc@millsaps.edu
www.millsaps.edu

Mississippi College
Department of Music

P.O. Box 4201
Clinton, MS 39058
Linda Edwards
601-925-3440
Fax: 601-925-3945
E-mail: music@mc.edu
www.mc.edu

Mississippi Gulf Coast College
Department of Music

Perkinston, MS 39573
Marilyn Lott
601-528-8408
E-mail: marilyn.lott@mgcc.edu
www.mgccc.edu

Mississippi State University
Department of Music

P.O. Box 9734
Mississippi State, MS 39762
662-325-3070
E-mail: musiced@colled.msstate.edu
www.msstate.edu

Bachelor of Arts in Music, Music Education, Minor in Music

Mississippi University for Women
Division of Fine and Performing Arts

1100 College St. MUW-70
Columbus, MS 39701
James O. Allen
662-329-7199
Fax: 662-241-7815
E-mail: jallen@muw.edu
www.muw.edu/fine_arts

Mississippi Valley State University
Department of Music

14000 Hwy. 82 West
Itta Bena, MS 38941
601-254-9041
www.mvsu.edu

Northeast Mississippi Community College
Department of Music

100 Cumminham Blvd.
Booneville, MS 38829
Jerry Rains
662-720-7320
E-mail: jcrains@nemcc.edu
www.nemcc.edu

Pearl River Community College
Department of Music

101 Hwy. 11 North
Box 5388
Poplaville, MS 39470
601-403-1180
Fax: 601-403-1138
E-mail: arawls@prcc.cc.ms.us
www.prcc.edu

Rust College
Department of Music

Holly Springs, MS 38635
Norman Chapman
601-252-4661
www.rustcollege.edu

University of Mississippi
Department of Music

164 Scruggs Building
P.O. Box 1848
University, MS 38677-1848
662-915-7268
Fax: 662-915-1230
E-mail: music@olemiss.edu
www.olemiss.edu/depts/music

B.A., B.M., M.M., and D.A.

The department of music at the University of Mississippi prepares professional musicians and educators, and has graduates teaching and performing throughout the nation. Over 160 students are enrolled as majors in the department of music. The size is ideal in affording a pleasant atmosphere and ensuring proper instrumentation for the larger ensembles as well as individual attention for students in private applied music study, in classes and in the many small ensembles. Performance facilities for music include: the Gertrude Ford Center, a 1,300-seat theatre/concert hall, the 240-seat Meek Auditorium, commonly used as a recital hall, the Fulton Chapel, a 650-seat concert hall used jointly by the department of theatre arts, Paris-Yates Chapel, seating 250, and the home of the university's 32 rank, 1642-pipe organ.

University of Southern Mississippi
Department of Music

118 College Dr.
Hattiesburg, MS 39406-0001
Charles Elliott
601-266-1000
E-mail: charles.elliott@usm.edu
www.usm.edu

William Carey College
Department of Music

498 Tuscan Ave.
WCU Box 14
Hattiesburg, MS 39401
Mark Hugh Malone
601-318-6175
E-mail: mark.malone@wmcarey.edu
www.wmcarey.edu

Population: 5,800,310 (2005 Estimate)
Capital City: Jefferson City
Bird: Bluebird
Motto: Salus Populi Suprema Lex Esto – The welfare of the people shall be the supreme law.
Flower: Hawthorn
Tree: Flowering Dogwood
Residents Called: Missourians
Origin of Name: Named after Missouri Indian tribe whose name means, "town of the large canoes."
Area: 69,709 square miles (21st largest state)
Statehood: August 10, 1821 (24th state)
Largest Cities: Kansas City, Saint Louis, Springfield, Independence, Columbia, Saint Joseph, Lee's Summit, Saint Charles, Saint Peters
College Band Programs: Central Missouri University, , University of Missouri-Columbia, University of Missouri-Rolla

Avila College
Department of Music

11901 Wornall Rd.
Kansas City, MO 64145-1007
Amity Bryson
816-501-3651
Fax: 816-501-2442
E-mail: brysonah@mail.avila.edu
www.avila.edu

Calvary Bible College and Theological Seminary
Department of Music

15800 Calvary Rd.
Kansas City, MO 64147
Paul Vander Mey
816-322-0110
Fax: 816-331-4474
E-mail: musicdept@calvary.edu
www.calvary.edu

B.Mus. in 1) Music Education (Vocal/Choral or
Instrumental); 2) Music Performance & Pedagogy
(piano or voice); and B.S. in 1) Church Music; 2)
Music & Youth Ministry

The institution is a Bible College with a high
quality, Christian, music/arts program in a small,
caring atmosphere. Music and arts faculty have
much experience and expertise. Personal attention and plenty of performance opportunities
abound. Strong emphasis in piano and voice.
Majors in: Music Performance & Pedagogy; Music
Education; Church Music; and Music & Youth
Ministry. Producing quality musicians to meet the
music needs of today.

Central Methodist College
Swinney Conservatory of Music

411 Central Methodist Square
Fayette, MO 65248
Ron Shroyer
660-248-6321
E-mail: rshroyer@centralmethodist.edu
www.centralmethodist.edu

Central Missouri State University
Department of Music

P.O. Box 800
Warrensburg, MO 64093
Dean Steven Boone
660-543-4364
E-mail: sboone@cmsu.edu
www.cmsu.edu/music

B.A in music, Bachelor odf Music Education

College of the Ozarks
Department of Music

P.O. Box 17
Point Lookout, MO 65726
Bruce Gerlach
417-334-6411
E-mail: gerlach@cofo.edu
www.cofo.edu

Cottey College
Department of Music

601 Laclede Ave.
Neosho, MO 64850-9165
Theresa Forrester Spencer
417-667-8181
Fax: 417-667-8103
www.cottey.edu

Culver Stockton College
Department of Fine Arts

One College Hill
Canton, MO 63435
573-288-6346
E-mail: finearts@culver.edu
www.culver.edu

Drury College
Department of Music

900 North Benton Ave.
Springfield, MO 65802-3712

Allin Sorenson
417-873-7291
E-mail: asorenso@drury.edu
www.drury.edu

Music, Music Education, Music Therapy

Evangel University
Department of Music

1111 North Glenstone Ave.
Springfield, MO 65802
Charity Fahlstrom
417-865-2815
Fax: 417-836-7665
E-mail: fahlstromc@evangel.edu
www.evangel.edu

Fontbonne College
Department of Fine Arts

6800 Wyndown Blvd.
St. Louis, MO 63105
314-889-1400
E-mail: fadmiss@fontbonne.edu
www.fontbonne.edu

Hannibal-LaGrange College
Department of Music

2800 Palmyra Rd.
Hannibal, MO 63401
Ray Carty
573-221-3675
Fax: 573-221-6594
E-mail: admissions@hlg.edu
www.hlg.edu

Church Music, Instrumental Performance,
Piano Performance, Vocal Performance, Music
Education

Hannibal-LaGrange College is a four-year college
of the liberal arts and sciences. Founded in 1858,
around 1,150 students come from 24 states and
18 countries to study.

Jefferson College
Department of Music

1000 Viking Dr.
Hillsboro, MO 63050-2440
636-797-3000
www.jeffco.edu

Lindenwood University
Department of Music

209 South KingsHwy.
Saint Charles, MO 63303
Joseph Alsobrook
636-949-4164
E-mail: jalsobrook@lindenwood.edu
www.lindenwood.edu

Maryville University
Department of Music

650 Mayville University Dr.
St. Louis, MO 63141
314-529-9300
www.maryville.edu

Mineral Area College
Department of Music

5270 Flat River Rd.
P.O. Box 1000
Park Hills, MO 63601
573-431-4593
www.mineralarea.edu

Missouri Southern State College
Department of Music

3950 East Newman Rd.
Joplin, MO 64801-1595
Rita Boyer
417-625-9318
Fax: 417-625-3030
E-mail: boyer-r@mssu.edu
www.mssu.edu

Missouri Western State College
Department of Music

4525 Downs Dr.
St. Joseph, MO 64507
Matt Gilmour
816-271-4421
E-mail: gilmour@missouriwestern.edu
www.missouriwestern.edu

Missouri Western State College has nearly 5,600 students. The department of music, led by chairperson Dr. F.M. Gilmour, has 125 majors in the diverse music offerings. Students can gain a degree and certification in music education with an instrumental or vocal certification (or both). They can also choose a bachelor of arts degree aimed at following different areas of music business: commercial music/jazz studies emphasis, commercial music/business emphasis, or commercial music/recording/studio emphasis. Missouri Western also offers a strong Bachelor of Arts degree in performance. Missouri Western has an excellent faculty and fine facilities. Outstanding band scholarships and talent awards are available.

Northwest Missouri State University
Department of Music

800 University Dr.
Maryville, MO 64468
660-562-1315
Fax: 660-562-1326
E-mail: music@nwmissouri.edu
www.nwmissouri.edu/~music

Bachelor of Arts, Bachelor of Science in Education, Instrumental k-12 and Vocal k-12

Northwest Missouri State University is located in Maryville, Missouri, a community of 11,000. Maryville is 45 miles from St. Joseph and approximately equidistant from Kansas City and Omaha. The university has a total enrollment of approximately 6,000 students. The College of Arts and Sciences has approximately 2,000 undergraduate and 190 graduate students. The

Department of Music enrolls approximately 110 majors, pursuing the B.S.Ed. or the B.A. degree in music. The department normally includes twelve full-time and four adjunct faculty members. For more information visit the department web site at www.nwmissouri.edu/dept/music.

Park University
Department of Music

8700 NW River Park Dr.
Parkville, MO 64152
Robert Pevitts
800-745-7275
E-mail: robert.pevitts@park.edu
www.park.edu

Rockhurst College
Department of Music

1100 Rockhurst Rd.
Kansas City, MO 64110
Peter J. Bicak
816-501-4682
E-mail: pete.bicak@rockhurst.edu
www.rockhurst.edu

Southeast Missouri State University
Department of Music

1 University Plaza MS7800
Cape Girardeau, MO 63701
573-651-2141
E-mail: bdelph@semo.edu
www.semo.edu

The department of music at Southeast offers both the variety of performing and learning experiences found at a large university, and the individual attention and relaxed atmosphere expected of a small college. Southeast is fully accredited by the National Association of Schools of Music. The department of music has over 120 music majors and has full and adjunct instructors in each area. Our full and adjunct faculty represents all areas of musical study, including performance, composition, electronic music and world music. This outstanding group of educators has performed both nationally and abroad with recognition in Canada, China, England, Ireland, Japan, Scotland and the Ukraine. The overall student to faculty ratio is 18:1, which provides students with the attention and instruction that they deserve and expect. Southeast Missouri State University is a public university founded in 1873, that has evolved into a comprehensive state university with more than 150 academic programs. Located in Cape Girardeau, "on the banks" of the Mississippi River, Southeast has nearly 400 full-time faculty. Music faculty with degrees from universities such as Cornell, Julliard and the London College of Music work with students in size-controlled classes. The department of music has over 15 ensembles, encompassing every performance area. Scholarship assistance is available through competitive auditions held each spring semester, by appointment.

Southwest Baptist University
Department of Music

1600 University Ave.
Bolivar, MO 65613
Jeffery Waters
417-328-1644
Fax: 417-326-1637
E-mail: jwaters@sbuniv.edu
www.sbuniv.edu

Southwest Missouri State University
Department of Music

901 South National Ave.
Springfield, MO 65897
James J. Burwinkel
314-977-3030
E-mail: burwinjj@slu.edu
www.slu.edu

St. Louis University
Department of Fine and Performance Art and Music

221 North Grand Blvd.
St. Louis, MO 63101

Suzanne Lee
314-977-2410
Fax: 314-977-2999
E-mail: leesr@slu.edu
www.slu.edu

Stephens College
Department of Perf Arts-Music

1200 East Broadway
Columbia, MO 65215
Pam Ellsworth
573-876-7117
www.stephens.edu

Three Rivers Community College
Department of Music

2080 Three Rivers Blvd.
Poplar Bluff, MO 63901
Cindy White
573-840-9639
Fax: 573-840-9603
E-mail: cwhite@trcc.cc.mo.us
www.trcc.cc.mo.us

Truman State University
Division of Fine Arts

100 East Normal St.
Kirksville, MO 63501-4221
Kristin Baer
660-785-4114
Fax: 660-785-7456
E-mail: kimbaer@truman.edu
www.truman.edu

University of Missouri at Columbia
Department of Music

135 Fine Arts Building
Columbia, MO 65211.
Melvin Platt
573-882-2606

Fax: 573-884-7444
E-mail: Plattm@missouri.edu
www.missouri.edu

M., BS Ed, BA, MM, Med

University of Missouri at Kansas City
Conservatory of Music

4949 Cherry St.
Kansas City, MO 64015
James Elswick
816-235-2900
Fax: 816-235-5264
E-mail: pembrookr@umkc.edu

www.umkc.edu/conservatory

Bachelors through Doctoral Degrees; Performance, Music Education, Music Therapy, Composition, Music Theory, Music History, Music, Dance

Now entering its second century, the Conservatory continues as the outstanding comprehensive education center for music and dance in the Midwest. As a major player and contributor in the cultural growth of Kansas City and the region, the Conservatory provides students of music and dance with opportunities that are hard to find anywhere else.

University of Missouri at St. Louis
Department of Music

8001 Natural Bridge Rd.
St. Louis, MO 63121
Lonard Ott
314-516-5981
Fax: 314-516-6593
E-mail: leonard_ott@umsl.edu
www.umsl.edu/~music

Washington University
Department of Music

One Brookings Dr.
Campus Box 1032
St. Louis, MO 63130
Kathleen Boldaun
314-935-5517
Fax: 314-935-4034
E-mail: kbolduan@wusl.edu
www.artsci.wustl.edu/~music

Webster University Leigh Gerdine College of Fine Arts
Department of Music

470 East Lockwood Ave.
St. Louis, MO 63119
Micheal Parkinson
314-968-7032
Fax: 314-963-5048
E-mail: parkinmi@webster.edu
www.webster.edu/depts/finearts/music

BM: composition, performance (orchestral instruments, guitar, voice, piano, organ), jazz studies (performance & music technology), BMEd (instrumental and vocal), BA in Music, MM in performance (voice, piano, organ, guitar), orchestral performance, church music, composition, and jazz studies; Certificate in Music Entrepreneurship, Minor in Music

Webster University Department of Music offers state of the art degrees in classical and jazz music. Located in St. Louis, one of the nation's great art centers, students work with renowned artists including members of the St. Louis Symphony. Students may also study at Webster-Vienna to gain a great international music education.

William Jewell College
Department of Music

500 College Hill
Liberty, MO 64068
Ian Coleman
816-781-7700
E-mail: colemani@william.jewell.edu
www.jewell.edu

William Woods University
Visual and Performing Arts

1 University Ave.
Fulton, MO 65251
800-995-3159
www.wmwoods.edu

Minor in Music

Population: 935,670 (2005 Estimate)
Capital City: Helena
Bird: Western Meadowlark
Motto: Oro y plata – Gold and Silver
Flower: Bitterroot
Tree: Ponderosa pine
Residents Called: Montanans
Origin of Name: Based on Spanish word for "mountainous"
Area: 147,046 square miles (4th largest state)
Statehood: November 8,1889 (41st state)
Largest Cities: Billings, Missoula, Great Falls, Butte, Bozeman, Helena, Kalispell, Havre, Anaconda, Miles City
College Band Programs: Montana State University

Dawson Community College
Department of Music

300 College Dr.
P.O. Box 421
Glendive, MT 59330
406-377-3396
Fax: 406-377-8132
www.dawson.cc.mt.us

Montana State University at Billings
Department of Music

1500 North 30th St.
Billings, MT 59101
406-657-2158
E-mail: berickson@msubillings.edu
www.msubillings.edu

Montana State University at Bozeman
Department of Music

186 Howard Hall
P.O. Box 173420
Bozeman, MT 59717
Kim Eggemeyer
406-994-3562
Fax: 406-994-6656
E-mail: keggemeyer@montana.edu
www.montana.edu/music

B.A. in music, B.M.E., and M.M.

The Montana State University Department of Music annually enrolls approximately 100 music majors and an additional 2,000 non-majors in a variety of academic, performance, and pedagogical activities. While its primary role is to develop and maintain programs, which prepare students for careers in music teaching, the department of music provides a musical environment in which students pursue the music arts. A faculty comprised of outstanding musician/teachers provides instruction in music. The department of music is an asset to the cultural and intellectual life of Montana State University and the community of Bozeman. Students, faculty, ensembles, and guest artists present more than 100 recitals and concerts annually. Many performing ensembles, ranging from the Chamber Orchestra, Wind Ensemble, and Chorale, to the Studio Jazz Lab and the "Spirit of the West" Marching Band, provide opportunities for all university students to actively continue their music endeavors. Many of these ensembles have represented the department of music at national conferences and through the international tours. The department of music is a wonderful environment in which to study and perform. Come to Montana State University - Bozeman and continue to make music with us.

University of Montana
Department of Music

Missoula, MT 59812
Stephen Kalm
406-243-6880
Fax: 406-243-2441
E-mail: griz.music@umontana.edu
www.sfa.umt.edu/music

Western Montana College
Fine Arts Department

710 S. Atlantic St.
Dillon, MT 59725
Jeri Bonnin
866-UMW-MONT
E-mail: J_bonnin@umwestern.edu
www.umwestern.edu

NEBRASKA

Population: 1,758,787 (2005 Estimate)
Capital City: Lincoln
Bird: Western Meadowlark
Motto: Equality before the law
Flower: Goldenrod
Tree: Eastern Cottonwood
Residents Called: Nebraskans
Origin of Name: Name based on an Oto Indian word that means "flat water," referring to the Platte River.
Area: 77,358 square miles (16th largest state)
Statehood: March 1, 1867 (37th state)
Largest Cities: Omaha, Lincoln, Bellevue, Grand Island, Kearney, Fremont, Hastings, North Platte, Norfolk, Columbus
College Band Programs: University of Nebraska-Lincoln

Central Community College Platte
Department of Music

P.O. Box 1027
4500 63rd St.
Columbus, NE 68602-1027
Rex Hash
308-398-4222
Fax: 308-398-7399
www.cccneb.edu

Chadron State College

Memorial Hall
1000 Main St.
Chadron, NE 69337
William Winki
308-432-6375
Fax: 308-432-6464
E-mail: wwinkle@csc.edu
www.csc.edu

College of St. Mary
Department of Music

1901 South 72nd St.
Omaha, NE 68124-2301
Patricia Will
402-399-2622
Fax: 402-399-2341
www.csm.edu

Concordia College
Department of Music

800 North Columbia Ave.
Seward, NE 68434-1556
Charles Ore
402-643-3651
Fax: 402-643-4073
www.cord.edu/music

Creighton University
Music Program

2500 California Plaza
Omaha, NE 68178
Frederick Hanna
402-280-1124
E-mail: fhanna@creighton.edu
www.creighton.edu

Dana College
Music Department

2848 College Dr.
Blair, NE 68008
Richard Palmer
800-444-7310
Fax: 402-426-7332
E-mail: rpalmer@dana.edu
www.dana.edu

Doane College
Department of Music

1014 Boswell Ave.
Crete, NE 68333
Jay Gilbert
800-333-6263
Fax: 402-862-8600
E-mail: jgilbert@doane.edu
www.doane.edu

Grace University
Department of Music

1311 South 9th St.
Omaha, NE 68108-3629
Greg Zielke
402-449-2800
E-mail: gdzielke@graceu.edu
www.graceuniversity.edu

Hastings College
Department of Music

710 North Turner
Hastings, NE 68902
Robin Koozer
800-532-7642

www.hastings.edu

Midland Lutheran College
Department of Music

900 NorthClarkson
Fremont, NE 68025
Eric Richards
402-941-6390
E-mail: richards@mic.edu
www.mlc.edu

Nebraska Wesleyan University
Department of Music

5000 St. Paul
Lincoln, NE 68504
402-465-7501
www.nebwesleyan.edu

Nebraska Wesleyan University is a private liberal
arts college, accredited by NCA and NASM. It
features a small student/teacher ratio, 13
performing ensembles and 21 full- and part-time
artist faculty.

Northeast Community College
Department of Music

801 East Benjamin Ave.
Norfolk, NE 68702
Linda Boullion
402-844-7354
Fax: 402-844-7402
E-mail: lindab@northeastcollege.com
www.northeastcollege.com

Peru State College
Department of Music

P.O. Box 10
600 Hoyt St.
Peru, NE 68421
402-872-2237
Fax: 402-872-2412
E-mail: Btrail@oakmail.peru.edu
www.peru.edu

Union College
Department of Music

3800 South 48th St.
Engel Hall
Lincoln, NE 68501
Daniel Lynn
402-486-2553
Fax: 402-486-2528
E-mail: dalynn@ucollege.edu
www.ucollege.edu

University of Nebraska
School of Music

P.O. Box 880100
Lincoln, NE 68588
Susan Tribby
402-472-6845
Fax: 402-472-8962
E-mail: music2unl.edu
www.music.unl.edu

University of Nebraska at Kearney
Department of Music and Performing Arts

2506 12th Ave.
Kearney, NE 68849
Valerie Cisler
308-865-8473
Fax: 308-865-8806
E-mail: cislerv@unk.edu
www.unk.edu

University of Nebraska at Omaha
Department of Music

6001 Dodge St.
Omaha, NE 68182
James R. Saker
402-554-2251
Fax: 402-554-2252
E-mail: jsaker@mail.unomaha.edu

www.unomaha.edu

Bachelor of Music (Education, Performance, Composition, Music Technology), MM Music Education, Performance, Conducting

A vibrant, metropolitan university in the state's largest city, the University of Nebraska at Omaha (UNO)has an enrollment of 16,000 students, and is a residential campus with several new and beautifully appointed residence halls. The campus is located in the heart of Omaha, a sophisticated city of more than 500,000. Omaha consists of a diverse community with a myriad of interesting neighborhoods. Music-making in Omaha is represented by an active Symphony and Opera Company, and many community and semi-professional performing groups. UNO is in a unique position to take advantage of these resources. The Department of Music is one of five academic units within the College of Communication, Fine Arts, and Media. It is located in the beautifully landscaped Janet A. and Willis S. Strauss Performing Arts Center, which is nestled near the focal point of the campus, a campanile that houses a carillon of forty-seven bells. The complex itself boasts a tunable recital hall which seats 500, impressive acoustic isolation, and well-equipped classrooms and rehearsal spaces. The center serves as a nexus of musical activity not only for the university, but for the city of Omaha as well. The Department of Music has a faculty of 40 full and part time members and is a fully accredited member of the National Association of Schools of Music.

Wayne State College
Fine Arts Division

1111 Main St.
Wayne, NE 68787
Linc Morris
800-228-9972
Fax: 402-375-7180
E-mail: admit1@wsc.edu
www.wsc.edu

Western Nebraska Community College
Department of Music

1601 E. 27th St.
Scottsbluff, NE 69361
Dale Skornia
308-635-6046
Fax: 308-635-6100
E-mail: dskornia@hannibal.wncc.cc.ne.us
www.wncc.net

York College
Department of Music

1125 East 8th
York, NE 68467
Clark Roush
402-363-5610
Fax: 402-363-5712
E-mail: croush@york.edu
www.york.edu

Population: 2,414,807 (2005 Estimate)
Capital City: Carson City
Bird: Mountain Bluebird
Motto: All for our country
Flower: Sagebrush
Tree: Single leaf pinon and Bristlecone pine
Residents Called: Nevadans
Nickname: The Silver State
Area: 110,567 square miles (7th largest state)
Statehood: October 31, 1864 (36th state)
Largest Cities: Las Vegas, Reno, Henderson, North Las Vegas, Sparks, Carson City, Elko, Boulder City, Mesquite, Fallon
College Band Programs: University of Nevada-Las Vegas

University of Nevada
at Las Vegas
College of Fine and
Performing Arts

4505 South Maryland Pkwy.
Las Vegas, NV 89154
Jonathan Good
702-895-3332
Fax: 702-895-4239
www.unlv.edu

University of Nevada at Reno
Department of Music

Reno, NV 89557
Melissa Choroszy
775-784-4700
E-mail: choroszy@admin.unr.edu
www.unr.edu/artsci/music

NEW HAMPSHIRE

Population: 1,309,940 (2005 Estimate)
Capital City: Concord
Bird: Purple Finch
Motto: Live free or die
Flower: Purple lilac
Tree: White birch
Residents Called: New Hampshirites
Nickname: The Granite State
Area: 9,351 square miles (46th largest state)
Statehood: June 21, 1788 (9th state)
Largest Cities: Manchester, Nashua, Concord, Derry, Rochester, Salem, Dover, Merrimack, Londonderry, Hudson
College Band Programs: Dartmouth College, University of New Hampshire

Colby-Sawyer College
Department of Fine and Performing Arts

541 Main St.
New London, NH 03257
Loretta Barnett
603-526-3668
E-mail: lbarnett@colby-sawyer.edu
www.colby-sawyer.edu

Dartmouth College
Department of Music

Hinman P.O. Box 6187
Hanover, NH 03755
603-646-1110
E-mail: contact@dartmouth.edu
www.dartmouth.edu

Franklin Pierce College
Department of Music

20 College Rd.
Rindge, NH 03461
800-437-0048
Fax: 603-899-4372
www.fpc.edu

Keene State College
Department of Music

229 Main St.
Keene, NH 03435
Peggy Richmond
603-358-2276
Fax: 603-358-2767
E-mail: mrichmon@keene.edu
www.keene.edu

B.M., B.A.

Keene State College has approximately 100 music majors, 9 full-time music faculty and 15 adjunct music faculty on a liberal arts college campus of 5,000 students. The music programs are accredited by the NASM. The music major program at Keene State College provides preparation for a wide range of career opportunities. In the Bachelor of Music degree program, students may choose teaching in the public school, teaching in privately owned studios, or professional performance. In the Bachelor of Arts degree programs, students may pursue interests in four specializations: Music Theory, Music Composition, Music history and literature, or (for elementary education majors) Music for Classroom Teachers. Entrance to any of these programs is contingent upon passing an audition on a traditional instrument or voice.

Plymouth State University
Department of Music, Dance, and Theatre

17 High St.
Plymouth, NH 03264-1595
Jonathan C. Santore
603-535-2334
Fax: 603-535-2645
E-mail: MTD-Dept@plymouth.edu
www.plymouth.edu/mtd

BS Music Ed; BA Music in Music Technology, Piano Performance and Pedagogy, Vocal Performance and Pedagogy, and Contract option

Music students at PSU receive a great deal of individualized attention from master teachers, with abundant performing opportunities in all the performing arts.

St. Anselm College
Department of Fine Arts and Music

100 St. Anslem Dr.
Manchester, NH 03102
603-641-7370
Fax:
E-mail: finearts@anselm.edu
www.anselm.edu

University of New Hampshire
Paul Creative Arts Center

PCAC 30 College Rd.
Durham, NH 03824
Isabel Gray
603-862-2404
Fax: 603-862-3155
E-mail: music.info@unh.edu
www.unh.edu/music

Population: 8,717,925 (2005 Estimate)
Capital City: Trenton
Bird: Eastern Goldfinch
Motto: Liberty and Prosperity
Flower: Violet
Tree: Red Oak
Residents Called: New Jerseyites
Nickname: The Garden State
Area: 8,722 square miles (47th largest state)
Statehood: December 18, 1787 (3rd state)
Largest Cities: Newark, Jersey City, Paterson, Elizabeth, Edison Township, Woodbridge, Township, Dover Township, Hamilton, Trenton, Camden
College Band Programs: Princeton University, Rutgers University

Bergen Community College
Music discipline, Arts and Communication Department

400 Paramus Rd.
Paramus, NJ 07652
Linda Marcel
201-447-7143
E-mail: lhodge@bergen.edu
www.bergen.edu

A.A.S. General Music, Music Technology, Music Business, Certificate Programs in Music Business and Music Technology

Bergen Commuity College offers applied music in all areas of performance, a state of the art music technology program, recording facilities, and dynamic music business program.

Caldwell College
Department of Music

9 Ryerson Ave.
Caldwell, NJ 07006
Robert Bednar
973-618-3000
E-mail: RBednar@caldwell.edu
www.caldwell.edu

Camden County College
Department of Music

P.O. Box 200
Blackwood, NJ 08012
Judith Rowlands
856-227-7200
Fax: 856-374-4969
www.camdencc.edu

Centenary College
Department of Music

400 Jefferson St.
Hackettstown, NJ 07840-2184
908-852-1400
www.centenarycollege.edu

College of New Jersey
Department of Music

P.O. Box 7718
Ewing, NJ 08628
Suzanne L. Hickman
609-771-2551
E-mail: hickman@tcnj.edu
www.tcnj.edu/~music

College of St. Elizabeth
Department of Music

2 Convent Rd.
Morristown, NJ 07960-6989
Teresa Walters
973-290-4216
E-mail: twalters@cse.edu
www.cse.edu

County College of Morris
Department of Music

214 Center Grove Rd.
Randolph, NJ 07869-2086
Susuan Cook
973-325-4300
E-mail: scook@ccm.edu
www.ccm.edu

Drew University
Department of Music

36 Madison Ave.
Madison, NJ 07940
Norman Lowrey
973-408-3421
E-mail: nlowrey@drew.edu
www.depts.drew.edu

Fairleigh Dickinson University Madison
Department of Fine Arts

Madison, NJ 07940
Louis Gordon

201-593-8638
www.fdu.edu

Georgian Court College
Department of Art and Music

900 Lakewood Ave.
Lakewood, NJ 08701
Kathie Gallant
732-987-2624
Fax: 732-987-2058
E-mail: malamutm@georgian.edu
www.georgian.edu

Bachelor of Arts in Music

In the Department of Music at Georgian Court University, every student gets to shine. Classes are small and student-focused, so each student enjoys individualized attention and a personalized education. Combine that with GCU's beautiful campus and caring atmosphere, and you have all you need to achieve your goals.

Kean University
Department of Music

1000 Morris Ave.
Union, NJ 07083
Thomas Connors
908-737-4330
Fax: 908-737-4333
E-mail: tconnors@kean.edu
www.kean.edu

Monmouth University
Department of Music and Theatre Arts

400 Cedar Ave.
West Long Branch, NJ 07764
732-571-3442
www.monmouth.edu

Montclair State University
Department of Music

Cali School of Music

One Normal Ave.
Upper Montclair, NJ 07043
Robert Aldridge
973-655-7212
Fax: 973-655-5279
E-mail: aldridger@mail.montclair.edu
www.montclair.edu/music

The department of music at Montclair State University has been training professional musicians for more than 45 years. Just 14 miles from Manhattan, our program attracts a distinguished faculty and guest artists to teach and perform every semester, while enabling students to take advantage of New York City's concerts, open rehearsals and extensive resources. The department offers undergraduate and graduate degrees in performance, theory/composition, music education and music therapy. Instruction is based on a rigorous traditional approach, combined with methodologies from the most up-to-date research available. Our philosophy is that students should be exposed to all facets of music, including performance, theory and music history, regardless of their particular concentration. Professional development is key to the music program. While activities such as ensemble and performance preparation are part of the required curriculum, additional experiences are offered through special programs and affiliations of the faculty. The department sponsors a full roster of 12 performing ensembles and more than 100 concerts each year. Facilities include three concert halls, faculty teaching studios, practice rooms, an electronic music studio and a computer/MIDI-keyboard lab. The department is fully accredited by the National Association of Schools of Music (NASM). The music therapy program is approved by the National Association for Music Therapy.

New Jersey City University
Department of Music, Dance, and Theatre

2039 Kennedy Blvd.
Jersey City, NJ 07305
Edward Raditz
201-200-3151

Fax: 201-200-3130
E-mail: eraditz@njcu.edu
www.njcu.edu

Princeton University
Department of Music

Woolworth Center of Musical Studies
Princeton, NJ 08544-1007
Scott Burnham
609-258-4241
Fax: 609-258-6793
E-mail: sburnham@princeton.edu
www.music.princeton.edu

Ramapo College
of New Jersey
School of
Contemporary Arts

505 Ramapo Valley Rd.
Mahwah, NJ 07430
201-684-7500
www.ramapo.edu

Raritan Valley
Community College
Department of Performance
Arts and Music

P.O. Box 3300
Somerville, NJ 08876
Roger Briscoe
908-218-8876
Fax: 908-595-0213
E-mail: rbriscoe@raritanval.edu
www.raritanval.edu

A.A. Liberal Arts: Music / A.A.S. Music

RVCC is one of 21 community colleges in NJ; we
serve two counties--Somerset and Hunterdon,
although we have students from other counties.
We provide the first two-years of collegiate study
in music. Performance opportunities include
private instruction, and The Master Chorale, The
Central Jersey Symphony Orchestra, the RVCC
Jazz Ensemble, and other smaller ensembles

Richard Stockton College
Music Sub-Track Area

P.O. Box 195
Pomona, NJ 08240
609-652-1776
www.stockton.edu

Rowan University
Wilson Hall

201 Mullica Hill Rd.
Glassboro, NJ 08028
robert Rawlins
856-256-4651
Fax: 856-256-4644
E-mail: music@rowan.edu
www.rowan.edu/mars

Rutgers University
Camden Department of
Fine Arts and Music Program

Music Program
Camden, NJ 08102
Lois Fromer
732-932-9190
Fax: 732-932-1517
E-mail: fromer@rci.rutgers.edu
www.rutgers.edu

Rutgers University
at New Brunswick
Department of Music

81 George St.
New Brunswick, NJ 08901
Antonius Bittmann
732-932-9302
www.rutgers.edu

Seton Hall University
Department of Art and Music

400 South Orange Ave.
South Orange, NJ 07079
973-761-7966
Fax: 973-275-2368
E-mail: museumgrad@shu.edu
www.shu.edu

Trenton State College
Department of Music

P.O. Box 7718
2000 Pennington Rd.
Ewing, NJ 08628
James Lentini
609-771-2278
E mail: lentini@tcnj.edu
www.tcnj.edu

Westminister Choir College
Department of Music

2083 Lawrenceville Rd.
Lawrenceville, NJ 08648
Katherine Shields
800-826-4647
Fax: 609-921-2538
E-mail: wccadmission@rider.edu
www.rider.edu

William Paterson University
Department of Music

300 Pompton Rd.
Wayne, NJ 07470
Diane Falk Romaine
973-720-2315
Fax: 973-720-2217
E-mail: falkd@wpunj.edu
www.wpunj.edu

Population: 1,928,384 (2005 Estimate)
Capital City: Santa Fe
Bird: Roadrunner
Motto: Crescit eundo – It grows as it goes
Flower: Yucca flower
Tree: Pinon
Residents Called: New Mexicans
Origin of Name: Named by the Spanish for lands north of the Rio Grande River.
Area: 121,593 square miles (5th largest state)
Statehood: January 6, 1912 (47th state)
Largest Cities: Albuquerque, Las Cruces, Santa Fe, Rio Rancho, Roswell, Farmington, Alamogordo, Clovis, Hobbs, Carlsbad
College Band Programs: New Mexico State University

NEW MEXICO

College of Santa Fe
Department of Performing Arts

17600 St. Michaels Dr.
Sante Fe, NM 87505-7615
Steven Miller
505-473-6196
Fax: 505-473-6021
E-mail: cmp@csf.edu
www.cfs.edu

Eastern New Mexico University
School of Music

Portales, NM 88130
Denise Hobbs
505-562-2985
Fax: 505-562-2118
E-mail: Denise.Hobbs@enmu.edu
www.enmu.edu

The Eastern New Mexico University School of Music is located on a beautiful and scenic campus in Portales. Professional programs in music prepare students for careers in performance, public school or private studio teaching, music theatre, music business and graduate school. Degrees offered include: bachelor of music education (choral/instrumental) with K-12 certification; bachelor of music performance (piano, instrumental or vocal); bachelor of music with music theatre emphasis; bachelor of science in music; bachelor of science in music with elective studies in business. One hundred percent placement rate for music education graduates.

New Mexico Junior College
Department of Music

5317 Lovington Hwy.
Hobbs, NM 88240
Ronnie Gray
505-392-5338 x354
E-mail: Rgray@nmjc.edu
www.nmjc.edu

New Mexico State University
Department of Music

P.O. Box 3001
3F
Las Cruces, NM 88003
Greg Fant
505-646-2421
Fax: 505-646-8199
E-mail: gfant@nmsu.edu
www.nmsu.edu/~music

San Juan College
Department of Music

4601 College Blvd.
Farmington, NM 47402
Keith Cochrane
505-566-3386
Fax: 505-566-3385
E-mail: cochreanek@sanjuancollege
www.sjc.cc.nm.us

Associate of Arts

University of New Mexico
Department of Music

College of Arts and Science
Ortega Hall 201
Albuquerque, NM 87131
Vera Norwood
505-277-4621
Fax: 505-277-3163
E-mail: vnorwood@unm.edu
www.unm.edu

Population: 19,254,630 (2005 Estimate)
Capital City: Albany
Bird: Bluebird
Motto: Excelsior
Flower: Rose
Tree: Sugar maple
Residents Called: New Yorkers
Origin of Name: Named after England's Duke of York.
Area: 54,475 square miles (27th largest state)
Statehood: July 26, 1788 (11th state)
Largest Cities: New York, Buffalo, Rochester, Yonkers, Syracuse, Albany, New Rochelle, Mount Vernon, Schenectady, Utica
College Band Programs: Columbia University, Cornell University, Syracuse University, SUNY-Buffalo

Binghamton University
Department of Music

P.O. Box 6000
Binghamton, NY 13902
Cheryl McGowan
607-777-2589
Fax: 607-777-4425
E-mail: cmcgowan@binghamton.edu
music.binghamton.edu

Bachelor of Arts, Bachelor of Music, Master of Music

Borough of Manhattan Community College
Department of Music and Art

199 Chambers St.
New York, NY 10007
Howard Meltzer
212-220-1464
E-mail: Hmeltzer@bmcc.cuny.edu
www.bmcc.cuny.edu/music-art/index.html

Associate in Arts

Bronx Community College
Department of Music and Art

University Ave. at West 181 St.
Bronx, NY 10453
Ruth Bass
718-289-5252
Fax: 718-289-6433
E-mail: curt.belsch@bcc.cuny.edu
www.bcc.cuny.edu/artmusic

Brooklyn Queens Conservatory of Music
58 Seventh Ave.
Brooklyn, NY 11217
Alan Fox
718-622-3300

E-mail: afox@bqcm.org
www.bcqm.org

Broome Community College
Department of Music

P.O. Box 1017
Binghamton, NY 13902
Michael Kinney
607-778-5323
Fax: 607-778-5150
E-mail: kinney_m@sunybroome.edu
www.sunybroome.edu/arts/music

Canisius College
Department of Fine Arts and Music

2001 Main St.
Lyons Hall Room 405
Buffalo, NY 14208
Penelope Lips
716-888-2536
Fax: 716-888-2402
E-mail: caryj@canisius.edu
www.canisius.edu/finearts/music/music.asp

Cayuga County Community College
Department of Music

Franklin St.
Auburn, NY 13021
David Richards
315-255-1743
Fax: 315-255-1743
www.cayuga-cc.edu

Chautauqua Institution
Department of Fine and Performing Arts

P.O. Box 1098
Chautauqua, NY 14722
Sarah Malinoski

716-357-6233
Fax: 716-357-9014
E-mail: music@ciweb.org
music.ciweb.org

City University of New York
Brooklyn College
Conservatory of Music

2900 Bedford Ave.
Brooklyn, NY 1121
Bruce MacIntyre
718-951-5286
Fax: 718-951-4502
E-mail: brucem@brooklyn.cuny.edu
www.bcmusic.org

Bachelor of Arts, Bachelor of Music, Master of
Music, Master of Arts, Advanced Certificate in
Music Education

City University of New York
City College of New York
Department of Music

138th St. & Convent Ave.
New York, NY 10031
Stephen Jablonsky
212-650-7663
Fax: 212-650-5428
E-mail: music@ccny.cuny.edu
www.ccny.cuny.edu/music

Bachelor of Arts; Bachelor of Fine Arts

City University of New York
College of Staten Island
Department of Performing
& Creative Arts˙

2800 Victory Blvd.
Staten Island, NY 10314
Syliva Kahan
718-982-2520
Fax: 718-982-2537
E-mail: kahan@mail.csi.cuny.edu
www.csi.cuny.edu

City University of New York
Graduate Center
Department of Music

365 Fifth Ave.
New York, NY 10016
212-817-8590
Fax: 212-817-1529
E-mail: music@gc.cuny.edu
www.web.gc.cuny.edu/music

Ph.D. - D.M.A. Program in Music

City University of New York
Hunter College
Department of Music

695 Park Ave.
New York, NY 10021
Paul F. Mueller
212-772-5020
Fax: 212-772-5022
E-mail: pmueller@hunter.cuny.edu
www.hunter.cuny.edu

City University of New York
John Jay College
Department of Art Music
and Philosophy

899 Tenth Ave.
New York, NY 10033
Laure Greenberg
212-237-8325
E-mail: Lgreenberg@jjay.cuny.edu
johnjay.jjay.cuny.edu/amp/

City University of New York-
Lehman College

Department of Music
250 Bedford Park Blvd.
MU316
Bronx, NY 10468
Bernard Shockett
718-960-8376
Fax: 718-960-7248
E-mail: music.department@lehman.cuny.edu

www.cuny.edu/deanhum/music/

Bachelor of Science; Master's in Applied Music
and Teaching

City University of New York Medgar Evers College
Department of Mass Communications, Creative and Performing Arts, and Speech

1650 Bedford Ave.
B-1010
Brooklyn, NY 11225-2010
Iola Thompson
718-270-4927
Fax: 718-270-4828
E-mail: ithompson@mec.cuny.edu
www.mec.cuny.edu

City University of New York York College
Department of Fine and Performing Arts

94 - 20 Guy R. Brewer Blvd.
AC-1B09
Jamaica, NY 11451
James Como
718-262-2400
E-mail: como@york.cuny.edu
www.york.cuny.edu

Bachelor of Arts

Colgate University
Department of Music

13 Oak Dr.
Hamilton, NY 13346
Joseph Swain
315-228-7642
Fax: 315-228-7557
E-mail: jswain@mail.colgate.edu
www.colgate.edu

A.B. with concentration in Music

Concordia College
Concordia Conservatory of Music

171 White Plains Rd.
Bronxville, NY 10708
Kathleen Suss
914-395-4507
Fax: 914-395-4500
E-mail: kbs@concordia-ny.edu
www.concordia-ny.edu/attendingconcordia/
conservatory.htm

Cornell University
Department of Music

101 Lincoln Hall
Ithaca, NY 14853
Rebecca Harris-Warrick
607-255-4097
Fax: 607-254-2877
E-mail: musicinfo@cornell.edu
www.arts.cornell.edu/music

Bachelor of Arts; PhD. In Musicology; Doctor of
Musical Arts in Composition; Doctor of Musical
Arts in Performance Practice

Corning Community College
Department of Music

1 Academic Dr.
Corning, NY 14830
Lee Martin
607-962-9CCC
Fax: 607-962-9456
E-mail: martin@corning-cc.edu
www.corning-cc.edu

No formal music major program, but they do
offer enough music courses for any student who
may want to concentrate in music.

Daemen College
Department of Music

4380 Main St.
Amherst, NY 14226
Deborah Mikolajczyk

800-462-7652
Fax: 716-839-8516
E-mail: dpappas@daeman.edu
www.daeman.edu

Dalcroze Institute

250 West 94th St., #15C
New York, NY 10025
Robert Abramson
212-866-0105
Fax: 212-580-0891
E-mail: Rabramson@juilliard.edu
www.dalcrozeinstitute.com

Dutchess Community College
Department of Music and Performing Arts

53 Pendell Rd.
Poughkeepsie, NY 12601-1595
Joe Cosentino
845-431-8618
E-mail: cosentin@sunydutchess.edu
faculty.sunydutchess.edu/conner

One-year Music Performance Certificate; Two-year A.S. Degree in the Performing Arts

Eastman School of Music University of Rochester

26 Gibbs St.
Rochester, NY 14604
800-388-9695
Fax: 585-232-8601
E-mail: admissions@esm.rochester.edu
www.esm.rochester.edu

BM, BA/BS, FORTE Program, Take Five, Double Degree; MA, MM, DMA, PHD, Double Degree, Transfer Credit

Elmira College
Department of Music

One Park Place

Elmira, NY 14901
800-935-6472
E-mail: admissions@elmira.edu
www.elmira.edu/academics/majors/jusic/

Bachelor of Arts

Erie Community College City Campus
Department of Liberal Arts and Science

121 Ellicott St.
Buffalo, NY 14203
716-842-2770
www.ecc.edu

Associate in Arts

Erie Community College North Campus
Department of Liberal Arts and Science

6205 Main St.
Williamsville, NY 14221
716-634-0800
www.ecc.edu

Associate in Arts

Erie Community College South Campus
Department of Liberal Arts and Science

4041 Southwestern Blvd.
Orchard Park, NY 14127
716-648-5400
www.ecc.edu

Associate in Arts

Finger Lakes Community College - Wayne County Campus Center
Department of Music

1100 Technology Pkwy.

Newark, NY 14513
315-331-9098
E-mail: newark@flcc.edu
www.flcc.edu/newark

Associate in Science

Finger Lakes Community College Canandaigua Campus
Department of Music

4355 Lakeshore Dr.
Canandaigua, NY 14424
716-394-3500
Fax: 716-394-5005
E-mail: admissions@flcc.edu
www.flcc.edu

Associate in Science

Finger Lakes Community College-Geneva Campus Center
Department of Music

63 Pulteney St.
Geneva, NY 14456
315-789-6701
E-mail: geneva@flcc.edu
www.flcc.edu/geneva

Associate in Science

Five Towns College
Department of Music

305 North Service Rd.
Dix Hills, NY 11746
Music Department
631-424-7000
E-mail: admissions@ftc.edu
www.ftc.edu

Master of Music; Bachelor of Music

Fordham University
Department of Art and Music

Faculty Memorial Hall 447
Bronx, NY 10458
Jack Spalding
718-817-4890
Fax: 718-817-4929
www.fordham.edu

Hamilton College
Department of Music

198 College Hill Rd.
Clinton, NY 13323
315-859-4261
E-mail: music@hamilton.edu
www.hamilton.edu

Hartwick College
Department of Music

One Hartwick Dr.
Oneonta, NY 13820
Lynda Clark
607-431-4800
Fax: 607-431-4102
E-mail: clarkl@hartwick.edu
www.hartwick.edu

Bachelor of Arts, Bachelor of Science.

Hebrew Union College Jewish Institute of Religion
School of Sacred Music

One West 4th St.
New York, NY 10012
212-824-2279
Fax: 212-388-1720
E-mail: cantorial@huc.edu
www.huc.edu

Hobart and William Smith College
Department of Music

629 South Main St.
Geneva, NY 14456
Robert Cowles

315-781-3404
Fax: 315-781-3403
E-mail: cowles@hws.edu
academics.hws.edu/music/

Bachelor of Arts in Music.

Hofstra University
Department of Music

101B Lowe
Hempstead, NY 11549
David Fryling
516-463-5490
Fax: 516-463-6393
E-mail: music@hofstra.edu
www.hofstra.edu

Bachelor of Arts in Music; Bachelor of Science in Music; Master of Science and Master of Arts in Music Education.

Houghton College
Department of Music

One Willard Ave.
Houghton, NY 14744
585-567-9400
E-mail: music@houghton.edu
www.houghton.edu

Bachelor of Arts; Bachelor of Music; Masters of Arts; Masters of Music

Institute of Audio Research
School of Audio Engineering and Music Production

64 University Place
New York, NY 10003-4595
212-777-8550
Fax: 212-677-6549
E-mail: contact@audioschool.com
www.audioschool.com

Ithaca College
School of Music

3322 Whalen Center

Ithaca, NY 14850
Townsend A. Plant
607-274-3171
E-mail: tplant@ithaca.edu
www.ithaca.edu/music/

Bachelor of Arts; Bachelor of Music; Master of Music; Master of Science in Music

Jamestown Community College Jamestown Campus
Department of Music

525 Falconer St.
P.O. Box 20
Jamestown, NY 14702
Michael F. Kelly
716-665-5220
E-mail: mikekelly@mail.sunyjcc.edu
www.sunyjcc.edu/jamestown/music/

Two year AAS Degree in Music

Jewish Theological Seminary of America
Jewish Music

3080 Broadway
New York, NY 10027
Hazzan Henry Rosenblum
212-678-8037
Fax: 212-678-8989
E-mail: cantorial@jtsa.edu
www.jtsa.edu

Bachelor of Arts

Juilliard School of Music
Music Division

60 Lincoln Center Plaza
New York, NY 10023
Lee Cioppa
212-799-5000 x 223
E-mail: admissions@juilliard.edu
www.juilliard.edu

Bachelor of Music; Master of Music; Artist Diploma; Doctor of Musical Arts.

Keuka College
Humanities & Fine
Arts Division

Keuka Park, NY 14478
315-279-5674
www.keuka.edu

Kingsborough
Community College
Communications and
Performing Arts

2001 Oriental Blvd.
Brooklyn, NY 11235
David Frankel
718-368-5591
Fax: 718-368-4879
E-mail: dfrankel@kbcc.cuny.edu
www.kbcc.cuny.edu

LaGuardia
Community College
Department of Humanities
and Performing Arts

31-10 Thomson Ave.
Long Island City, NY 11101
718-482-5000
E-mail: admissions@lagcc.cuny.edu
www.lagc.cuny.edu

Long Island University
at Brooklyn
Humanities

1 University Plaza
Brooklyn, NY 11201
718-488-1011
www.brooklyn.liu.edu

Long Island University
at CW Post
Department of Music

720 Northern Blvd.
Brookville, NY 11548
Chris Culver
516-299-2474
Fax: 516-299-2884
E-mail: music@cwpost.liu.edu
www.cwpost.liu.edu/cwis/cwp

Bachelor of Science in Music; Bachelor of Music;
Master of Arts; Master of Science in Music.

Manhattan School of Music
120 Claremont Ave.

New York, NY 10027
Amy Anderson
917-493-4501
E-mail: aanderson@msmnyc.edu
www.msmnyc.edu

Manhattanville College
Fine Arts and Music

2900 Purchase St.
Purchase, NY 10577
914-694-2200
Fax: 914-694-2386
www.mville.edu

Mannes College of Music
150 West 85th St.
New York, NY 10024
212-580-0210 x8802
E-mail: mannesadmissions@newschool.edu
www.mannes.newschool.edu

Mercy College
Bronx Campus
1200 Waters Place
Bronx, NY 10461
877-MERCY-GO
www.mercy.edu

Mercy College
Dobbs Ferry Campus
555 Broadway

Dobbs Ferry, NY 10522
877-MERCY-GO
Fax: 914-674-7488
www.mercy.edu

Mercy College
Mercy Manhatten

66 West 35th St.
New York, NY 10001
800-MERCY-NY
www.mercy.edu

Mercy College
Yorktown Campus

2651 Strang Blvd.
Yorktown Heights, NY 10598
800-MERCY-NY
www.mercy.edu

Molloy College
Department of Music

1000 Hempstead Ave.
Rockville Center, NY 11570
Brendan Droge
516-678-5000 x6751
www.molloy.edu

Bachelor of Fine Arts in Music; Bachelor of Science in Music Education

Monroe Community College

1000 East Henrietta Rd.
Rochester, NY 14623
585-292-2000
www.monroecc.edu
Music A.S.

Nassau Community College
Department of Music

1 Education Dr.
Garden City, NY 11530
516-572-7345
E-mail: admissions@ncc.edu
www.ncc.edu

Nazareth College
Department of Music

4245 East Ave.
Rochester, NY 14618
James Douthit
585-389-2700
Fax: 585-389-2939
E-mail: jdouthi2@naz.edu
www.naz.edu

Bachelor of Music; Master of Science.

New York University
The Steinhardt School
Music and Performing
Arts Professions

35 West 4th St., Suite 777
New York, NY 10012
Lawrence Ferrara
212-998-5424
Fax: 212-995-4147
E-mail: lf2@nyu.edu
www.nyu.edu

Bachelor of Music; Bachelor of Science in Music; M.A. in Music; M.M. in Music; Ph.D. in Music

Niagara County Community College
Department of Music

3111 Saunders Settlement Rd.
Sanborn, NY 14132
Lois Hall
716-614-5965
Fax: 716-614-6700
E-mail: hall@niagaracc.suny.edu
www.niagaracc.suny.edu

Nyack College
Department of Music

1 South Blvd.
Nyack, NY 10960
Glenn Koponen
845-358-1710

E-mail: admissions@nyack.edu
www.nyackcollege.edu

Bachelor of Arts; Bachelor of Music; Bachelor of
Sacred Music

Onondaga Community College
Department of Music

4585 West Seneca Turnpike
Syracuse, NY 13215
David Abrams
315-498-2256
Fax: 315-498-2792
E-mail: music@sunyocc.edu
www.sunyocc.edu

Associate of Applied Science degree in Music
(1-year program)

Orange County Community College
Department of Arts and Communications

115 South St.
Middletown, NY 10940
Mark Strunksy
845-341-4030
E-mail: mstrunsk@sunyorange.edu
orange.cc.ny us

Queens College
Aaron Copland School of Music

65-30 Kissena Blvd.
Flushing, NY 11367
Edward Smaldone
718-997-3800
Fax: 718-997-3849
E-mail: edward.smaldone@qc.cuny.edu
www.qc.cuny.edu/music/

Bachelor of Arts; Bachelor of Music; B.A./M.A.
Program

Queensborough Community College
Department of Music

22205 56th Ave.
Bayside, NY 11364
Joseph Nagler
718-631-6393
Fax: 718-631-6041
E-mail: jnagler@qcc.cuny.edu
www.qcc.cuny.edu

A.S. in Fine and Performing Arts; A.A.S. in Music
Electronic Technology

Robert Wesleyan College
Department of Music

2301 Westside Dr.
Rochester, NY 14624
Kristyn Kuhlman
585-594-6000
www.roberts.edu

Rockland Community College
Department of Music

145 College Rd.
Suffern, NY 10901
Patricia Maloney-Titland
845-574-4000
www.sunyrockland.edu

Russell Sage College
Department of Creative and Performing Arts

45 Ferry St.
Troy, NY 12180
888-VERY-SAGE
www.sage.edu

Minor in Music

Sarah Lawrence College
Admissions Office

1 Mead Way

Bronxville, NY 10708
800-888-2858
Fax: 914-395-2515
E-mail: slcadmit@sarahlawrence.edu
www.sic.edu

Schenectady County Community College
Department of Music

78 Washington Ave.
Schenectady, NY 12305
William Meckley
518-381-1231
E-mail: mecklewa@gw.sunyscc.edu
www.sunyscc.edu

Associate of Science; Associate in Applied Science; Music Certificates

Skidmore College
Department of Music

815 North Broadway
Saratoga Springs, NY 12866
Thomas Denny
518-580-5320
Fax: 518-580-5320
E-mail: tdenny@skidmore.edu
www.skidmore.edu

Bachelor of Arts in Music

St. Bonaventure University
Department of Visual & Performing Arts

P.O. Drawer AU
St. Bonaventure, NY 14778
Les Sabina
716-375-2000
Fax: 716-375-2690
E-mail: lsabina@sbu.edu
www.sbu.edu/academics_arts.html

St. Lawrence University
Department of Music

20 Ramoda Dr.
Canton, NY 13617
Perry Goldstein
631-632-7330
Fax: 631-632-7404
E-mail: perry.goldstein@stonybrook.edu
www.sunysb.edu/music

Stony Brook is a mid-size research university. The Department of Music offers conservatory-level training in a university setting. The University is close to New York City and its cultural resources.

Stony Brook University
Department of Music

Stony Brook, NY 11794-5475
Daniel Weymouth
631-632-7330
Fax: 631-632-7404
E-mail: Daniel.Weymouth@StonyBrook.edu
www.sunysb.edu/music

Suffolk County Community College
Department of Music

533 College Rd.
Seldon, NY 11784
631-451-4000
www.sunysuffolk.edu

SUNY at Adelphi University
Department of Music

1 South Ave.
P.O. Box 701
Garden City, NY 11530
Lyndon-Gee, Christopher
516-877-4290
Fax: 516-877-4926
E-mail: lyndongee@adelphi.edu
www.adelphi.edu

SUNY at Albany
Department of Music

1400 Washington Ave.
Performing Arts Center, Room 310
Albany, NY 12222
Bernadette Socha
518-442-4187
Fax: 518-442-4182
E-mail: musinfo@albany.edu
www.albany.edu/music/

SUNY at Buffalo
Department of Music

222 Baird Hall
Buffalo, NY 14260
Susan Clark Manns
716-645-2765
Fax: 716-645-3824
E-mail: scmanns@buffalo.edu
www.music.buffalo.edu

Bachelor of Music; Bachelor of Arts; Master of
Music; Master of Arts; Ph.D.

SUNY at Cobleskill
Department of Humanities

State Route 7
Cobleskill, NY 12043
Susan Zimmermann
518-255-5350
E-mail: zimmerSJ@cobleskill.edu
www.cobleskill.edu

SUNY at Cortland
Department Performing Arts

P.O. Box 2000
Cortland, NY 13045
Karen Zimmerman
607-753-2811
E-mail: zimmermank@cortland.edu
www.cortland.edu

SUNY at Fredonia
School of Music

280 Central Ave.
Fredonia, NY 14063

716-673-3151
E-mail: music@fredonia.edu
www.fredonia.edu

SUNY at Geneseo
School of The Arts

Music Program/One College Cir.
Geneseo, NY 14454
Patricia Baird
585-245-5824
Fax: 582-245-5826
E-mail: baird@geneseo.edu
sota@geneseo.edu

Bachelor of Music, Bachelor of Musical Theater

Public Ivy: SUNY Geneseo has carved an impressive niche among the nation's public colleges. The most selective of the State University of New York's comprehensive colleges, and considered to be SUNY's Honors College, Geneseo offers a professionally focused education that's comparable in quality to the educational experience available at many of the nation's finest private colleges and universities.

SUNY at New Paltz
School of Fine and Performing Arts

1 Hawke Dr.
New Paltz, NY 12561
Carole Cowan
845-257-2700
Fax: 845-257-3121
E-mail: cowanc@newpaltz.edu
www.newpaltz.edu/music/

Bachelor of Arts; Bachelor of Science; Master of Science.

SUNY at Oneonta
Department of Music

Ravine Pkwy.
Oneonta, NY 13820
Robert S. Barstow
607-436-3500
E-mail: music@oneonta.edu
www.oneonta.edu/academics/music/

SUNY at Oswego
Department of Music

7060 Route 104
Oswego, NY 13126
Juan LaManna
315-312-2130
E-mail: jlamanna@oswego.edu
www.oswego.edu

Bachelor of Arts in Music

SUNY at Plattsburgh
Department of Music

101 BRd. St.
Plattsburgh, NY 12901
Jo Ellen Miano
518-564-2472
Fax: 518-564-2197
E-mail: mianoj@plattsburgh.edu
www.plattsburgh/edu

Bachelor of Arts in Music

SUNY at Potsdam
The Crane School of Music

44 Pierrepont Ave.
Potsdam, NY 13676
Alan Solomon
315-267-2000
E-mail: solomon@potsdam.edu
www.potsdam.edu

SUNY at Purchase College
Conservatory of Music

735 Anderson Hill Rd.
Purchase, NY 10577
Maggie Smith
914-251-6702
Fax: 914-251-6739
E-mail: music@purchase.edu
www.purchase.edu/music

Bachelor of Music, Master of Music, Performer's
Certificate, Artist Diploma

Music Conservatory set on Performing Arts

campus approximately 40 minutes from
New York City. Our majors include Classical
Composition,Instrumental Peformance, Jazz
Studies, Studio Composition, Studio Production
and Voice and Opera Studies.

SUNY at Stony Brook
Department of Music

3304 Staller Center
Stony Brook, NY 11794
Daniel Weymouth
631-632-7330
Fax: 631-632-7404
E-mail: Daniel.Weymouth@StonyBrook.edu
www.stonybrook.edu

Bachelor of Arts; Master of Arts; Master of Music;
Ph.D.; Doctor of Music Arts.

Syracuse University
College of Visual and Performing Arts: Setnor School of Music

200 Crouse College
Syracuse, NY 13244
Carole Brzozowski
315-443-5889
Fax: 315-443-1935
E-mail: brzoz@syr.edu
www.syr.edu

Bachelor of Music; Bachelor of Arts; Master of
Music; Master of Science; Ph.D.

Teachers College Columbia University
Program in Music Education

525 West 120th St.
520A Horace Mann
New York, NY 10027
Harold Abelels
212-678-3283
Fax: 212-678-4048
E-mail: abeles@tc.edu
www.tc.edu

Master of Arts; Master of Education; Doctor of
Education; Doctor of Education in College Teaching of Music

The New School for Jazz and Contemporary Music
Jazz Admissions Department

55 W. 13th St., 5th Floor
New York, NY 10011
Teri Lucas
212-229-5896 x4589
Fax: 212-229-8936
E-mail: LucasT@newschool.edu
www.jazz.newschool.edu

BFA Jazz Performance, BA/BFA in Liberal Arts
and Jazz

The quality and uniqueness of the program lie
in its artist-as-mentor classroom approach, its
progressive curriculum and focus on small-group
performance, and its community of exceptionally
talented students.

Tompkins Cortland Community College
Department of Music

170 North Rd.
P.O. Box 139
Dryden, NY 13053
607-844-8211
www.sunytccc.edu

Ulster County Community College
Visual and Performing Arts and Communications

Cottekill Rd.
Stone Ridge, NY 12484
Martha Robinson
845-687-5110
E-mail: robinsom@sunyulster.edu
www.sunyulster.edu

Union College
Department of Music

807 Union St.
Schenectady, NY 12308
www.union.edu

Utica College
Department of Music

1600 Burrstone Rd.
Utica, NY 13502
315-792-3006
Fax: 315-792-3003
www.utica.edu

Vassar College
Department of Music

124 Raymond Ave.
Box 18
Poughkeepsie, NY 12604
845-437-7000
www.vassar.edu

Villa Maria College
Music and Music Business

240 Pine Ridge Rd.
Buffalo, NY 14225
Carmen Jude Aquila
716-961-1882
E-mail: aquila@villa.edu
www.villa.edu

Wagner College
Department of Music

One Campus Rd.
Staten Island, NY 10301
Shirley Bock
718-390-3313
E-mail: sbock@wagner.edu
www.wagner.edu

Wells College
Department of Music

170 Main St.
Aurora, NY 13026
Crawford R. Thorburn
315-364-3347
E-mail: cthoburn@wells.edu
www.wells.edu

Westchester Conservatory of Music

216 Central Ave.
White Plains, NY 10606
Dave Barnes
914-761-3900
E-mail: dbarnes@musiced.org
www.musicconservatory.org

Non-profit NASM-accredited community music school.

Population: 8,683,242 (2005 Estimate)
Capital City: Raleigh
Bird: Cardinal
Motto: Esse Quam Videri – To be, rather than to seem
Flower: Dogwood
Tree: Pine
Residents Called: North Carolinians
Origin of Name: Taken from "Carolus," the Latin word for Charles and named after England's King Charles I.
Area: 53,821 square miles (28th state)
Statehood: November 21, 1789 (12th state)
Largest Cities: Charlotte, Raleigh, Greensboro, Durham, Winston-Salem, Fayetteville, Cary, High Point, Wilmington, Asheville
College Band Programs: Appalachian State University, Duke University, East Carolina University, Elizabeth City State University, Fayetteville State University, North Carolina Central University, North Carolina State University, University of North Carolina-Chapel Hill

Appalachian State University
Department of Music

Hayes School Of Music
813 Rivers St.
Boone, NC 28608
828-262-3020
Fax: 828-262-6446
E-mail: music@appstate.edu
www.music.appstate.edu

B.S., and M.M.

The Mariam Cannon School of Music is the prime purveyor of music for the University, presenting an exciting and stimulating array of cultural events throughout the year. The faculty of the Hayes School of music, composed of thirty-seven nationally recognized teachers, performers and composers, is a major element in sustaining the creative atmosphere that surrounds Appalachian. The community is treated to a broad spectrum of faculty and student programs including solo recitals, instrumental and vocal ensemble concerts, chamber music and opera. The Hayes School of Music is among the leading music education institutions in the region and maintains a reputation of excellence in undergraduate and graduate instruction. Young musicians pursue studies in music education, music therapy, music pe rformance, sacred music, composition/theory and music industry. Performances of the faculty and students of the Hayes School of Music are presented in the beautiful Rosen Concert Hall and the Recital Hall of the Broyhill Music Center.

Barton College
Department of Community and Performance Arts

P.O. Box 5000
Wilson, NC 27893-7000
252-399-6300
www.barton.edu

Bennett College
Department of Music

900 East Washington Ave.
Greensboro, NC 27410
David Pinnix

336-517-2316
Fax: 336-373-0569
www.bennett.edu

Brevard College
Department of Music

400 North BRd. St.
Breward, NC 28712
828-884-8211
E-mail: music@brevard.edu
www.brevard.edu

Campbell University
Department of Music

P.O. Box 128
Buies Creek, NC 27506
Ran Whitley
910-893-1495
Fax: 910-893-1515
www.campbell.edu

Catawba College
Department of Music

2300 West Innes St.
Salisbury, NC 28144
Renee McCachren
704-637-4426
E-mail: rmccachr@catawba.edu
www.catawba.edu

Chowan College
Department of Music

One University Place
Murfreesboro, NC 27855
252-398-6500
www.chowan.edu

In a small, nurturing environment, the department of music offers qualified students the opportunity to become well-trained musicians capable of pursuing graduate studies in music or professional careers in a variety of music-related fields. The degree programs stress training in basic musical disciplines, proficiency in applied and theoretical areas as well as the completion of a liberal arts core curriculum. The department also provides all college students and community members the opportunity to enrich their musical experiences through participation in choral and instrumental ensembles, to increase their knowledge in music appreciation classes and to attend musical performances. The department of music aggressively supports the cultural life of the college and community.

Coastal Carolina Community College
Department of Music

444 Western Blvd.
Jacksonville, NC 28546
Sue Flaharty
910-455-1221
Fax: 910-455-7027
E-mail: admissions@coastal.cc.nc.us
www.coastalcarolina.org

BA with major in music; emphasis in performance, history, theory, or composition

Our small department offers close interaction with faculty and many opportunities to study and perform a wide range of music. We expose students to traditions both inside and outside Western art music. As a liberal arts institution, students can pursue a variety of interests and hone their skills in critical thinking, writing, and speaking.Our program prepares students for a number of life paths both inside and outside music. Graduates have pursued careers and graduate study in music performance, arts administration, ethnomusicology, entertainment law, and even biomedical research.

College of the Albemarle
Department of Music

Elizabeth City, NC 27909
Hank Rion
252-335-0821
Fax: 252-335-2011
E-mail: hrion@albemarle.edu
www.albemarle.cc.nc.us

Davidson College
Department of Music

P.O. Box 7131

Davidson, NC 28035
Katy Hoffler
704-894-2357
Fax: 704-892-2593
E-mail: kahoffler@davidson.edu
www.davidson.edu

Duke University
Department of Music

P.O. Box 90665
Durham, NC 27701
Department Head
919-660-3300
Fax: 919-660-3301
www.duke.edu

For students seeking a professional career in music or pursuing music as an avocation, Duke offers: a curriculum that combines theory, history, and performance; a low student-faculty ratio; a distinguished faculty of scholars, composers, and performers with expertise in a broad range of subjects; 13 different vocal and instrumental performing groups, open to major and non-majors alike; opportunities to work with renowned visiting artists and composers; annual concert series focusing on a wide variety of periods and styles; a music library with more than 85,000 books, scores, journals, and microfilms, housed in the Mary Duke Biddle Music Building; superb practice facilities and a wide-ranging collection of historical instruments. At the graduate level, the department of music offers programs leading to the A.M. and Ph.D. in composition and musicology, and the A.M. in performance practice. The programs include courses, seminars, and independent study in composition, ethnomusicology, music history, music theory and analysis, performance practice and interpretation, and interdisciplinary studies.

East Carolina University
School of Music

102 A. J. fletcher Music Center
Greenville, NC 27858
252-328-6851
www.music.ecu.edu

The East Carolina University School of Music is one of the largest, most noted and comprehensive music programs in the southeast. The successful record of our graduates in a broad range of careers is our highest achievement and a continuing source of pride. The school is housed in the A.J. Fletcher Music Center, a facility designed exclusively for music. All music classes are held in the center, which features two large rehearsal halls and a 300-seat recital hall. Within the center are two electronic piano labs, five organs, more than 50 practice rooms, faculty studios, the music library and the center for music technology. The music library's collection contains more than 61,000 books, scores, periodicals and media materials representative of all types and periods of music. The state-of-the-art Center for Music Technology is an outstanding resource and teaching facility. Our artists-teachers provide students with valuable musical experience and a solid foundation for success in the music profession. Eastern Music Festival Piedmont Jazz Festival P.O. Box 22026 Greensboro, NC 2742 Jazz Festival Hotline 336-271-2600 www.easternmusicfestival.com.

Elizabeth City State University
Department of Music

237 Fine Arts Building
Campus Box 831
Elizabeth City, NC 27909
Gloria Knight
252-335-3359
Fax: 252-335-3779
E-mail: gjknight@mail.ecsu.edu
www.ecsu.edu

Elon University
Department of Music

100 Campus Dr.
Campus Box 2700
Elon, NC 27244
Stephen Futrell
800-334-8448
Fax: 336-278-5609
E-mail: sfutrell@elon.edu
www.elon.edu/music

B.S. in Music Education, B.A. in Music Performance, B.A. Music, music minor, Jazz Studies

The Elon University Music Department's mission is to provide a dynamic, challenging and intellectually rich environment where students are actively engaged and encouraged to develop creativity and excellence in the study and performance of diverse musical styles. By offering career-oriented/professional programs in music education, and music performance, the Music Department prepares students for graduate school or careers in performance and/or teaching. Elon's Fine Arts Center boasts numerous Steinway concert grand pianos; McCrary Theatre, a fully equipped theatre and concert hall; Yeager Recital Hall, with digital recording capabilities; modular practice rooms; and a music technology lab. Newly renovated Whitley Auditorium houses a new, custom-built Cassavant pip organ. Performance and experiential learning opportunities include a variety of instrumental and/or choral ensembles; recording projects in Elon's digital recording facility featuring ProTools recording;/editing software; and Elon's nationally recognized Study Abroad program. At Elon, students gain real-world skills and experiences in a liberal arts setting.

Fayetteville State University
Department of Fine Arts

1200 Murchison Rd.
Fayetteville, NC 28301
Don N. Parker
910-672-1253
www.uncfsu.edu

Music Education Major

Gaston College
Department of Music

201 Hwy. 321 South
P.O. Box 45
Dallas, NC 28034
704-922-6200
www.gaston.cc.nc.us

Greensboro College
Department of Music

815 West Market St.
Greensboro, NC 27401
336-272-7102
Fax: 336-378-0154
E-mail: admissions@gborocollege.edu

www.gborocollege.edu

Bachelor of Music Education, Bachelor of Arts in Music, Bachelor of Science in music, a Certificate in Church Music and a Minor in Music

Greensboro College has been known for over 150 years for the quality of its music programs and graduates. Located in the heart of a city that boasts of its cultural offerings, students enjoy not only concerts and recitals on campus but those offered throughout the city as well as in neighboring Piedmont Triad communities. With a student population a little over 1,200, class size is small and allows for individual attention to student needs. Private lessons are taught in all classical orchestral instruments, piano, organ, and voice. Within the context of the valuable liberal arts undergraduate education, the curricula for the Bachelor of Arts in Music, the Bachelor of Science in Music, and the Bachelor of Music Education allows for focused study in music along with a disciplined pursuit of knowledge. Students are also given a wide range of music experiences and ensembles also including marching band, opera workshop and clinics with internationally renowned musicians.

Guilford College
Department of Music

5800 West Friendly Ave.
Greensboro, NC 27410
Timothy H. Lindeman
336-316-2500
E-mail: tlindema@guilford.edu
www.guilford.edu

BA

Small, liberal arts residential college found by Society of Friends in the 19th century.

Guilford Technical Community College
Dept of Communications and Fine Arts

P.O. Box 309
Jamestown, NC 58401
336-334-4822
www.technet.gtcc.cc.nc.us

Jamestown College
Department of Music

6000 College Lane
Jamestown, NC 58401
William Wojnar
701-252-3467
Fax: 701-253-4318
E-mail: wojnar@acc.jc.edu
www.jc.edu

Johnson C. Smith University
School of Music And Fine Arts

100 Beatties Ford Rd.
Charlotte, NC 28216
704-378-1000
www.jcsu.edu

Lees-McRae College
Dept of Performing Arts

P.O. Box 128
Banner Elk, NC 28604
Janet Speer
828-898-8721
Fax: 828-898-8814
E-mail: speerj@lmc.edu
www.lmc.edu

Lenoir Community College
Dept of Arts and Sciences

P.O. Box 188
231 Hwy. 58 South
Kinston, NC 28502-0188
Kim Waller
252-527-6223
E-mail: kturnage@lenoircc.edu
www.lenoir.cc.nc.us

Livingstone College
Department of Music

701 W. Monroe St.
Salisbury, NC 28144

704-216-6000
www.livingstone.edu

Mars Hill College
Department of Music

100 Athletic St.
Mars Hill, NC 28754
Joel Reed
828-689-1131
E-mail: jreed@mhc.edu
www.mhc.edu/music

Meredith College
Department of Music

3800 Hillsborough St.
Raleigh, NC 27607
David Lynch
919-760-8536
E-mail: lynchd@meredith.edu
www.meredith.edu

Meredith College, an accredited institutional member of NASM, offers about 95 majors, 40 faculty; a comprehensive private college for women; strong programs in choral music, voice, piano, strings, woodwinds, orchestra. Several competitive scholarships are available to entering freshmen music majors.

Methodist College
Department of Music

5400 Ramsey St.
Fayetteville, NC 28311
Jane Gardner
910-630-7101
E-mail: gardiner@methodist.edu
www.methodist.edu/music

Mitchell Community College
Department of Music

500 West BRd. St.
Statesville, NC 28677
704-878-3200
www.mitchell.cc.nc.us

Montreat College
Department of Music

310 Gaither Cir.
Montreat, NC 28757
James D. Southerland
828-669-8012 x3641
E-mail: jsoutherland@montreat.edu
www.montreat.edu

Mount Olive College
Music Program

634 Henderson St.
Mount Olive, NC 28365
Alan Armstrong
919-658-2502
Fax: 919-658-7180
www.mountolive.edu

North Carolina A and T State University
Department of Music

1601 East Market St.
Greensboro, NC 27411
Music Department
336-334-7926
E-mail: music@ncat.edu
www.ncat.edu

North Carolina Central University
Department of Music

1801 Fayetteville St.
Durham, NC 27707
919-530-6100
E-mail: dmccullers@nccu.edu
www.nccu.edu

North Carolina School of the Arts
School of Music

1533 South Main St.
Winston-Salem, NC 27117

Thomas Clark
336-770-3251
Fax: 336-770-3248
E-mail: tclark@ncarts.edu
www.ncarts.edu

North Carolina
Wesleyan College
Department of Music

3400 North Wesleyan Blvd.
Rocky Mount, NC 27804
Micheal McAllister
919-985-5100
Fax: 919-977-3701
www.ncwc.edu

Peace College
Department of Music

15 East Peace St.
Raleigh, NC 27604
Virginia Vance
919-508-2296
E-mail: vvance@peace.edu
www.peace.edu

Pembroke State university
Department of Music

P.O. Box 1510
Pembroke, NC 28372
910-521-6230
Fax: 910-521-6390
E-mail: music@uncp.edu
www.uncp.edu

Pheiffer University
Department of Music

P.O. Box 960
48380 US Hwy.52 North
Misenheimer, NC 28109
Jean Raines
704-463-1360 x2305
Fax: 704-463-1363
E-mail: jraines@pfeiffer.edu
www.pfeiffer.edu

Piedmont Baptist College
Department of Music

420 South BRd. St.
Winston-Salem, NC 27101
Jeff Crum
800-937-5097
E-mail: crumj@pbc.edu
www.pbc.edu

Queens University
of Charlotte
Department of Music

1900 Selwyn Ave.
Charlotte, NC 28274
Julie Dean
704-337-2213
E-mail: deanjm@queens.edu
www.queens.edu

Bachelor of Music in Performance, Music
Therapy and Bachelor of Arts in Music

Rockingham
Community College
Department of Music

P.O. Box 38
Wentworth, NC 27375
336-342-4261
Fax: 336-349-9986
E-mail: admissions@rockinghamcc.edu
www.rcc.cc.nc.us

Salem College
School of Music

610 South Church St.
Winston-Salem, NC 27108
Reeves Shulstad
336-721-2637
E-mail: shulstad@salem.edu
www.salem.edu

Shaw University
Department of Visual and Performing Arts

118 East South St.
Raleigh, NC 27601
Mildred H. Hooker
919-546-8452
E-mail: mhooker@shawu.edu
www.shawuniversity.edu

Southeast Baptist Theology Seminary
Department of Music

P.O. Box 1889
Wake Forest, NC 27588
919-761-2280
E-mail: admissions@sebts.edu
www.sebts.edu

St. Augustine's College
Department of Music

1315 Oakwood Ave.
Raleigh, NC 27610
Katherine Boyes
919-516-4158
E-mail: kboyes@st-aug.edu
www.st-aug.edu

University of North Carolina at Asheville
Department of Music

1 University Heights
CPO 2290
Asheville, NC 28804-6432
Patrick Hill
828-251-6432
E-mail: music@unca.edu
www.unca.edu/music

BA General, BA Jazz Studies, BS Music Technology

UNCA offers three degree programs: The Bachelor of Science in Music Technology; the Bachelor of Arts in Music/Jazz Studies track, and the Bachelor of Arts in Music/General Studies track. All programs are grounded in a nationally acclaimed liberal arts curriculum. This special feature of the UNCA experience helps students prepare not only for entry-level jobs but also, and more importantly, for leadership roles in the music professions of the twenty-first century.

University of North Carolina at Chapel Hill
Department of Music

CB #3320 Hill Hall
Chapel Hill, NC 27599-3320
919-962-1039
Fax: 919-962-3376
www.unc.edu/depts/music

University of North Carolina at Charlotte
Department of Music

9201 University City Blvd.
Room 340- Robinson Hall
Charlotte, NC 28223
704-547-2472
Fax: 704-687-6806
E-mail: dlshrops@email.uncc.edu
www.uncc.edu

University of North Carolina at Greensboro
Department of Music

220 Music Building
Greensboro, NC 27402-6170
Dianna Carter
336-334-5789
E-mail: dtcarter@uncg.edu
web.uncg.edu

University of North Carolina at Wilmington
Department of Music

601 South College Rd.
Wilmington, NC 28403-5975
Daniel Johnson

910-962-3390
Fax: 910-962-7106
E-mail: johnsond@uncw.edu
www.uncwil.edu

BA, BM in performance, BM in music education

UNC Wilmington students study with internationally recognized artists and teachers while enjoying small class sizes and extensive performance opportunities. With a new state-of-the-art facility for music and other arts programs opening the fall of 2006, it would be difficult to find more diversified and challenging undergraduate programs in an ideal learning environment than the music programs at UNCW.

Wake Forest University
Department of Music

P.O. Box 7345
Winston-Salem, NC 27109
Carol Brehm
336-758-5364
Fax: 336-758-4935
E-mail: music@wfu.edu
www.wfu.edu

The Department of Music is comitted to honor the ideals of liberal learning. These include the transmission of cultural heritages, the teaching of music using a variety of modes of learning, the development of critical appreciation of aesthetic values found in the art of music, the advancement of music through in-depth study, scholarly research, and creative exploration, the development of individual artistic potential, and the application of musical knowledge in the service of humanity.

Warren Wilson College
Department of Music

P.O. Box 9000
Asheville, NC 28815
828-298-3325
www.warren-wilson.edu
Minor in Music

Western Carolina University
Department of Music

Cullowhee, NC 28723

Sheila Frizzell
828-227-7242
Fax: 828-227-7162
E-mail: sfrizzell@email.wcu.edu
www.wcu.edu

Wilkes Community College
Department of Music

P.O. Box 120
1328 Collegiate Dr.
Wilkesboro, NC 28697
Blair Hancock
336-838-6230
www.wilkescc.edu

Wilmington Academy of Music

1635 Ellington Ave.
Wilmington, NC 28401
910-392-1590
www.academyofmusic.com

Wingate University
Department of Music

P.O. Box 3031
Wingate, NC 28174
Ron Bostic
704-233-8312
E-mail: robost@windgate.edu
www.wingate.edu/home.asp

Winston-Salem State University
Dept of Fine Arts and Music

601 Martin Luther King Jr. Dr.
Carolina Hall Suite 130
Winston-Salem, NC 27110
Merdis J McCarter
336-750-2403
Fax: 336-750-2405
E-mail: mccarterm@wssu.edu
www.wssu.edu

Population: 636,677 (2005 Estimate)
Capital City: Bismarck
Bird: Western Meadowlark
Motto: Liberty and union, now and forever, one and inseparable.
Flower: Wild Prairie Rose
Tree: American Elm
Residents Called: North Dakotans
Origin of Name: Dakota is the Sioux Indian word for "friend."
Area: 70,704 square miles (19th largest state)
Statehood: November 2, 1889 (39th state)
Largest Cities: Fargo, Bismarck, Grand Forks, Minot, Mandan, Dickinson, Jamestown, West Fargo, Williston, Wahpeton
College Band Programs: North Dakota State University, University of Mary

Bismarck State College
Department of Music

Leach Music Center 171
Bismarck, ND 58506
Thomas Porter
701-224-5438
E-mail: Thomas.Porter@bsc.nodak.edu
www.bismarckstate.edu

Dickinson State University
Department of Fine Arts and Music

291 Campus Dr.
Dickinson, ND 58601
701-227-2308
Fax: 701-227-2006
www2.dsu.nodak.cdu

Bachelor of Science in Composite Music, Choral Music, Minor in Instrumental Music, Choral Music

Minot State University
Division of Music

500 University West
Minot, ND 58707
Sandra Starr
701-858-3837
Fax: 701-858-3823
E-mail: sandra.starr@minotstateu.edu
www.minotstateu.edu

University of Mary
Department of Music

7500 University Dr.
Bismarck, ND 58504
Scott Prebys
701-255-7500
Fax: 701-255-7685
E-mail: sprebys@umary.edu
www.umary.edu

Music, and Music Teaching

University of North Dakota at Grand Forks
Department of Music

Hughees Fine Arts Center Room 110
3350 Campus Rd. Stop 7125
Grand Forks, ND 58202
701-777-2644
E-mail: tamara.mulske@und.nokak.edu
www2.und.edu

Music, Music Education, Music Education - Instrumental, Music Education; Choral, Music Performance, Music Therapy

Valley City State University
Department of Music

101 College St. SW
Valley City, ND 58072
Diana Skroch
701-845-7272
Fax: 701-845-7275
E-mail: diana_skroch@mail.vcsu.nodak.edu
www.vcsu.edu

K-12 Certification/ Music in B.S. Ed. Major Music/ (B.A., B.S.); Minor Music/ (B.A., B.S., B.S. in Ed.); Composite Major Music/(B.S. in Ed.)

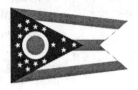

Population: 11,464,042 (2005 Estimate)
Capital City: Columbus
Bird: Cardinal
Motto: With God all things are possible
Flower: Scarlet Carnation
Tree: Buckeye
Residents Called: Ohioans
Origin of Name: From the Iroquois Indian word for "good river."
Area: 44,828 square miles (34th largest state)
Statehood: March 1, 1803 (17th state)
Largest Cities: Columbus, Cleveland, Cincinnati, Toledo, Akron, Dayton, Parma, Youngstown, Canton, Lorain
College Band Programs: Bowling Green State University, Miami University, Kent State University, Ohio Northern University, Ohio State University, Ohio University, University of Cincinnati, University of Toledo

OHIO

Antioch College
Department of Music

795 Livermore St.
Yellow Springs, OH 45387
937-769-1000
E-mail: admissions@antioch-college.edu
www.antioch-college.edu

Ashland University
Department of Music

401 College Ave.
Ashland, OH 44805
Donald Sloan
419-289-4142
E-mail: dsloan@ashland.edu
www.ashland.edu

Athenaeum of Ohio
Department of Music

6616 Beechmont Ave.
Cincinnati, OH 45230
Anthony DiCello
513-231-2223
Fax: 513-231-3254
E-mail: tdicello@mtsm.org
www.mtsm.org

Baldwin-Wallace College
Conservatory of Music

275 Eastland Rd.
Berea, OH 44017
Anita S. Evans
440-826-2362
Fax: 440-826-3239
E-mail: aevans@bw.edu
www.bw.edu/academics/conservatory

The Conservatory of Music is within a liberal arts college near Cleveland. Bachelor of Music degrees are conferred in performance, musical theatre, music therapy, composition, theory, history and literature. Also offered is the bachelor of music education degree and music management program. The conservatory provides personal attention from esteemed faculty and numerous performance opportunities.

Bluffton University
Department of Music

1 University Dr.
Bluffton, OH 45817
Lucia Unrau
800-488-3257
E-mail: unraul@bluffton.edu
www.bluffton.edu

Bowling Green State University
College of Musical Arts

110 McFall Center
Bowling Green, OH 43403
Kathleen Moss
419-372-2531
E-mail: kmoss@bgsu.edu
www.bgsu.edu

Bachelor of Music; Master of Music; Doctor of Musical Arts

Capital University
Conservatory of Music

1 College and Main
Columbus, OH 43029
William B. Dederer
614-236-6474
www.capital.edu

Case Western Reserve University
Department of Music

10900 Euclid Ave.
Cleveland, OH 44106
Georgia J. Cowart
216-368-2400
E-mail: georgia.cowart@case.edu
music.cwru.edu

Cedarville University
Department of
Music and Art

251 North Main St.
Cedarville, OH 45314
Doug Atkins
937-766-7728
Fax: 937-766-7661
E-mail: atkinsd@cedarville.edu
www.cedarville.edu

Central State University
Department of Fine
and Performing Arts

P.O. Box 1004
Wilberforce, OH 45384
937-376-6011
E-mail: info@centralstate.edu
www.centralstate.edu
Bachelor of Music

Cincinnati Christian University
Music and Worship Studies

2700 Glenway Ave.
Cincinnati, OH 45204
800-949-9CCU x8165
E-mail: musicworship@ccuniversity.edu
www.ccuniversity.edu

Cleveland Institute of Music
11021 East Blvd.
Cleveland, OH 44106
216-791-5000
Fax: 216-791-3063
E-mail: admission@cim.edu
www.cim.edu

Cleveland State University
Department of Music

2121 Euclid Ave.
MU332
Cleveland, OH 44115

Alexandra Vago
216-687-5039
E-mail: a.vago@csuohio.edu
www.csuohio.edu/music/

College of Mount St. Joseph
Department of Music

5701 Delhi Rd.
Cincinnati, OH 45233
513-244-4200
Fax: 513-244-4601
www.msj.edu

College of Wooster
Department of Music

525 East University St.
Scheide Music Center
Wooster, OH 44691
Brian Dykstra
330-263-2033
E-mail: bdykstra@wooster.edu
www.wooster.edu/music/

Cuyahoga Community College - Metropolitan Campus
Department of Music

2900 Community College Ave.
Cleveland, OH 44115
216-987-4000
E-mail: webmail@tri-c.edu
www.tri-c.edu/metro/

Cuyahoga Community College - Western Campus
Department of Music

11000 Pleasant Valley Rd.
Parma, OH 44130
216-987-5000
E-mail: webmail@tri-c.edu
www.tri-c.edu/west/

Dana School of Music

One University Plaza
Youngstown, OH 44555
Michael Crist
330-941-3636
Fax: 330-941-1490
E-mail: mrcrist@ysu.edu
www.fpa.ysu.edu/music/

Bachelor of Music; Bachelor of Arts; Master of
Music.

Denison University
Department of Music

P.O. Box M
Granville, OH 43023
Pam Hughes
740-587-0810
E-mail: hughes@denison.edu
www.denison.edu/music/

Heidelberg College
Department of Music

310 East Market St.
Tiffin, OH 44883
Douglas McConnell
419-448-2073
Fax: 419-448-2124
E-mail: dmcconne@heidelberg.edu
www.heidelberg.edu

BM: Performance, Music Education Composi-
tion/Theory, Music Industry; BA/BS Music Major;
Music Minor

The Department of Music enjoys a tradition of
excellence dating back to 1885. It is led by a
distinguished faculty who combine a personal commitment to teaching with professional
achievements in performance, research and
composition. The low student-teacher ratio allows
for personal attention to student progress and development. Heidelberg's program features a wide
variety of performances, including solo recitals
and ensembles. Faculty, Guest Artist programs
and an annual New Music Festival are among the
100 events sponsored by the Department each
year. The program enjoys full accreditation from
NASM and also features an outstanding placement record for students in the job market and
graduate schools.

Hiram College
Department of Music

P.O. Box 67
Hiram, OH 44234
Tina Dreisbach
330-569-5294
Fax: 330-569-6093
E-mail: music@hiram.edu
www.hiram.edu

Bacalaureate

John Carroll University
Music Performance Area and Fine Arts

20700 North Park Blvd.
University Heights, OH 44118
Cynthia Caporella
216-397-4721
Fax: 216-397-1822
E-mail: ccaporella@jcu.edu
www.jcu.edu

Kent State University
The Hugh A. Glauser School of Music

P.O. Box 5190
Kent, OH 44242
Joseph Knott
330-672-2172
Fax: 330-672-7837
E-mail: mhyatt@kent.edu
www.kent.edu/music/

Kenyon College
Department of Music

Gambier, OH 43022
Benjamin Locke
740-427-5197
Fax: 740-427-5512

E-mail: lockeb@kenyon.edu
www.kenyon.edu/music.xml

Bachelor of Arts

Lake Erie College
Department of Fine and Performing Arts

391 West Washington St.
Painesville, OH 44077
Professor Paul Gothard III
440-375-7030
E-mail: pgothard@lec.edu
www.lec.edu

Bachelor of Arts; Bachelor of Fine Arts.

Lorain County Community College
Division of Arts and Humanities

1055 North Abbe Rd.
Elyria, OH 44035
Robert Beckstrom
800-995-LCCC
E-mail: rbecks@loraincc.edu
www.loraincc.edu

Lourdes College
Department of Music

6832 Convent Blvd.
Sylvania, OH 43560
Karen Thornton Biscay
419-824-3772
E-mail: kbiscay@lourdes.edu
www.lourdes.edu

Malone College
Department of Fine Arts

515 25th St., NW
Canton, OH 44709
Cynthia Bridges
330-471-8231
Fax: 330-471-8478

E-mail: cbridges@malone.edu
www.malone.edu

The Department of Fine Arts offers the BA in Music, Music Ministry, and Commercial Music Technology and the BS in Music Education. Vocal and Instrumental Ensembles as well as private instruction provide opportunities for students to develop particular talents. Malone's music programs prepare students for positions in public schools, churches, private teaching and music technology. Malone, a member of the Council for Christian Colleges and Universities, is recognized by the prestigious Templeton Foundation as a leader in character development.

Marietta College
The Edward E. MacTaggart Department of Music

215 5th St.
Marietta, OH 45750
740-376-4688
Fax: 740-376-4529
E-mail: music@marietta.edu
www.marietta.edu

BFA Musical Theatre, BA Music

Located in Marietta, Ohio, at the confluence of the Muskingum and Ohio rivers, Marietta College is a four-year liberal arts college. Tracing its roots to the Muskingum Academy begun in 1797, the College was officially chartered in 1835. Today Marietta College serves a body of 1,300 full-time undergraduates hailing from 42 states and 14 countries. The college offers 39 majors and has been listed among Baron,s Best Buys in College Education, Peterson,s Competitive Colleges, and has been recognized as one of the top regional comprehensive colleges by U.S News and World report. The Edward E. MacTaggart Department of Music at Marietta College offers exceptional training in a supportive environment for undergraduate students pursuing either a Bachelor of Fine Arts in Musical Theatre or a Bachelor of Arts in Music with emphasis in performance, composition, or historical research. A music minor is also available. Each year the Music Department awards numerous scholarships to deserving students who plan to participate in instrumental, vocal, and piano solo or ensemble performance. These renewable scholarships have values totaling up to $14,000 for four years. They are awarded to both music majors and non-majors alike, and may be combined with academic scholarships.

Miami University
Department of Music

119 Center for Performing Arts
Oxford, OH 45056
Richard D. Green
513-529-3014
Fax: 513-529-3027
E-mail: greenrd@muohio.edu
www.muohio.edu/music

Bachelor of Music in Music Performance, Bachelor of Music in Music Education, Bachelor of Arts in Music, Master of Music in Music Education

Mount Union College
Department of Music

1972 Clark Ave.
Alliance, OH 44601
James Perone
330-823-2128
E-mail: dorseysw@muc.edu
www.muc.edu

Mount Vernon Nazarene College
Department of Music

800 Martinsburg Rd.
Mount Vernon, OH 43050
Robert Tocheff
740-392-6868 x3001
E-mail: btocheff@mvnu.edu
www.mvnu.edu

Bachelor of Arts

Muskingum College
Department of Music

163 Stormont

New Concord, OH 43762
Jenny Hulboy
740-826-8182
Fax: 740-826-8109
E-mail: music@muskingum.edu
www.muskingum.edu

Bachelor of Arts in Music; Bachelor of Arts in Music Education

Muskingum College is a liberal arts college with a full program in music including two undergraduate degree programs and one graduate degree program. A minor in music is also offered and scholarships are available for majors, minors, and participants.

Oberlin Conservatory of Music
Conservatory Admissions

39 West College St.
Oberlin, OH 44074
Michael Manderen
440-775-8413
Fax: 440-776-6972
E-mail: conservatory.admissions@oberlin.edu
www.oberlin.edu/con

The Oberlin Conservatory provides thorough and professional music training. Its faculty consists of highly regarded musicians who maintain active careers as performers, composers, theoreticians and historians. Founded in 1865, the conservatory is internationally recognized as one of the finest music schools in the United States. A conservatory student's program includes private study and solo and ensemble performance, plus courses in music history and music theory. Individual instruction is highly valued, and there is one faculty member for every eight students. Most faculty members live in Oberlin, so teachers and students get to know one another in the studio and outside academic contexts - over coffee at the De Café, at post-concert receptions, at parties at professors' homes, at various campus events. The Oberlin Conservatory is a division of Oberlin College, making it a major music school linked with a preeminent liberal arts college. Degree candidates in the conservatory take at least 20 percent of their courses in non-music subjects in the College of Arts and Sciences, and most may elect up to 40 percent. This approach provides balance between intense professional training and broad general education.

Ohio Dominican College
Department of Music

1216 Sunbury Rd.
Columbus, OH 43219
800-955-OHIO
Fax: 614-251-0156
E-mail: admissions@ohiodominican.edu
www.ohiodominican.edu

Minor in Music

Ohio Northern University
Department of Music

525 South Main St.
Ada, OH 45810
419-772-2260
E-mail: admissions-ug@onu.edu
www.onu.edu

Bachelor of Music; Bachelor of Arts.

Ohio State University
School of Music

110 Weigel Hall
1866 College Rd.
Columbus, OH 43210
614-292-6571
Fax: 614-292-1102
www.osu.edu

Bachelor of Music; Bachelor of Arts; Master of Music; Master of Arts; Doctor of Musical Arts; Doctor of Philosophy

Ohio State University at Lima
Department of Music

4240 Campus Dr.
Lima, OH 45804
Bev Bletstein
419-995-8289

E-mail: bletstein.1@osu.edu
lima.osu.edu

Ohio University
School of Music

Robert Glidden Hall
Athens, OH 45701
Allyn Reilly
740-593-4244
Fax: 740-593-1429
E-mail: reillya@ohio.edu
www.ohio.edu

Bachelor of Music; Master of Music.

Ohio University Lancaster

1570 Granville Pike
Lancaster, OH 43130
740-654-6711
E-mail: lancaster@ohio.edu
www.lancaster.ohiou.edu

Ohio University Zanesville

1425 Newark Rd.
Zanesville, OH 43701
740-453-0762
www.zanesville.ohiou.edu

Ohio Wesleyan University
Department of Music

61 South Sandusky St.
Sanborn Hall
Delaware, OH 43015
Nancy Gamso
740-368-3700
Fax: 740-368-3723
E-mail: music@owu.edu
music.owu.edu

Bachelor of Music; Bachelor of Arts.

Otterbein College
Department of Music

One Otterbein College
Westerville, OH 43081

Ann Dunnigton
614-823-1508
E-mail: adunnington@otterbein.edu
www.otterbein.edu/music

Bachelor of Arts; Bachelor of Fine Arts; Bachelor of Music.

Recording Workshop
455 Massieville Rd.
Chillicothe, OH 45601
Dena Brookover
800-848-9900
Fax: 740-663-2427
E-mail: info@recordingworkshop.com
www.recordingworkshop.com

Shawnee State
Community College
Department of Music

940 2nd St.
Portsmouth, OH 45662
Leslie Williams
614-354-3205
Fax: 614-335-2416

Shawnee State University
Fine, Digital, and
Performing Arts

940 Second St.
Portsmouth, OH 45662
740-351-4SSU
Fax: 740-351-3159
E-mail: To_SSU@shawnee.edu
www.shawnee.edu

Music Minor

Shawnee State University
Department of Music

Portsmouth, OH 45662
Jerry Holt
614-354-3205
Fax: 614-355-2416
www.shawnee.edu

Sinclair Community College
Department of Fine and
Performing Arts

444 West Third St.
Dayton, OH 45402
Robert Ruckman
800-315-3000
E-mail: robert.ruckman@sinclair.edu
www.sinclair.edu

Terra Community College
Department of Music

2830 Napolean Rd.
Fremont, Ohio 43420
419-334-8400
www.terra.edu

The University of Akron
School of Music

Akron, OH 44325
Dr. William K. Guegold
330-972-7590
Fax: 330-972-6409
E-mail: WGuegold@AOL.com
www.uakron.edu/faa/schools/music.html

BM, BFA, MM, MFA, MA, DMA, PhD, AD

University of Cincinnati
College Conservatory
of Music (CCM)

3245 Emery Hall
Cincinnati, OH 45221
CCM Admissions
513-556-9479
Fax: 513-556-1028
E-mail: ccmadmis@uc.edu
www.ccm.uc.edu

The College Conservatory of Music (CCM) has been called "One of this country's leading conservatories" by the New York Times. A $93.2 million village for the performing and electronic media was completed in 1999. CCM offers programs in music performance, music education, conducting, acting, musical theater, voice, stage production, television and audio. More than 1,000 performances take place each year, with opportunities for all student instrumentalists to perform with orchestras, wind symphonies, and large and small chamber ensembles. The prestigious faculty attract students from all over the world. CCM offers quality education at an affordable price with over $4 million available in scholarship awards. Visit the Web site for further information and listen to students perform.

University of Dayton
Department of Music

300 College Park
Dayton, OH 45469
Donna Cox
937-229-3936
Fax: 937-229-3916
E-mail: donna.cox@notes.udayton.edu
www.udayton.edu/~music

The University of Dayton Department of Music is fully accredited by the National Association of Schools of Music. Students have a distinctive opportunity to enrich their backgrounds in music, as well as enjoy the wide variety of liberal arts offerings by the university. Performance opportunities include Pride of Dayton Marching Band, symphonic wind ensemble, university concert band, Dayton Jazz Ensemble, jazz lab band, jazz combos, Flyer Pep Band, indoor drum line, University Chorale, choral union, Ebony Heritage Singers, musical theatre, opera workshop, Hands in Harmony (sign-sing), and a wide variety of chamber ensembles. The Dayton area provides rich, cultural opportunities for the university student, including the Dayton Philharmonic Orchestra, Dayton Opera, and the Dayton Bach Society (chorus). Opening in 2002, the brand new Shuster Performing Arts Center, downtown Dayton, will be a state-of-the-art performance facility. Music education and music therapy majors will find a variety of field experience opportunities in the immediate area. A large number of area schools have high-quality music education programs, providing the music education major with quality experiences. For the therapy major, there are plenty of area hospitals, assisted-care facilities, schools, and other programs for practicum experiences.

University of Findlay
Department of Music

1000 N. Main St
Findlay, OH 45840-3695
Michael Anders
419-434-4531
Fax: 419-434-4822
E-mail: anders@findlay.edu
www.findlay.edu

Minor in Musical Arts

Although the University of Findlay does not offer a professional degree in music, it has a long tradition of training excellent musicians from other academic areas, as well as fostering extensive performance opportunities for students pursuing degrees in all academic disciplines. The mission of the UF Music Department is "to effectively train the avocational musician to the highest level possible and foster an appreciation for the musical arts in all persons through live performances, applied music study, and traditional and non-traditional classroom experiences." Performance opportunities at UF include, among others, the Concert-Chorale, University Singers, Marching Band, Wind Ensemble, Jazz Ensemble, annual spring musical production, and applied music study in 20 different fields of study (including all areas of voice, piano, strings, woodwinds, brass, percussion, and composition). UF is the ideal choice for the student who is seeking nurturing, yet rigorous, musical training while pursuing a professional degree within another academic area.

University of Toledo
College of Arts and Sciences-Music Department

2801 West Bancroft
Toledo, OH 43606
419-530-2448
E-mail: utmusic@utoledo.edu
www.utoledo.edu

Bachelor of Education; Bachelof or Music; Bachelor of Arts

Walsh University

2020 East Maple St. NW
Canton, OH 44720
800-362-9846
E-mail: brfreshour@walsh.edu
www.walsh.edu

Wilberforce University

Wilberforce, OH 45384
www.wilberforce.edu

Bachelor of Science; Bachelor of Arts

Wittenberg University
Department of Music

P.O. Box 720
Springfield, OH 45501
Kenneth Scheffel
800-677-7558
Fax: 937-327-7347
E-mail: kscheffel@wittenbertg.edu
www.wittenberg.edu

Wright State University
Department of Music

3640 Colonel Glenn Hwy.
Dayton, OH 45435
Herbert Dregalla
937-775-2346
Fax: 937-775-3786
E-mail: music@wright.edu
www.wright.edu

Xavier University
Department of Music

1530 Dana Ave.
Cincinnati, OH 45207
Kaleel Skeirik
513-745-3803
E-mail: skeirik@xu.edu
www.xu.edu

Youngstown State University
Dana School of Music

One University Plaza
Youngstown, OH 44555
Michael Crist
330-941-3636
Fax: 330-941-1490
E-mail: mrcrist@ysu.edu
www.ysu.edu

Population: 3,547,884 (2005 Estimate)
Capital City: Oklahoma City
Bird: Scissor-tailed Flycatcher
Motto: Labor omnia vincit – Labor conquers all things
Flower: Mistletoe
Tree: Redbud
Residents Called: Oklahomans
Origin of Name: Based on Choctaw Indian words for "red man."
Area: 69,903 square miles (20th largest state)
Statehood: November 16, 1907 (46th state)
Largest Cities: Oklahoma City, Tulsa, Norman, Lawton, Broken Arrow, Edmond, Midwest City, Enid, Moore, Stillwater
College Band Programs: University of Oklahoma

Bartlesville Wesleyan College
Music Program

2201 Silver Lake Rd.
Bartlesville, OK 74006
918-335-6200
Fax: 918-335-6229
E-mail: info@okwu.edu
www.okwu.edu

Cameron University
Department of Music

2800 West Gore Blvd.
120 Music Building
Lawton, OK 73505
John Moots
580-581-2440
Fax: 580-581-5764
E-mail: johnmoo@cameron.edu
www.cameron.edu

Carl Albert State College
Communications and Fine Arts

1507 South McKenna
HC 305
Poteau, OK 74953
Bob Hendricks
918-647-1242
E-mail: bhendricks@carlalbert.edu
www.carlalbert.edu

East Central University
Department of Music

1100 East 14th St.
Ada, OK 74820
Mark Hollingsworth
580-332-8000
E-mail: mholling@ecok.edu
www.ecok.edu

Eastern Oklahoma State College
Social Science and Music Division

1301 West Main
Mitchell Building
Wilburton, OK 74578
Marilynn Duncan
918-465-1809
E-mail: mduncan@eosc.edu
www.eosc.edu

Langston University
Department of Music

P.O. Box 728
Langston, OK 73050
Mark Davis
405-466-3428
Fax: 405-466-3391
E-mail: admissions@lunet.edu
www.lunet.edu

Northeastern Oklahoma A&M College
Department of Fine Arts

200 I St., NE
Miami, OK 74354
918-540-6291
www.neoam.cc.ok.us

Northeastern State University
Department of Performing Arts

600 North Grand Ave.
Tahlequah, OK 74464
918-456-5511
www.nsuok.edu

Northwestern Oklahoma State University
Department of Music

709 Oklahoma Blvd.
Alva, OK 73717
Kathryn Lindberg
580-327-8191
E-mail: kalindberg@nwosu.edu
www.nwosu.edu

Oklahoma Baptist University
Division of Music

500 West University
Shawnee, OK 74804
800-654-3285
www.okbu.edu

Oklahoma Christian University
Department of Music

P.O. Box 11000
Oklahoma City, OK 73136
405-425-5530
E-mail: music@oc.edu
www.oc.edu

Oklahoma City University
Wanda L. Bass School of Music

2501 North Blackwelder
Oklahoma City, OK 73106
Mark Edward Parker
405-208-5000
E-mail: mparker@okcu.edu
www.okcu.edu/music

Oral Roberts University
Department of Music

7777 South Lewis Ave.
Tulsa, OK 74171
J. Randall Guthrie
918-495-7500
E-mail: music@oru.edu
www.oru.edu

Panhandle State University
Department of Fine Arts and Music
P.O. Box 430
Goodwell, OK 73939
580-349-2611
E-mail: opsu@opsu.edu
www.opsu.edu

Phillips University
Department of Music

P.O. Box 2127
Enid, OK 73702
580-237-4433
E-mail: admin@phillips.edu
www.phillips.edu

Rose State College
Department of Music

6420 SE 15th St.
Midwest, OK 73110
405-733-7380
Fax: 405-736-0370
E-mail: pcooksey@rose.edu
www.rose.cc.ok.us/hudiv/Music.html

Southwestern Oklahoma State University
Department of Music

100 Campus Dr.
Weatherford, OK 73096
Bob Klaassen
580-774-3708
Fax: 580-774-3714
E-mail: Bob.Klaassen.swosu.edu
www.swosu.edu/deps/music

BM degrees in Performance, Music Education, Music Business & Music Therapy; MM degrees in Performance & Music Education

St. Gregorys University
Department of Music

1900 W MacArthur St.
Shawnee, OK 74804

405-878-5461
Fax: 405-878-5198

University of Oklahoma
School of Music

500 West Boyd St.
Room 138
Norman, OK 73019
Carl Rath
405-325-2081
Fax: 405-325-7574
E-mail: oumusic@ou.edu
www.ou.edu

The school of music is located in a brand new building, Catlett Music Center. There is one concert hall, which is named Paul F. Sharp Concert Hall. This hall seats about 1,000 people. Our recital hall, Pitman Recital Hall, holds about 200 people. We currently have about 350 undergraduate students and 200 graduate students.

University of Science and Arts of Oklahoma
Department of Music

P.O. Box 82345
Chickasha, OK 73018
Dan Hanson
405-574-1297
Fax: 405-574-1220
E-mail: dhanson@usao.edu
www.usao.edu

University of Tulsa
Department of Music

600 South College Ave.
Tulsa, OK 74112
Frank Ryan
918-631-2262
Fax: 918-631-3589
E-mail: frank-ryan@utulsa.edu
www.cas.utulsa.edu/music

The School of Music is dedicated to providing professional, comprehensive musical education for students preparing for careers in the field of music and, as part of a comprehensive university, to enriching the curriculum with special course offerings and a variety of ensemble experiences available to all students. The School of Music offers both liberal arts and professional degree programs. The B.A. degree (bachelor of arts) is offered in both general music studies and also with a special emphasis on jazz studies. In cooperation with the School of Art, the Department of Theatre and the College of Business Administration, the B.A. degree is also offered with a major in arts administration. The B.M. degree (bachelor of music) is offered with majors in performance, music composition and music theory. The B.M.E. degree (bachelor of music education) is offered in instrumental and vocal music, and in vocal music with piano as the principal instrument. Additionally, the bachelor of music education is offered in all three of these areas with an emphasis on jazz techniques. Students may also receive a minor in music by completing 12 to 15 hours of selected music courses.

Western Oklahoma State College
Department of Music

2801 N. Main St.
Altus, OK 73521-1310
Karla Shelby
580-477-2000
Fax: 580-477-7777
E-mail: karla.shelby@wosc.edu
www.wosc.edu

Population: 3,641,056 (2005 Estimate)
Capital City: Salem
Bird: Western Meadowlark
Motto: Alis Volat Propiis – She Flies With Her Own Wings
Flower: Oregon Grape
Tree: Douglas Fir
Residents Called: Oregonians
Origin of Name: Origin and meaning of name unknown. May have been derived from that of the Wisconsin River shown on a 1715 French map as, "Ouaricon-sint."
Area: 98,386 square miles (9th largest state)
Statehood: February 14, 1859 (33rd state)
Largest Cities: Portland, Eugene, Salem, Gresham, Hillsboro, Beaverton, Medford, Springfield, Bend, Corvallis
College Band Programs: Oregon State University, University of Oregon

Blue Mountain Community College
Department of Music

P.O. Box 100
BMCC Music Instructor
Pendleton, OR 97801-1000
Margaret Mayer
541-278-5174
E-mail: mmayer@bluecc.edu
www.bluecc.edu

Britt Institute

216 West Main St.
Medford, OR 97501
541-779-0847
Fax: 541-776-3712
www.brittfest.org

Clackamas Community College
Department of Music

19600 South Molalla Ave.
Oregan City, OR 97054
503-657-6958
clackamas.cc.or.us

Eastern Oregon University
Department of Music

One University Blvd.
La Grande, OR 97850-2899
541-962-3555
Fax: 541-962-3596
E-mail: admissions@eou.edu
www.eou.edu

George Fox University
Department of Music

414 North Meridian St.
Newberg, OR 97132
503-538-8383
www.georgefox.edu

Lewis and Clark College
Department of Music

0615 Palatine Hill Rd.
MSC 18
Portland, OR 97219
503-768-7460
Fax: 503-768-7475
E-mail: music@lclark.edu
www.lclark.edu

Linfield College
Department of Music

900 SE Baker St.
McMinnville, OR 97128-6894
503-883-2275
Fax: 503-883-2647
E-mail: admission@linefield.edu
www.linfield.edu

Marylhurst College
Department of Music

17600 Pacific Hwy. (Hwy 43)
P.O. Box 261
Maryhurst, OR 97036-0261
503-699-6263
Fax: 503-636-9526
www.marylhurst.edu

Oregon State University
Department of Music

101 Benton Hall
Corvallis, OR 97331
541-737-4061
www.oregonstate.edu

Pacific University
Department of Music

2043 College Way
Forest Grove, OR 97116
503-352-2216
Fax: 503-352-2910

E-mail: music@pacificu.edu
www.pacificu.edu

Portland State University
Department of Music

P.O. Box 751
231 Lincoln Hall
Portland, OR 97207
503-725-3011
Fax: 503-725-8215
www.pdx.edu

Reed College
Department of Music

3203 SE Woodstock Blvd.
Portland, OR 97202-8199
503-771-1112
Fax: 503-777-7769
www.web.reed.edu

Southern Oregon University
Department of Music

1250 Siskiyou Blvd.
Ashland, OR 97520
541-552-6411
www.sou.edu

Umpqua Community College
Department of Music

1140 College Rd.
P.O. Box 967
Roswebug, OR 97470-0226
503-440-7743
E-mail: Lavera.Nordling@empqua.edu
www.umpqua.edu

University of Oregon
School of Music

1225 University of Oregon
Eugene, OR 97403
Laurie Goren
541-346-3761

Fax: 541-346-0723
E-mail: amclucas@oregon.uoregon.edu
www.music.uoregon.edu

The University of Oregon is a fully-accredited institution for degrees in music through the doctoral level, offering major programs in music performance, music education, composition, theory, jazz studies and music technology. Facilities include 540-seat Beall Concert Hall, acclaimed for its superb acoustics; microcomputer laboratory; Clavinova digital keyboard lab; and three studios for creating electro-acoustic music.

University of Portland
Department of Music

5000 North Willamette Blvd.
Portland, OR 97203
503-943-7760
Fax: 503-943-8079
college.up.edu

Warner Pacific College
Department of Music

2219 SE 68th Ave.
Portland, OR 97203
503-517-1020
E-mail: admiss@warnerpacific.edu
www1.warnerpacific.edu

Western Oregon University
Department of Music

345 North Monmouth Ave.
Monmouth, OR 97361
503-838-8327
Fax: 503-838-9696
E-mail: registar@wou.edu
www.wou.edu

Willamette University
Department of Music

900 St. State
Salem, OR 97301
503-370-6255
www.willamette.edu

Population: 12,429,616 (2005 Estimate)
Capital City: Harrisburg
Bird: Ruffed Grouse
Motto: Virtue, Liberty, and Independence
Flower: Mountain Laurel
Tree: Eastern Hemlock
Residents Called: Pennsylvanians
Origin of Name: Named in honor of Admiral William Penn, father of the state's founder, William Penn.
Area: 46,058 square miles (33rd largest state)
Statehood: December 12, 1787 (2nd state)
Largest Cities: Philadelphia, Pittsburgh, Allentown, Erie, Upper Darby Township, Reading, Scranton, Bethlehem, Lower Merion Twp, Lancaster
College Band Programs: Carnegie-Mellon University, Indiana University of Pennsylvania, Lehigh University, Millersville University, Pennsylvania State University, University of Pennsylvania, University of Pittsburgh, West Chester University

Albright College
Department of Music

13th and Bern St.
P.O. Box 15234
Reading, PA 19612
Adlai Binger
610-921-7715
E-mail: abinger@alb.edu
www.alb.edu

Allegheny College
Department of Music

Arnold Hall
520 North Main
Meadville, PA 16335
Lowell Helper
814-332-3304
E-mail: lhelper@alleg.edu
www.alleg.edu

Bloomsburg University
Department of Music

400 East Second St.
Bloomsburg, PA 17815
570-389-4284
Fax: 570-389-4289
E-mail: lfisher@bloomu.edu
www.bloomu.edu

Bryn Mawr College
Arts Program

101 North Merion Ave.
Bryn Mawr, PA 19010
610-526-5000
www.brynmawr.edu

Bucknell University
Department of Music

701 Moore Ave.
Lewisburg, PA 17837
570-577-2000
www.bucknell.edu

Carnegie-Mellon University
School of Music

5000 Forbes Ave.
Pittsburgh, PA 15131
Michele McGregor
412-268-4118
E-mail: mtmcgreg@andrew.cmu.edu
www.cmu.edu

Chestnut Hill College
Department of Music

9601 Germantown Ave.
Philadelphia, PA 19118
215-248-7194
Fax: 215-248-7155
E-mail: kmcclosk@chc.edu
www.chc.edu

Clarion University of Pennsylvania
Department of Music

227 Marwick-Boyd
Clarion, PA 16214
Jeffrey Wardlaw
814-393-2287
Fax: 814-393-2723
E-mail: jwardlaw@clarion.edu
www.clarion.edu

Curtis Institute of Music
Admissions Office

1726 Locust St.
Philadelphia, PA 19103
Music Department
215-893-5252
Fax: 215-893-9065
E-mail: admissions@curtis.edu
www.curtis.edu

Delaware Valley College
Department of Music

700 East Butler Ave.
Doylestown, PA 18902-2607
215-489-2233
Fax: 215-489-4950
E-mail: schmidtj@devalcol.edu
www.devalcol.edu

Dickinson College
Waidner Admissions House

P.O. Box 1773
Carlisle, PA 17013-2896
Robert Pound
717-243-5121
E-mail: pound@dickinson.edu
www.dickinson.edu

Duquesne University
Mary Pappert School of Music

600 Forbes Ave.
Pittsburgh, PA 15282
Nicholas Jordanoff
412-396-5983
Fax: 412-396-5719
E-mail: jordanof@duq.edu
www.music.duq.edu
Bachelor's and Master's

A Catholic university with an enrollment of 10,000 with 10 schools of study. The School of Music offers undergraduate degrees in Music Education, Music Therapy, Music Performance with three tracks-classical, jazz, sacred music, and Music Technology with three tracks- performance, composition, and sound recording. The master's degree offers Music Education, Music Performance, Music Technology, Theory and Composition.

Edinboro University of Pennsylvania
Heather Hall

Edinboro, PA 16444
Gary Grant
814-732-2555

E-mail: ggrant@edinboro.edu
www.edinboro.edu

The music department at Edinboro University provides music students with a wealth of opportunities in musical performance and study. Many of our graduates teach in elementary and secondary schools, while others go on to graduate study, or pursue careers in the music industry or performance.

Franklin and Marshall College
Department of Music

P.O. Box 3003
Lancaster, PA 17604-3003
Bruce Gustafson
717-291-4346
www.fandm.edu

B.A., music major, music minor-general; music minor performance

At Franklin and Marshall, we believe that music has a central place in liberal arts education. Our purpose is to provide students the means of opportunity to interact on intellectual and aesthetic levels with the art of music. Those taking music courses work closely with faculty members, and all students have access to professionally directed instrumental and choral ensembles. The newly renovated Barshinger Center provides a worlclass concert hall to serve as the centerpiece of the College's thriving music program. The setting is elegant and acoustically vibrant and serves as a venue for visiting musicians of higher caliber.

Geneva College
Department of Music

3200 College Ave.
Beaver Falls, PA 15010
Donald B. Kephart
724-846-5100
Fax: 724-847-6687
E-mail: dbk@geneva.edu
www.geneva.edu

PENNSYLVANIA

Gettysburg College
Department of Music

P.O. Box 403
300 N. Washington St.
Gettysburg, PA 17325
John William Jones
717-337-6131
Fax: 717-337-6099
E-mail: jjones@gettysburg.edu
www.gettysburg.edu

Grove City College
Department of Music

100 Campus Dr.
Grove City, PA 16127
724-458-2000
www.gcc.edu

Haverford College
Department of Music

370 Lancaster Ave.
Haverford, PA 19041
Nancy Merriam
610-896-1011
E-mail: nmerriam@haverford.edu
www.haverford.edu

Immaculata College
Department of Music

1145 King Rd.
Immaculata, PA 19345
610-647-4400
www.immaculata.edu

Indiana University of Pennsylvania
Department of Music

101 Cogswell Hall
Indiana, PA 15705
Lorraine Wilson
724-357-2390
Fax: 724-357-1324

E-mail: lpw@iup.edu
www.arts.ipu

Juniata College
Department of Music

1700 Moore St.
Huntingdon, PA 16652
814-641-3000
E-mail: info@juniata.edu
www.juniata.edu

Lafayette College
Department of Music

Easton, PA 18042
J. Larry Stockton
610-330-5356
Fax: 610-330-5355
E-mail: stocktoj@lafayette.edu
www.lafayette.edu

LaSalle University
Department of Fine Arts

1900 West Olney Ave.
Philadelphia, PA 19141
Patricia Haberstroh
215--951-1149
E-mail: haverstr@lasalle.edu
www.lasalle.edu

Lebanon Valley College
Department of Music

101 N. College Ave.
Annville, PA 17003-1400
Mark Mecham
717-867-6275
Fax: 717-867-6390
E-mail: music@lvc.edu
www.lvc.edu

BA in music, Music Business, BM in Music recording Tech., BS and Masters in Music Ed.,

Lebanon Valley College is a Private-Liberal Arts College founded in 1866. The department of music (one of the largest on campus) offers four undergraduate music degree programs and a Summers only Masters degree in Music Education. An institutional member of the National Associaiton of Schools of Music since 1941; LVC is also accredited by the Middle States Association of Colleges and Schools and the Pennsylvania Department of Education.

Lehigh University
Department of Music

420 E. Packer Ave.
Bethlehem, PA 18015
Paul Salerni
610-758-3839
E-mail: pfs0@lehigh.edu
www.lehigh.edu

Lehigh offers a liberal arts degree with concentrations in performance, history and literature, theory and composition. The program is designed to allow students to double major in other fields. The new arts center has a 1,000-seat concert hall. Outstanding student ensembles include philharmonic orchestra, university choir, jazz, opera and music theatre and marching band.

Lincoln University
Department of Music

1570 Baltimore Pike
P.O. Box 179
Lincoln University, PA 19352
Kathy Madron
610-932-1254
E-mail: madron@lincoln.edu
www.lincoln.edu

Lycoming College
Department of Music

700 College Place
Williamsport, PA 17701
Gary M. Boerckel
570-321-4094
E-mail: boerckel@lycoming.edu
www.lycoming.edu

Mansfield University
Department of Music

Mansfield, PA 16933
570-662-4000
www.mansfield.edu

Marywood University
Department of Music

2300 Adams Ave.
Scranton, PA 18509
Joseph Fields
570-348-6268
Fax: 570-961-4721
E-mail: music@marywood.edu
www.marywood.edu

The programs in music provide a framework for students to master the professional and leadership skills necessary for various careers in music, while at the same time enabling them to develop their highest potential. The strength of the programs lies in a solid core of music classes required of all music students along with comprehensive musical development, which permits a student to specialize in a chosen field. The music department has the following facilities in the performing arts center: 1,100-seat theater, performing arts studio seating 125, digital piano lab, two harpsichords, two harps, practice facilities - including a complement of band and orchestra instruments, multiple copies of orchestral scores, choral library, vocal solo library, small library of reference books, curriculum lab and learning center, two microcomputer labs, biofeedback lab and multiple organs.

Mercyhurst University
School of Music

501 East 38th St.
Erie, PA 16546
Albert Glinsky
814-824-2000
www.mercyhurst.edu

Millersville University
Department of Music

P.O. Box 1002
Millersville, PA 17551
Micheal Houlahan
717-872-3357
Fax: 717-871-2304
E-mail: Micheal.Houlahan@millersville.edu
muweb.millersville.edu

Moravian College
Department of Music

1200 Main St.
Bethlehem, PA 18018
610-861-1300
www.moravian.edu

Muhlenberg College
Department of Music

2400 Chew St.
Allentown, PA 18104-5586
484-664-3100
www.muhlenberg.edu

Penn State School of Music
School of Music

233 Music Building
Music Buildling 1
University Park, PA 16802
Russell Bloom
814-865-0431
Fax: 814-865-6785
E-mail: music-ug-adm@psu.edu
www.music.psu.edu

B.M., B.A., B.M.A., B.S. in music education,
twelve graduate degrees, and six integrated
undergraduate-graduate degrees

The Penn State School of music has experienced
significant growth in both quantity and quality
over the past several years, and prides itself
on providing a wide range of degree offerings,
from the Bachelor's degrees in performance,
music education, and music arts to the doctor
of philosophy degree in music education. Over
300 students currently major in music at the
University Park campus. The faculty consists of
50 full-time artist/teachers. In addition to providing professional instruction for music majors the
School of Music Faculty is committed to enriching the arts experience for the entire University
community, both through performance and
instruction. Each semester, nearly 150 student
and faculty performances are scheduled in Penn
State facilities: the 500-seat Esber Recital Hall,
the 900-seat Schwab Auditorium, and the 2,300-
seat Eisenhower Auditorium in addition to other
venues. In addition, dozens of performances are
presented throughout the Commonwealth, the
nation, and abroad.

Penn State University Abington
Department of Music

1600 Woodland Rd.
Abington, PA 19001-3918
215-881-7300
Fax: 215-881-7623
E-mail: kws3@psu.edu
www.abington.psu.edu

Penn State University Altoona
Department of Music

124 Arts Center
Altoona, PA 16601-3760
814-949-5296
Fax: 814-949-5368
E-mail: ahzl@psu.edu
www.psu.edu

Penn State University Monaca
Department of Music

Brodhead Rd.
Monaca, PA 15061
724-773-3898

Penn State University
University Park
School of Music

233 Music Building
University Park, PA 16802-1901
814-865-0431
Fax: 814-865-6785
www.psu.edu

Phhiladelphia Biblical University
Department of Music

200 Manor Ave.
Langhorne, PA 19047
215-752-5800
www.pbu.edu

Saint Vincent College
Department of Music

300 Fraser Purchase Rd.
Latrobe, PA 15650-2690
724-532-6600
www.stvincent.edu

Seton Hill University
Department of Music

Seton Hill Dr.
Greensburg, PA 15601
Kim McCarty
800-826-2634
Fax: 724-830-1294
E-mail: admit@setonhill.edu
www.setonhill.edu

Bachelor of Music in Music Education, Music Therapy, Performance, Sacred Music. Bachelor of Arts in Music

Seton Hill University is a Catholic Liberal Arts University located in Greensburg, Pennsylvania, 30 miles east of Pittsburgh. The Music Program is a fully accredited institutional member of the National Association of Schools of Music and the Music Therapy degree is approved by the American Music Therapy Association.

Slippery Rock University
Department of Music

225 Swope Music Hill
slippery Rock, PA 16057
Maribeth Knaub
724-738-2063
www.sru.edu

Susquehanna University
Department of Music

514 University Ave.
Selinsgrove, PA 17870
570-372-4281
Fax: 570-372-2789
www.susqu.edu/music

B.M. in Performance, Music Education, and Church Music; B.A. in Music

Located in central Pennsylvania, Susquehanna has an enrollment of approximately 1,900 students from 30 states and a dozen countries. Our music program has over 100 majors with a faculty of 10 full-time and 17 part-time members. We are pleased to offer our students several music majors and minors to choose from within the framework of a liberal arts institution. More than a dozen performing ensembles are available for students to participate in, regardless of major. Countless non-music majors take lessons and perform in ensembles throughout the department and are integral members of our program. Minors in music technology, theory/literature, and performance are also available. In February 2003, our new Center for Music and Art was dedicated. These facilities include the 320-seat Sretansky Concert Hall, 32 practice rooms and renovated classroom and teaching space. Susquehanna's Department of Music is fully accredited by the National Association of Schools of Music.

Swarthmore College
Department of Music and Dance

500 College Ave.
Swarthmore, PA 19081
610-328-8000
www.swarthmore.edu

Technology Institute for Music
Office of Music Activities

305 Maple Ave.
Wyncote, PA 19095
610-519-7214
Fax: 610-519-7596
www.ti-me.org

Temple University
Boyer College of Music

Philadelphia, PA 19122
Robert Stroker
215-204-8301
Fax: 215-204-4957
E-mail: music@temple.edu
www.temple.edu/music

Temple University's Esther Boyer College of Music offers comprehensive, professional education in music - baccalaureate through doctorate - for performers, educators, therapists, and scholars. Students enjoy a 10:1 student to faculty ratio. Our world-renowned faculty includes many members of the Philadelphia Orchestra, as well as many other noted recording and performing artists. Students also enjoy the cultural advantages of the City of Philadelphia.

The Music Academy
Music Department

519 West College Ave.
State College, PA 16801
814-238-3451
www.musicacademy.org

Thiel College
Department of Music

75 College Ave.
Greenville, PA 16125
800-24-THIEL
www.thiel.edu

University of Pennsylvania
Department of Music

School of Arts and Sciences
Philadelphia, PA 19104
215-898-9664
www.sas.upenn.edu

University of Pittsburgh
Department of Music

110 Music Building
Pittsburgh, PA 15260
Rose Booth
412-624-4126
E-mail: rbooth@pitt.edu
www.music.pitt.edu

University of the Arts
College of the Performing Arts

Office of Admissions
320 South Broad St.
Philadelphia, PA 19102
Barbara Elliot
800-616-ARTS
www.uarts.edu

B.M. in Jazz Studies (performance or concentration), Master of Music in Jazz Studies (performance), Master of Arts in Teaching in Music Education

The School of Music at the University of the Arts is distinguished by its emphasis on Jazz and American music idioms. The school offers Bachelor and Master degrees in Jazz studies, and a Master of Arts in Teaching in Music Education. There are three large ensembles, and more than 40 small jazz groups performing all styles of traditional, contemporary, and Latin jazz. Faculty include world-renowned artists Carl Allen, Jimmy Bruno, Charles Fambrough, John Fedchock, Tim Hagans, Jeff Jarvis, Pat Martino, John Swana, and Gerald Veasley. Alumni include Stanley Clarke, Kenny Barron, Robin Eubanks, Gerry Brown, Lew Tabackin, and TV/FIL composers Edd Kalehoff and John Davis. Recent guest artists include Patti Austin, Jack DeJohnette, Kurt Elling, John Faddis,

Chris Potter, McCoy Tyner, Dave Weckl, and the Yellojackets. The school of music continues to grow its long-held tradition of excellence which Grammy-winning saxophonist Michael Brecker called "...one of the premier schools of jazz in the universe as we know it". Uarts, located in the heart of downtown Philadelphia on the Avenue of the Arts, is the nation's only university devoted exclusively to education and training in performing, visual and media arts.

Valley Forge Christian College
Department of Music

1401 Charlestown Rd.
Phoenixville, PA 19460
610-935-0450
Fax: 610-917-2069
www.vfcc.edu

Wikes University
Department of Music

84 West South St.
Wilkes-Barre, PA 18766
800-WILKES-U
www.wilkes.edu

York College
Division of Music

York, PA 17405
717-846-7788
www.ycp.edu

Population: 1,076,189 (2005 Estimate)
Capital City: Providence
Bird: Rhode Island Red
Motto: Hope
Flower: Violet
Tree: Red Maple
Residents Called: Rhode Islanders
Origin of Name: Possibly named in honor of the Greek Island of Rhodes or was named "Roode Eylandt" by Adriaen Block, Dutch explorer, because of its red clay.
Area: 1,545 square miles (the smallest state)
Statehood: May 29, 1790 (13th state)
Largest Cities: Providence, Warwick, Cranston, Pawtucket, East Providence, Woonsocket, Coventry, North Providence, Cumberland, West Warwick
College Band Programs: Brown University

Brown University
Orwig Music Building

1 Young Orchard Ave.
Providence, RI 02912
James Baker
401-863-3234
Fax: 401-863-1256
E-mail: music@brown.edu
www.brown.edu

Providence College
Department of Music

549 River Ave.
Smith Center for the Arts G04
Providence, RI 02918
401-865-2183
Fax: 401-865-2761
www.providence.edu

The Department of Music offers a Bachelor of Arts in Music, a Bachelor of Arts in Music/Music Education and a minor in music

The department of Music offers the study of music in a balanced and creative atmosphere that emphasizes the theoretical, historical, and educational foundations of music in a Liberal Arts context. Ample opportunity is provided for vocal and instrumental study and performance on an individual basis as well as in a variety of choral and instrumental ensembles. The music degree has five areas of specialization: History/Literature; Theory Composition; Performance; Jazz and Church Music. It is possible to double major, combining music with another department. The music education degree program balances the requirements of both music and education departments with the College's Liberal Arts program. This K-12 music education program prepares students for certification. Requirements for the minor include history, theory, private study, and participation in an ensemble. A new center for the Arts will be completed for the 2004-2005 academic year and will include performance areas, classrooms, offices and student practice rooms.

Rhode Island College
Nazarian Center for the Performing Arts

600 Mount Pleasant Ave.
Providence, RI 02908-1991
Robert Franzblau
401-456-9883
www2.ric.edu

Bachelor of Music, Bachelor of Science in Music Education, Bachelor of Arts, Minor in Music, Minor in Jazz Studies, Master of Music Education, Master of Arts in Teaching

University of Rhode Island
Department of Music

105 Upper College Rd.
Suite 2
Kingston, RI 02881
Gerard Heroux
401-874-5584
Fax: 401-874-2772
E-mail: muslib@uri.edu
www.uri.edu/artsci/mus

Population: 4,255,083 (2005 Estimate)
Capital City: Columbia
Bird: Great Carolina Wren
Motto: Animis Opibusque Parati / Dum Spiro Spero – Prepared in mind and resources / While I breathe, I hope
Flower: Yellow Jessamine
Tree: Sabal Palmetto
Residents Called: South Carolinians
Origin of Name: Named in honor of England's King Charles I
Area: 32,007 square miles (40th largest state)
Statehood: May 23, 1788 (8th state)
Largest Cities: Columbia, Charleston, North Charleston, Greenville, Rock Hill, Mount Pleasant, Spartanburg, Sumter, Hilton Head Island, Florence
College Band Programs: Clemson University, Furman University, University of South Carolina-Columbia

Anderson College
Department of Music

316 Blvd.
Anderson, SC 29621
800-231-2002
E-mail: dlarson@andersonuniversity.edu
www.ac.edu

Benedict College
Department of Music

1600 Harden St.
Columbia, SC 29204
803-253-5260

Bob Jones University
Division of Music

P.O. Box 34533
Greenville, SC 29614
David Christ
864-242-5100
Fax: 864-467-9302
www.bju.edu

Bob Jones University is a Christian liberal arts university (fundamental in doctrine and evangelistic in emphasis) offering more than 100 majors. A music faculty of over 60 includes specialists in all fields. The faculty's training represents leading graduate schools and conservatories from around the world. Students have excelled in contests on the local, state, regional, and national level. Our facilities are unsurpassed in Christian education and serve approximately 250 music majors, 150 music minors.

Charleston Southern University
Horton School of Music

P.O. Box 118087
Charleston, SC 29423-808
843-853-7966

Claflin University
Department of Music

400 Magnolia St.
Orangeburg, SC 29115
800-922-1276
www.claflin.edu

Clemson University
Department of Performing Arts

211 Brooks Center
Clemson, SC 29634-0525
Richard E. Goodstein
864-656-3043
Fax: 864-656-1013
E-mail: perf-arts-l@clemson.edu
www.clemson.edu/Perf-Arts

B.A.

Clemson University features a distinctive B.A. degree, which combines the disciplines of music and theater. The curriculum includes hands-on experiences in performing arts production technologies with classes in performance and arts history and theory in order to prepare students for entry into a wide variety of traditional, commercial, and community-based barriers. Students can choose from among 75 minors in order to customize their degree to their individual interests. The degree emphasizes multidisciplinary and collaborative performing arts and service learning as partners to traditional performance studies. The production studies in performing arts degree is designed to provide students with diverse and essential skills and experiences that are marketable in today's international, multicultural workplace. Housed in the beautiful Brooks Center for the Performing Arts, the Clemson University Department of Performing Arts features state-of-the-art technology, including the 1,000-seat Brooks Theatre, a new ProTools recording studio and a 12-station music technology lab.

Coker College
Department of Music

300 East College Ave.
Hartsville, SC 29550
843-383-8000

College of Charleston
Simons Center for the Arts

66 George St.
Charleston, SC 29424
Music Department
843-805-5507
www.cofc.edu

Columbia College
Department of Music

P.O. Box 3122
Columbia, SC 29230
803-754-4100

Converse College
School of Music

580 East Main St.
Spartanburg, SC 29302
800-766-1125
E-mail: music@converse.edu
www.converse.edu

Established in 1889, Converse College is a liberal arts college for women with a professional school of music. The Petrie School of Music is an accredited, charter member of the National Association of Schools of Music (NASM). Majors include performance (all instruments), music education, piano pedagogy, composition, theory and music history. The B.A. degree is offered with concentrations in general music or music business. Double major opportunities are also available. The low 7:1 student-faculty ratio allows students to learn in small classes and receive individualized instruction from a distinguished faculty of artists who are active in performance, composition and research. The faculty is complemented by a guest artist series featuring acclaimed musicians in master classes and concerts. The curriculum is enhanced by two nationally-recognized performance halls, one of the largest music libraries in the southeast, teaching studios and classrooms, 30 practice rooms, music technology labs, Steinway pianos, Casavant and Schantz pipe organs, and instrument collections for student use. Performing opportunities include Converse Sinfonietta, festival orchestra, wind ensemble, chamber winds, chorale, festival chorus, opera theatre, a student recital series and numerous chamber ensembles.

Furman University
Department of Music

3300 Poinsett Hwy.
Greenville, SC 29613
Marcella Frese
864-294-2086
Fax: 864-294-3035
E-mail: marcella.frese@furman.edu
www.MusicAtFurman.com

BM in Performance, Ed, Theory, Composition, Church Music; BA

Lander University
Department of Music

320 Stanley Ave.
Greenwood, SC 29649
864-388-8000
www.lander.edu

Limestone College
Department of Music

1115 College Dr.
Gaffney, SC 29340
Walt Griffin
800-795-7151
www.limestone.edu

Newberry College
Department of Music

2100 College St.
Newberry, SC 29108
Katie Youell

800-845-4900
Fax: 803-321-5175
E-mail: katie.youell@newberry.edu
www.newberry.edu

Bachelor Of Artsdegrees offered in Applied
Music,Music Theory, & Church Music ; Bachelor
of Music Performance ; Bachelor of Music
Education with Specialization in Choral Music or
Instrumental Music (Band)

Newberry College's Music Department offers a
challenging and diverse curriculum with minors
in everything from Church Music to Jazz Studies. We allow students to develop their musical
talents, not only as a means of entertainment,
but also as a method of self-expression. Newberry
College is fully accredited by the National Association of Schools of Music and our graduates
go on to pursue rewarding careers or graduate
studies at some of the most prestigious American
conservatories.

Presbyterian College
Department of Music

503 South BRd. St.
Clinton, SC 29325
Porter Stokes
864-833-2820
E-mail: pstokes@presby.edu
www.presby.edu

South Carolina
State University
Department of Visual
and Performing Arts

300 College St. NE
Orangeburg, SC 29117
Frank Mundy
803-536-8815
Fax: 803-536-8765
E-mail: mundyfm@scsu.edu
www.scsu.edu

University of South Carolina
at Aiken
Department of Fine Arts

471 University Pkwy.
Aiken, SC 29801
803-648-6851
www.usca.edu

University of South Carolina
at Columbia
School of Music

813 Assembly St.
Columbia, SC 29208
Jennifer Jablonski
803-777-6614
Fax: 803-777-6508
E-mail: jjablonski@sc.edu
www.music.sc.edu

Undergraduate: BA in Music, BM in Music
with emphases in: Composition, Jazz Studies,
Music, Music Education, Music Theory, Music
Performance, Piano Pedagogy. Master of Music
in Composition, Conducting, Jazz Studies, Music
History, Music Theory, Opera Theatre, Music
Performance, Piano Pedagogy, Music Educa-
tion. Doctorate of Musical Arts in Composition,
Conducting, Performance, and Piano Pedagogy.
Doctor of Philosophy in Music Education

The University of South Carolina School of
Music offers more then 20 bachelor, master and
doctorate music degrees. Out-of-state students
are granted a heavily reduced tuition rate along
with USC music scholarships awards. Founded
in 1801 as the flagship institution of the state of
South Carolina, USC offers more than 70 undergraduate majors, 150 master's programs, and 60
doctoral programs to more than 25,000 students
from all 50 states and more than 100 countries.

Winthrop University
Department of Music

129 Conservatory of Music
Rock Hill, SC 29733
Debi Barber
803-323-2255
Fax: 803-323-2343
E-mail: barberdg@winthrop.edu
www.winthrop.edu

BA Music; BME (Choral or Instrumental Certification), BM Performance, MME, MM Performance, MM Conducting (Wind or Choral), MAT
(initial certification in music

Nearly 6,500 students pursue 37 undergraduate
and 25 graduate degrees and options at Winthrop
University, a state-assisted university located in
Rock Hill, S.C., a city of 60,000 in the Charlotte,
N.C. metropolitan area. Winthrop has received
100 percent national accreditation in all eligible
programs, the first comprehensive learning
institution among South Carolina's senior colleges to reach that level of national accreditation.
Winthrop has been identified in the US News
and World Report ranking as a top 10 Southern
regional university for 14 consecutive years.
The university boasts a 14:1 student to faculty
ratio, with average class size ranging from 17-26
students. The campus features state-of-the art
learning facilities, including SMART classrooms
and high speed Internet access from all campus
buildings and residence hall rooms. Its athletic
teams compete in NCAA Division I. In its pursuit
of its goal of national caliber education, Winthrop
demonstrates the characteristics which make
it distinctive among universities of its kind: a
carefully selected student body of high academic
achievement and cultural diversity; a challenging
and comprehensive curriculum of the arts, sciences, and professions; a residential educational
experience emphasizing personal identity and
close relationships; and a highly qualified faculty
dedicated to teaching and public service. Winthrop is an institutional member of the National
Association of Schools of Music (NASM).

Population: 775,933 (2005 Estimate)
Capital City: Pierre
Bird: Ring-necked Pheasant
Motto: Under God the people rule
Flower: Pasque Flower
Tree: Black Hills Spruce
Residents Called: South Dakotans
Origin of Name: South Dakota is the land of the famous Sioux or Dacotah Indians. Dakota Territory and later South Dakotans were named for the tribe.
Area: 77,121 square miles (17th largest state)
Statehood: November 2, 1889 (40th state)
Largest Cities: Sioux Falls, Rapid City, Aberdeen, Watertown, Brookings, Mitchell, Pierre, Yankton, Huron, Vermillion

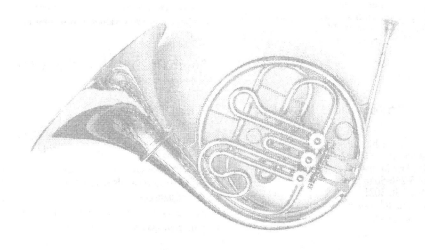

SOUTH DAKOTA

Augustana College
Department of Music

2001 South Summit Ave.
Sioux Falls, SD 57197
Janet Brown
605-274-5297
Fax: 605-274-5288
E-mail: janet.brown@augie.edu
www.augie.edu

Music, B.A. Instrumental Emphasis, Music education major, Minor

Black Hills State University
Department of Music

1200 University St.
Spearfish, SD 57799
800-ALL-BHSU
www.bhsu.edu

B.S. in Education: Music; B.S. in Liberal Arts: Music

Black Hills State University is a small liberal arts university in a beautiful and scenic location with many skiing, biking and hiking trails nearby. A new music facility has recently been completed with a new recital hall, band room, choir room, recording studio and practice rooms. The program features individual faculty mentoring by experienced teachers and a cooperative group spirit among the students. BHSU has long been a center for teacher education, and is fully accredited by NCATE. The music program is fully accredited by the National Associated of Schools of Music as well. Students who choose the non-teaching music program often minor in Entrepreneurial Studies of Business.

Dakota State University
Music Department

820 N. Washington
Madison, SD 57042
Dr. Eric Johnson
605-256-5646 Fax:
605-256-5021
E-mail: johnsone@columbia.dsu.edu
www.dsu.edu

Mount Marty College
Department of Music

1105 West 8th St.
Yankton, SD 57078
800-658-4552
www.mtmc.edu

Northern State University
Department of Music

1200 S. Jay St.
Aberdeen, SD 57401
605-626-2497
Fax: 605-626-2263
E-mail: lafavea@northern.edu
www.northern.edu/music/index.htm

BA in Music, BME (Bachelor of Music Education) in Instrumental, Vocal, or Composite

The NSU department of music is a fully accredited institutional member of NASM. The beautiful campus setting is the ideal place to refine and develop musical skills and abilities with a world class faculty of artist/teachers. The band performed for the Presidential Inaugural Parade in 2000 and has also performed at the Kennedy Center. The choir has performed at Carnegie Hall and recently completed a European Tour. The Marching Band will be performing in Hawaii for the 65th Pearl Harbor Memorial Parade. Outstanding facilities, faculty, and students, combined with a very reasonable cost, make NSU a very attractive option for music study.

South Dakota State University
Department of Music
Box 2212
Lincoln Music Hall
Brookings, SD 57007
David Reynolds
605-688-5188
Fax: 605-688-4307
E-mail: paul.reynolds@sdstate.edu
www.sdstate.edu

BA in Music; BME (Bachelor of Music Education) in Instrumental, Vocal, or Composite

University of Sioux Falls
Department of Music

1101 West 22nd St.
Sioux Falls, SD 57105
800-888-1047
www.usiouxfalls.edu

University of South Dakota
Department of Music

414 East Clark St.
Vermillion, SD 57069
605-677-5274
Fax: 605-677-5988
E-mail: lschou@usd.edu
www.usd.edu/cfa/Music

BM in Music Education, BM in Performance, MM
in Music Education, MM in Performance, MM
in Music History, and MM in History of Musical
Instruments

Population: 5,962,959 (2005 Estimate)
Capital City: Nashville
Bird: Mockingbird
Motto: Agriculture and Commerce
Flower: Iris
Tree: Tulip Tree
Residents Called: Tennesseans
Origin of Name: Named after Cherokee Indian villages called "Tanasi"
Area: 42,146 square miles (36th largest state)
Statehood: June 1, 1796 (16th state)
Largest Cities: Memphis, Nashville, Knoxville, Chattanooga, Clarksville, Murfreesboro, Jackson, Johnson City, Kingsport, Franklin
College Band Programs: Middle Tennessee State University, University of Tennessee

Austin Peay State University
Department of Music

P.O. Box 4625
MMC 139
Clarksville, TN 37044
931-221-7818
E-mail: oturug@apsu.edu
www.apsu.edu

Belmont University
School of Music

1900 Belmont Blvd.
Nashville, TN 372123757
615-460-6408
www.belmont.edu/music

B.M., B.A., and M.M.

Belmont's School of Music offers its students a winning combination of large university resources and personal, small college service. Our world-class instructors, wide variety of degrees and state-of-the-art studio resources and performance halls place us among the best music schools in the country - yet our students also benefit from a sense of community rare in large universities. Located at the end of history music row, near the heart of Nashville, TN, Belmont's quiet, neighborhood campus provides a peaceful, inspiring environment for musicians to participate and learn.

Bethel College
Division of Humanities
325 Cherry Ave. Suite 201
McKenzie, TN 38201
731-352-4002
www.bethel-college.edu

Bryan College
Department of Music

P.O. Box 7000
Dayton, TN 37321
423-775-7289

Fax: 423-775-7317
E-mail: Wilhoime@Bryan.edu
www.bryan.edu

BS in Music: 10 tracks

Music Major has tracks in Music Education, Performance, Musical Theater, Church Music, Music Management, Piano Pedagogy.

Carson-Newman College
Department of Music

Jefferson City, TN 37760
Clark Measels
865-471-3328
E-mail: cmeasels@cn.edu
www.cn.edu

Columbia State Community College
Department of Music

P.O. Box 1315
Columbia, TN 38402
Mark Lee
931-540-2874
Fax: 931-540-2889
E-mail: lee@columbiastate.edu
www.coscc.cc.tn.us

David Lipscomb University
School of Music

3901 Granny White Pike
Nashville, TN 37204
615-966-5929
E-mail: music@lipscomb.edu
http://music.lipscomb.edu/

Dyersburg State Community College
Department of Music

1510 Lake Rd.
Dyersburg, TN 38024
Carol Ann Feathers

901-286-3256
E-mail: feather@dscc.edu
www.dscc.edu

East Tennessee State University
Department of Music

Box 70661
Johnson City, TN 37614-0054
423-439-4270
Fax: 423-439-4290
www.etsu.edu

Fisk University
Department of Humanities and Fine Arts

1000 Seventeenth Ave. North
Nashville, TN 37208-3051
615-329-8500
www.fisk.edu

Lambuth University
School of Music

705 Lambuth Blvd.
Jackson, TN 38301
800-LAMBUTH
www.lambuth.edu

Lee University
School of Music

1120 North Ocoee St.
Cleveland, TN 37320-3450
423-614-8240
E-mail: music@leeuniversity.edu .
www.leeuniversity.edu

B.A., B.M., B.M.E., B.S., and M.C.M.

The Lee University School of Music is an institutional member of the National Association of Schools of Music. The School of Music offers programs of study designed to prepare men and women for the performance or instruction of the music arts by developing skills needed to become music performers, educators, ministers, private instructors, or music business professionals. It serves its majors by providing intensive, personalized studio instruction and other specialized courses in vocal and instrumental music. The primary music facility, the Curtsinger Music Building, is a fully equipped educational facility which includes five classrooms, 19 teaching studios, 25 practice rooms, two rehearsal rooms for large ensembles, an audio library, a MIDI Lab, and an electronic piano lab.

Lipscomb University
Department of Music

3901 Granny White Pike
Nashville, TN 37204
800-333-4358
E-mail: music@lipscomb.edu
music.lipscomb.edu

B.A. in Music and B.S. in Music Teaching, Instrumental Teaching, Vocal Performance, Instrumental Performance, Piano Performance, and Theory/Composition. Minors are offered in General Music and Church Music. Music scholarships are available to majors, minors, and some other participants.

Maryville College

Admissions Office
502 East Lamar Alexander Pkwy.
Maryville, TN 37804
Ned Willard
800-597-2687
Fax: 865-981-8005
E-mail: ned.willard@maryvillecollege.edu
www.maryvillecollege.edu

BA, BM

Located in Maryville, Tenn., Maryville College is ideally situated between the Great Smoky Mountains National Park and Knoxville, the state's third largest city. Founded in 1819, it is the 12th oldest institution of higher learning in the south. With a focus on liberal arts, College faculty and staff are dedicated to teaching the skills and providing the opportunities for students to be successful and make a difference in the world. Affiliated with the Presbyterian Church (USA), the College is recognized in the John Templeton Foundation's Honor Roll for Character Building Colleges and its "Colleges that Encourage Character Development" guide. For 11 of the last 12 years, it has been ranked in the top 10 of U.S. News and World Report's listing of the best southern liberal arts colleges. Total enrollment for the fall 2005 semester was 1,146 students.

Middle Tennessee State University
School of Music

P.O. Box 47
MTSU
Murfreesboro, TN 37132
615-898-2469
E-mail: tmusselm@mtsu.edu
www.mtsu.edu/~music

Milligan College
Department of Music

P.O. Box 500
Milligan College, TN 37682
423-461-8700
E-mail: admissions@mulligan.edu
www.mulligan.edu

Navy Music Program
5722 Integrity Dr.

Millington, TN 38054
Mark Hammond
901-874-5784
www.bupers.navy.mil/navymusic

Rhodes College
Department of Music

111 Hassell Hall
Memphis, TN 38122
901-843-3775
www.rhodes.edu

The mission of the Rhodes Music Department is to foster creativity and to develop the skills of students, while instilling a passion for quality and an appreciation of the universal importance of the arts. Students are encouraged to become aware of the great variety of musical styles, both past and present, and to recognize the wide range of musical activity currently available. They are invited to explore their individual interests in music and to discover ways to apply their own musical capabilities within society. The Bachelor of Arts degree in music is a liberal arts degree designed to prepare students for graduate studies, to develop a satisfying avocation, and to serve as preparation for a wide range of careers. Students from various backgrounds are welcome to pursue this degree. Course offerings are in the areas of music theory, music history and literature, applied music and ensembles.

Sewanee, The University of the South
Department of Music

735 University Ave.
Sewanee, TN 37383
931-598-1000
www.sewanee.edu

Southern Adventist University
Department of Music

P.O. Box 370
Collegedale, TN 37315-0370
Scott Ball
423-236-2880
Fax: 423-236-1880
E-mail: sball@southern.edu
www.southern.edu

Tennessee State University
Department of Music

3500 John A. Merritt Blvd.
Nashville, TN 37209
615-963-5000
www.tnstate.edu

Tennessee Technological University
Dept of Music and Art

P.O. Box 5045
Cookeville, TN 38505
Arthur Labar
931-372-3161
Fax: 931-372-6279
E-mail: alabar@tntech.edu
www.tntech.edu

B.M. in Music Education or Music Performance

Accredited since 1967 by the National Association
of Schools of Music, the Department of Music
and Art has 24 full-time music faculty, 160
music majors, and offers the Bachelor of Music
degree in Music Education and the Bachelor of
Music degree in Performance with options in
composition, instrumental and vocal music, jazz
and piano.

Union University
Department of Music

1050 Union University Dr.
Jackson, TN 38305
731-661-5345
E-mail: rjoiner@uu.edu
www.uu.edu/dept/music

Union is a four-year, Christian liberal arts college
associated with Tennessee Baptist Convention.
The music department is housed in a new state-
of-the-art fine arts building.

University of Memphis
Department of Music

101 Wilder Tower
Memphis, TN 38152
901-678-2111
www.memphis.edu

University of Tennessee at Knoxville
School of Music

1741 Volunteer Blvd.
Knoxville, TN 37996-2600
Roger Stephens
865-974-3241
Fax: 865-974-1941

E-mail: music@utk.edu
www.music.utk.edu

University of Tennessee at Martin
Department of Music

102 Fine Arts Building
Martin, TN 38238
Jeremy Kolwinska
731-587-7402
E-mail: music@utm.edu
www.utm.edu

Vanderbilt University
Blair School of Music

2400 Blakemore Ave.
Nashville, TN 37212
615-322-7651
Fax: 615-343-0324
E-mail: Blair-web@vanderbilt.edu
www.vanderbilt.edu/blair

B.M. in Performance, composition, musical arts,
and teacher education

If you are looking for the perfect balance between
a finely tuned music school and a highly regarded
university, consider the Blair School of Music at
Vanderbilt University. Vanderbilt is one of only
three top twenty universities in the nation to
boast an acclaimed, accredited undergraduate
school of music, the only one whose school of
music is solely for undergraduates. The talented
musicians we attract expect the best. They want
conservatory quality music training with excellent
teachers, frequent performance opportunities,
and great facilities. They want to participate in
their school's top ensembles, so we deliberately
limit our admission numbers, because we are
selective, our students study and perform with
musicians who are equally dedicated. The stu-
dent-to-faculty ratio of 4:1 provides opportunities
to work closely with the world-class musicians
on our faculty. And for musicians, Nashville is an
ideal college town, home to a sizeable segment of
the global music industry in a progressive city.

Population: 22,859,968 (2005 Estimate)
Capital City: Austin
Bird: Mockingbird
Motto: Friendship
Flower: Bluebonnet
Tree: Pecan
Residents Called: Texans
Origin of Name: Based on a word used by Caddo Indians meaning "friends."
Area: 268,601 square miles (2nd largest state)
Statehood: December 29, 1845
Largest Cities: Houston, Dallas, San Antonio, Austin, El Paso, Fort Worth, Arlington, Corpus Christi, Plano, Garland, University of Texas-El Paso, University of Texas-Austin
College Band Programs: Baylor University, Rice University, Southern Methodist University, Stephen F. Austin State University, Texas A&M University, Texas A&M University-Kingsville, Texas Christian University, Texas Tech University, University of Houston

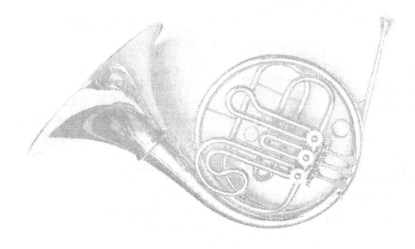

Abilene Christian University
Department of Music

ACU Box 28274
Abilene, TX 79699
325-674-2199
Fax: 915-260-2608
www.acu.edu

Alvin Community College
Department of Music

3110 Mustang Rd.
Alvin, TX 77511-4898
281-756-3587
Fax: 281-756-3880
E-mail: kmoody@alvincollege.edu
www.alvincollege.edu

Angelo State University
Dept of Art and Music

2601 West Ave. North
San Angelo, TX 76909
David Scott
325-942-2085 x 233
E-mail: david.scott@angelo.edu
www.angelo.edu

Austin College
Department of Music

900 North Grand Ave.
Suite 61587
Sherman, TX 75090-4400
Wayne Crannell
903-813-2251
Fax: 903-313-2273
E-mail: music@austincollegemusic.com
www.austincollegemusic.com

Austin College is a private, liberal arts college of which the music department is an important part, with four full-time and nine adjunct faculty. We offer three choral organizations, a full jazz band, and smaller ensembles for strings, brass, and winds. The college and community also support a regional volunteer and professional symphony orchestra that plays a full season of concerts in a renovated 1930s concert hall. The degree program includes courses in music theory, history, applied, and supporting electives for a major that is well-suited to continued graduate study.

Baylor University
School of Music

One Bear Place #97408
Waco, TX 76798
Celia Austin
254-710-1161
Fax: 254-710-1191
www.baylor.edu

Brazosport College
Department of Music

500 College Dr.
Lake Jackson, TX 77566-3136
Kate Funkhouser
979-230-3000
E-mail: Kate.Funkhouser@brazosport.edu
www.brazosport.edu

Del Mar College
Division of Arts and Sciences

101 Baldwin Blvd.
Corpus Christi, TX 78404-3897
Andy Wen
800-652-3357
E-mail: jkairies@delmar.edu
www.delmar.edu

East Texas Baptist University
Department of Music

1209 North Grove
Marshall, TX 75670
Marilyn Johnson
903-923-2158
E-mail: mjohnson@etbu.edu
www.etbu.edu

Eastfield College
Department of Music

3737 Motley Dr.
Mesquite, TX 75150-8342
Harrell C. Lucky
972-860-7135
E-mail: Harrell_Lucky@dccd.edu
www.efc.dccd.edu

Frank Phillips College
Department of Music

Borger, TX 79008
Judy Strecker
806-274-5311
Fax: 806-274-6835
E-mail: jstrecke@fpc.cc.tx.us
www.fpc.cc.tx.us

Hardin-Simmons University
School of Music

2200 Hickory
Box 16050
Abilene, TX 79698-6230
325-670-1206
www.hsutx.edu

Hill College
Department of Music

P.O. Box 619
Hillsboro, TX 76645-0619
Phillip Lowe
254-582-2555 x 270
Fax: 254-582--7591
E-mail: phillowe@hillcollege.edu
www.hillcollege.edu

Hill College is the home of an established music
program and provides music students with a
number of performance opportunities. These include band, jazz band, brass ensemble, choir and
vocal ensemble, and a community choir. Music
scholarships are available to interested students.

Houston Baptist University
School of Music

7502 Fondren Rd.
Houston, TX 77074
281-649-3000
www.hbu.edu

Howard College at Big Spring
Department of Music

1001 Birdwell Lane
Big Spring, TX 79720
Ross Litman
432-264-5145
E-mail: rlitman@howardcollege.edu
www.howardcollege.edu

Howard Payne University
School of Music And Fine Arts

1000 Fisk St.
Brownwood, TX 76801
Robert Tucker
325-649-8020
Fax: 325-649-8901
E-mail: rtucker@hputx.edu
www.hputx.edu

Huston-Tillotson College
Department of Music

900 Chicon St.
Austin, TX 78702
512-505-3000
Fax: 512-505-3190
http://cas.htu.edu

International Festival-Institute

P.O. Box 89
248 Jaster Rd.
Round Top, TX 78954-0089
979-249-3129
http://festivalhill.org

Jacksonville College
Department of Music

105 BJ Albritton Dr.
Jacksonville, TX 75766
903-586-2518
Fax: 903-586-0743
www.jacksonville-college.edu

Kilgore College
Department of Music

1100 Broadway Blvd.
Kilgore, TX 75662
Jeanne Johnson
903-983-8121
E-mail: jeannej@kilgore.edu
www.kilgore.edu

Lamar University
Department of Music
Theater and Dance

P.O. Box 10044
106 Music Building
Beaumont, TX 77710
Harry Bulow
409-880-2342
E-mail: harry.bulow@lamar.edu
www.lamar.edu

The department of music, theatre and dance at Lamar serves an average of 180 students, including about 125 music majors. Degrees offered include the bachelor of music degree with specializations in performance, composition and music education. Performing groups include a cappella choir, chamber orchestra, concert band, grand choir, jazz band, opera theatre and symphonic band, as well as numerous smaller ensembles (clarinet quartet, sax quartet, brass quintet, woodwind quintet, string quartet). Students may audition for competitive scholarships in varying amounts. Additional scholarship support is available from the university, based on academic achievement and student need.

Laredo Community College
Department of Music

1 West End Washington St.
Laredo, TX 78040
956-721-5330
Fax: 956-764-5924
E-mail: jcrabtree@;aredo.edu
www.laredo.edu

Lee College
Department of Music

P. O. Box 818
Baytown, TX 77522
281-425-6350
Fax: 832-556-4010
E-mail: dcorder@lee.edu
www.lee.edu/vpa/music

Lon Morris College
Department of Music

800 College Ave.
Jacksonville, TX 75766-2930
903-589-4000
Fax: 903-586-8562
E-mail: mrich@lonmorris.edu
www.lonmorris.edu

McLennan Community College
Department of Music

1400 College Dr.
Waco, TX 76708
Rob Page
254-299-8240
E-mail: rpage@mclennan.edu
www.mclennan.edu

McMurry University
Department of Music

Box 698
Abilene, TX 796987
Dianna Ellis

325-793-4860
E-mail: dellis@mcm.edu
www.mcm.edu

Midland College
Department of Music

3600 North Garfield SSt.
Midland, TX 79705-6329
Dale Beikirch
432-685-5539
E-mail: bfeeler@midland.edu
www.midland.edu

Midwestern State University
Department of Music

3410 Taft Blvd.
Wichita Falls, TX 76308
940-397-4267
Fax: 940 397 4511
E-mail: music.program@mwsu.edu
www.mwsu.edu

Navarro College
Department of Music

3200 West 7th Ave.
Corsicana, TX 751100-4818
903-874-6501
Fax: 903-874-4636
www.navarrocollege.edu

Odessa College
Department of Music

201 West University Blvd.
Odessa, TX 79764
Kathryn Hoppe
432-335-6630
E-mail: khoppe@odessa.edu

Our Lady of the Lake University
Department of Music

411 SW 24th St.

San Antonio, TX 78207
210-434-6711
Fax: 210-431-4090
www.ollusa.edu

Our Lady of the Lake University is a small Catholic college (enrollment of about 3,500) in San Antonio. It is sponsored by the Congregation of Divine Providence. The department seeks to involve as many students as possible in music courses and ensembles, regardless of major. Ensembles include vocal, mariachi, flute, clarinet, wind, brass, recorder and guitar ensembles. Currently a proposal is in process to establish a B.A. in music. Instructors are highly competent and include members of the San Antonio Symphony. Opportunities in San Antonio provide many on- and off-campus opportunities for performing and attending concerts. Current chair of the music department is Sister Madlyn Pape.

Panola College
Department of Fine Arts

1109 West Panola St.
Carthage, TX 75633-1149
Mike McGowan
903-693-2027
Fax: 903-693-1149
E-mail: mmcgowan@panola.edu
www.panola.edu

Paris Junior College
Department of Music

2400 Clarksville St.
Paris, TX 75460
903-785-7661
www.parisjc.edu

Rice University
Shepherd School of Music

2235 Alice Pratt Brown Hall
Houston, TX 77251
Matthew Loden
713-348-3032
E-mail: mloden@rice.edu
www.rice.edu

Sam Houston State University
School of Music

1751 Ave.
Huntsville, TX 77341
936-294-1360
www.shsu.edu/~music

San Antonio College
Department of Music

1300 San Pero Ave.
San Antonio, TX 78212
210-733-2731
Fax: 210-733-2985
E-mail: jhoward@accd.edu
www.accd.edu/sac

AA in Music

San Antonio College offers a comprehensive music program that includes a wide variety of lessons, nine ensembles, music lecture courses, and a well-articulated program for majors.

San Antonio College
Department of Music

1300 San Pedro Ave.
San Antonio, TX 78212-4299
Jessica Howard
210-733-2731
E-mail: jhoward@accd.edu
www.accd.edu/sac

San Jacinto College Central
Department of Music

13735 Beamer Rd.
Houston, TX 77089
Jeremy Garcia
281-929-4643
Fax: 281-922-3483
E-mail: jeremy.garcia@sjcd.edu
www.sjcd.edu

Associate of Arts (Music)

San Jacinto College South is a growing music department boasting an excellent music faculty, the latest technology in new facilities, and superb

instruction in small classes and/or private lessons.

Southern Methodist University
Division of Music

P.O. Box 750356
Dallas, TX 75275
214-768-1951
E-mail: music@smu.edu
www.smu.edu

Southwest Texas State University
School of Music

601 University Dr.
MUS 101
San Marcos, TX 78666-4616
Joseph Stuessy
512-245-2651
Fax: 512-245-8181
E-mail: js66@txstate.edu
www.txstate.edu

B.M., B.A., and M.M.

375 undergraduate and 65 graduate students are enrolled in the school of music. NASM accredited the school, which offers a unique opportunity for aspiring musicians who receive a comprehensive education from a faculty upholding high music standards. Jazz ensembles have performed at festivals in France, Switzerland, Italy and Holland. The orchestra toured in Austria, the Czech Republic, England, Germany, Poland and Scotland. The chorale performed at Carnegie Hall. The marching band appeared on television and marched at festivals in Ireland. Sound Recording Technology students participate in commercial recording sessions in a studio housing computer labs, digital editing stations and electronic audio labs while completing their degree.

Southwestern University
Department of Music

P.O. Box 770
Georgetown, TX 78627
Paul Gaffney

512-863-1379
Fax: 512-863-1422
www.southwestern.edu

St. Edwards University
Department of Music

3001 South Congress Ave.
Austin, TX 78704-6524
512-428-1297
www.stedwards.edu

St. Marys University
Department of Music

1 Camino Santa Maria St.
San Antonio, TX 78228-8562
John P. Moore
210-436-3421
Fax: 210-436-3640
E-mail: mujohn@stmarybr.cdu
www.stmarytx.edu

Stephen F. Austin State University
School of Music

P.O. Box 13043, SFA Station
Nacogdoches, TX 75962
936-468-4602
Fax: 409-468-5810
E-mail: randerson@sfasu.edu
www.finearts.sfasu.edu/music/music.html

BM with certification, in performance and in composition, MA, MA in Music Education, MM in performance and conducting

The SFA School of Music is noted as one of the finest training programs for public school teachers in the state. Boasting more than 300 music majors, the School is "Big enough to show you the world; small enough to discover the world in you!" With a 10:1 student:faculty ratio, the School retains faculty specialists on all instruments. Its ensembles have gained national and even international attention through performances at regional and national conventions and trips to Europe. Auditions are required for entrance into the music program.

Texas A&M University, Commerce
Department of Music

P.O. Box 3011
Commerce, TX 75429
Heather White
903-886-5286
E-mail: Heather_White@tamu-commerce.edu
www.tamu-commerce.edu

Texas Christian University
Department of Music

TCU Box 298000
Fort Worth, TX 76129
Andie Piehl
817-257-2787
www.cfac.tcu.edu

Texas Woman's University
Department of Performing Arts

304 Administration Dr.
P.O. Box 425768
Denton, TX 76204
James Chenevert
940-898-2505
www.twu.edu

Trinity University
Department of Music

715 Stadium Dr.
San Antonio, TX 78212
Ken Greene
210-999-8212
E-mail: kgreene2@trinity.edu
www.trinity.edu

Trinity Valley Community College
Department of Music

500 South Prairesville
Athens, TX 75751

903-677-TVCC
www.tvcc.edu

University of Texas at Arlington
Department of Music

700 Greek Row, Room 101
Box 19105
Arlington, TX 76019
Susan Collins
817-272-3471
Fax: 817-272-4343
E-mail: music@uta.edu
www.uta.edu/music

University of Texas at Austin
School of Music

1 University Station
E3100
Austin, TX 78712
512-471-7764
Fax: 512-471-7836
www.utexas.edu

University of Texas at El Paso
Department of Music

500 West University Ave.
El Paso, TX 79968
Ron Hufstad
915-747-5606
Fax: 915-747-5023
E-mail: rhufstad@utep.edu
www.utep.edu/music

Programs of study include music education, performance, theory and composition, conducting and music theater.

University of Texas at Houston
Moores School of Music

Suite 120
Houston, TX 77204
David Ashley White
713-743-3009
Fax: 713-743-3166
www.uth.tmc.edu

University of Texas at San Antonio
Department of Music

1604 Campus
One UTSA Cir.
San Antonio, TX 78249
Steve Hill
210-458-4355
Fax: 210-458-4381
E-mail: steve.hill@utsa.edu
www.utsa.edu

University of the Incarnate Word
Department of Music

4301 Broadway
San Antonio, TX 78209
Bill Gokelman
210-829-3848
E-mail: gokelman@uiwtx.edu
www.uiw.edu

West Texas A&M University
Department of Music and Dance

WTAMU Box 60907
Canyon, TX 79016
800-99-WTAMU
Fax: 806-651-5285
www.wtamu.edu

Population: 2,469,585 (2005 Estimate)
Capital City: Salt Lake City
Bird: California Seagull
Motto: Industry
Flower: Sego lily
Tree: Blue Spruce
Residents Called: Utahns
Origin of Name: Taken from the name of the Ute Indians, whose name means, "people of the mountains."
Area: 84,904 square miles (13th largest state)
Statehood: January 4, 1896 (45th state)
Largest Cities: Salt Lake City, West Valley City, Provo, Sandy, Orem, Ogden, West Jordan, Layton, Taylorsville, St. George
College Band Programs: University of Utah

Brigham Young University
School of Music

C-550 HFAC
Provo, UT 84602
801-422-8903
E-mail: music@byu.edu
www.byu.edu

Brigham Young University - founded, supported, and guided by The Church of Jesus Christ of Latter-day Saints - is dedicated to educating the whole person through a synthesis of spiritual and professional education. The university seeks to enhance not only the intellectual lives but also the social, cultural and spiritual lives of its students. Through these students, as well as its faculty and facilities, BYU symbolizes one of the Church's fundamental articles of faith: "We believe in being honest, true, chaste, benevolent, virtuous, and in doing good to all men...If there is anything virtuous, lovely, or of good report or praiseworthy, we seek after these things." The art of music - as expressed through performance, composition, and teaching or communication media - is built on a foundation of knowledge and skills. Knowledge comes from study and research in music theory, literature, history and performance practices as well as from study in other arts and sciences. Skills come from applying knowledge to the instrument or voice and developing the tools of musicianship. The mission of the School of Music is to offer quality instruction that will enable students to think clearly about diverse kinds of music and to create, perform and teach music well. We strive to develop strong moral character, leading students to lifelong learning and service. The School of Music is housed in the Harris Fine Arts Center, a comprehensive complex that includes five theatres, a piano lab, organ lab, computer music lab, recording studio, several libraries and many practice rooms and classrooms. Additional large rehearsal spaces and teaching studios for music, dance, theatre and media music students are found in the Knight Mangum Building. BYU's School of Music is comprehensive, with 50 full-time and 49 part-time faculty teaching private instruction, ensembles, education, music theory

and history and conducting, plus other exciting fields of study. Our focus is on cultivating individual talents and fostering some of the country's most respected music ensembles.

College of Eastern Utah
Department of Music

451 East 400 North
Price, UT 84501
435-637-2120
www.ceu.edu

University of Utah
School of Music

1375 E. Presidents Cir.
204 David Gardner Hall
Salt Lake City, UT 84112-0030
Carla Ray
801-581-6762
Fax: 801-581-5683
E-mail: carla.ray@music.utah.edu
www.music.utah.edu

BA in Music, BM, MM, MA in Musicology, Ph.D. in Composition or Music Education

Comprehensive Music School offering bachelor through doctorate.

Utah State University
Department of Music

4015 Old Main Hill
Logan, UT 84322
435-797-3015
E-mail: dorothyk@cc.usu.edu
www.music.usu.edu

Weber State University
Department of Music

Ogden, UT 84408-1905
801-626-6006
www.weber.edu

Bachelor of Music, Bachelor of Music Education,

Bachelor of Music in Performance, Bachelor of
Music in Keyboard Pedagogy, Bachelor of Music in
Vocal Pedagogy , Music Minor, Music Honors

Westminster College
Department of Music

1840 South 1300 East
Salt Lake City, UT 84105
801-484-7651
www.westminstercollege.edu
Minor only in Music

Population: 623,050 (2005 Estimate)
Capital City: Montpelier
Bird: Hermit Thrush
Motto: Freedom and unity
Flower: Red Clover
Tree: Sugar Maple
Residents Called: Vermonters
Origin of Name: Based on "verts monts," French for green mountains.
Area: 9,615 square mile (45th largest state)
Statehood: March 4, 1791
Largest Cities: Burlington, Essex, Rutland, Colchester, South Burlington, Bennington, Brattleboro, Hartford, Milton, Barre

Bennington College
Department of Music

One College Dr.
Bennington, VT 05201
802-442-5401
www.bennington.edu

Castleton State College
Department of Music

45 Alumni Dr.
Castleton, VT 05735
Ronald Sherwin
802-468-1119
Fax: 802-468-1440
E-mail: ronald.sherwin@castleton.edu
www.castleton.edu

Bachelor of Arts in Music Education (BAMUSED),
Bachelor of Arts in Music (BAMUS). Music Education majors specialize in Instrumental, Choral,
or Elementary Music; Minor in Music

Green Mountain College
Department of Visual and Performing Arts

Middlebury, VT 05753
Peter Hamlin
802-443-5221
Fax: 802-443-2057
E-mail: phamlin@Middlebury.edu
www.middlebury.edu

B.A., and Visual and Performing Arts with a music
concentration

Johnson State College
Department of Fine and Performing Arts

337 College Hill
Johnson VT 05656
Penny Howrigan
800-635-1310
Fax: 802-635-1230

E-mail: jscadmissions@jsc.vsc.edu
www.jsc.vsc.edu

B.A. Music, B.A. Music Education, B.A. Classical
Music, B.A. Jazz/Contemporary Studies, B.A.
Musical Theater

Johnson's beautiful hilltop 350-acre campus is
home to over 1,700 students, and offers easy access to six major ski resorts and endless outdoor
activities such as hiking, biking, and kayaking.
Students transferring to Johnson find it to be an
easy and seamless integration, both academically
and personally. The small class size (average size
is 17 students), numerous clubs, varsity sports,
and individual attention from faculty members
all combine to create the strong community that
is Johnson State College.

University of Vermont
Department of Music

384 South Prospect St.
Redstone Campus
Burlington, VT 05405
802-656-3040
Fax: 802-656-0759
E-mail: music@zoo.uvm.edu
www.uvm.edu/~music

Population: 7,567,465 (2005 Estimate)
Capital City: Richmond
Bird: Cardinal
Motto: Sic Semper Tyrannis – Thus Always to Tyrants
Flower: Dogwood
Tree: Dogwood
Residents Called: Virginians
Origin of Name: Named for England's "Virgin Queen," Elizabeth I.
Area: 42,769 square miles (35th largest state)
Statehood: June 25, 1788 (10th state)
Largest Cities: Virginia Beach, Norfolk, Chesapeake, Richmond, Newport News, Arlington, Hampton, Alexandria, Portsmouth, Roanoke
College Band Programs: James Madison University, Liberty University, University of Virginia, Virginia Tech

Armed Forces School of Music

1420 Gator Blvd.
Norfolk, VA 23521-2617
757-462-7501
Fax: 757-462-7294
www.npdc.navy.mil

Located aboard the Naval Amphibious Base in Norfolk, the Armed Forces School of Music provides specialized training for selected personnel of the Army, Navy, and Marine Corps, and is the first stop after basic training for instrumentalists and vocalists seeking to join the ranks of America's military bands. This unique facility, the largest of its kind in the world, provides basic to advanced levels of instruction geared toward preparing soldiers, sailors and marines for the challenges of performance within a wide variety of military ensembles. Graduates of the Armed Forces School of Music go on to become musical ambassadors throughout the United States and abroad as members of U.S. Army, Navy and Marine Corps bands.

Bridgewater College
Department of Music

402 East College St.
Bridgewater, VA 22812
540-828-8000
www.bridgewater.edu

The music department at Bridgewater College serves the various needs of the academic community with the Carter Center for worship and music as the site of most musical activity. Students from all majors are invited to participate in one or more of the choral, instrumental or chamber ensembles, and private study is available to singers and players. Students who choose music as a career may focus on performance and/or elect to gain certification to teach vocal or instrumental music in the public schools. A special concentration in church music is offered and supported by the College's strong choral tradition and outstanding rehearsal and performance facilities for organists. Regular study and performance tours to international centers of music are a part of the music curriculum.

Christopher Newport University
Department of Music

1 University Place
Newport News, VA 23606
Mark Reimer
757-594-7089
Fax: 757-594-7389
E-mail: reimer@cnu.edu
music.cnu.edu/contactus.html

College of William and Mary
Department of Music

P.O. Box 8795
Williamsburg, VA 23187
Katherine Preston
757-221-1075
Fax: 757-221-3171
E-mail: kkpres@wm.edu
www.wm.edu

Ferrum College
School of Arts and Humanities

P.O. Box 1000
Ferrum, VA 24088
Susan Spataro
540-365-4351
E-mail: sspataro@ferrum.edu
www.ferrum.edu

George Mason University
Dept of Performing Arts

417 Performing Arts Building
4400 University Dr. MSN 3E3
Fairfax, VA 22030
703-993-1380
Fax: 703-993-1394
E-mail: music@gmu.edu
www.gmu.edu/departments/music

B.M., B.A., M.M., D.A. and Ph.D.

Located 15 miles outside of the nation's capital, George Mason University is in the heart of one of the richest cultural centers in the US. The Music Department offers a B.M. in performance and music education; B.A. in music, minor in jazz studies, M.M. in performance, music education, conducting, and composition. Also offers a D.A. in community college education with a concentration in music, and a PhD. in education with a minor in music. Part of the college of visual and performing arts, the Music Department boasts over 50 nationally and internationally recognized full-time and part-time artist-faculty instructors. Continual seminars workshops, master classes, and courses in music and wellness are prominent features of the curriculum. Over 100 student and faculty performances are given annually on campus throughout the capital region. Venues include a 2,000-seat concert hall and a 500-seat theatre. In addition to the rigorous academic curriculum, the department hosts exciting national events including the National Trump Competition, Saxophone Symposium, and one of the nation's largest Orff Schulwerk Certification programs for music educations. Auditions required. For more information and audition dates contact the Music Department.

Hampton University
Department of Music

Armstrong Hall Room 137
Hampton, VA 23668
Shelia Maye
757-728-6508
Fax: 757-637-2445
E-mail: humusic@hamptonun.edu
www.hamptonu.edu

Hollins University
Department of Music

P.O. Box 9643
Roanoke, VA 24020
Judith Cline
540-362-6514
Fax: 540-362-6218
E-mail: jcline@hollins.edu
www.hollins.edu/undergrad/music/music.htm

James Madison University
School of Music

800 South Main St.
Harrisonburg, VA 22807
540-568-3851
www.jmu.edu/music

Liberty University
Department of Fine Arts

1971 University Blvd.
Lynchburg, VA 24506
Sandy Snell
434-582-2318
www.liberty.edu

Longwood College
Department of Music

Farmville, VA 23909
434-395-2504
E-mail: music@longwood.edu
www.longwood.edu

Mary Baldwin College
Department of Music

Mary Baldwin College
Staunton, VA 24401
Lise Keiter-Brotzman
540-887-7193
E-mail: lkeiter@mbc.edu
www.mbc.edu

Bachelor of Arts in Music, Bachelor of Arts in Arts

Mary Baldwin College offers a strong music program within a liberal arts setting. MBC is a Women's College, set in the heart of the beautiful Shenandoah Valley. Contact us for more information

Norfolk State University
Department of Liberal Arts

Norfolk, VA 23504

757-823-8544
Fax: 757-823-2605
www.nsu.edu

Old Dominion University
Department of Music

4810 Elkhorn Ave.
Norfolk, VA 23529
Dennis Zeisler
757-683-4061
Fax: 757-683-5056
E-mail: dzeisler@odu.edu
www.odu.edu/al/music

BM, BA, MME

Old Dominion University is an Urban University in the cultural area of Hampton Roads. Students benifit from a regional orchestra, opera, ballet and theater.

Randolph-Macon Woman's College
Admissions Department

2500 Rivermont Ave.
Lynchburg, VA 24503
Pat LeDonne
434-947-8100
Fax: 434-947-8138
E-mail: pledonne@rmwc.edu
www.rmwc.edu

Roanoke College
Department of Fine Arts

221 College Lane
Salem, VA 24153
540-375-2096
Fax: 540-375-2559
www.roanoke.edu

Shenandoah University
Department of Music

1460 University Dr.
Winchester, VA 22601
David Zerull

540-665-4639
E-mail: dzerull@su.edu
www.su.edu

Shenandoah Conservatory offers intense, specialized, professional training in instrumental and vocal music, theatre and dance. Students work with a faculty of active professionals as they develop artistically and intellectually for careers in the performing arts. Programs of study lead to over 30 degrees at the undergraduate and graduate levels. Shenandoah Conservatory offers dozens of ensemble experiences, from jazz to dance and opera. Students perform throughout the region, including regional concerts at the Kennedy Center in Washington, D.C., and at universities and public schools throughout the Mid-Atlantic region and New York. The Ohrstrom-Bryant Theatre/Ruebush Complex is a hub for vocal music programs and the theatre program. In addition to a 630-seat auditorium, the Ohrstrom-Bryant Theatre Complex houses the intimate Glaize Studio for children's theatre, as well as rehearsal space, make-up rooms, scene and costume shops. Ruebush Hall houses instructional space, faculty studios, practice rooms, choral and band rehearsal halls, a digital recording studio and a musical instrument digital interface (MIDI) laboratory. The newly renovated Armstrong Hall is home to the instrumental music programs with faculty and practice studios and a 550-seat auditorium. Singleton Hall houses the Dorothy Ewing Dance Studio, the dance program and a black box theatre.

Sweet Briar College
Department of Music

Sweet Briar, VA 24595
434-381-6100
E-mail: info@sbc.edu
www.sbc.edu

University of Mary Washington
Department of Music

1301 College Ave.
Fredericksburg, VA 22401
540-654-1012
www.umw.edu/music

University of Richmond
Department of Music

28 Westhampton Way
Richmond, VA 23173
Gene Anderson
800-700-1662
E-mail: ganderso@richmond.edu
www.music.richmond.edu

University of Virginia
McIntire Department of Music

P.O. Box 400176
Charlottesville, VA 22904
434-924-3052
Fax: 434-924-6033
E-mail: music@virginia.edu
www.virginia.edu/~music/index.html

Virginia Commonwealth University
Department of Music

922 Park Ave.
P.O. Box 842004
Richmond, VA 23284-2004
Calvin Sutton
804-828-1166
Fax: 804-237-0230
E-mail: music@vcu.edu
www.vcumusic.org

Bachelor of Music (Performance, Jazz Studies, Music Education), Bachelor of Arts in Music, Master of Music Education

The Department of Music is committed to the advancement of Western art music and jazz as academic disciplines, as fields of professional endeavor and as a viable presence in the community.

Virginia Tech
Department of Music

241 Squire Student Center
Blacksburg, VA 24061
540-231-5685
Fax: 540-231-5034
E-mail: music@vt.edu
www.music.vt.edu

The Virginia Tech Music Department provides high-quality training to a select number of music majors, as well as ensembles and courses for large numbers of non-music majors. Instruction takes place in a handsome modern facility which has superb rehearsal rooms, well-designed practice rooms and music teaching studios, a beautiful, acoustically engineered recital salon, and laboratories with state-of-the-art electronic equipment for music study, recording and digital music. The curriculum offers an excellent liberal arts education with a low professor/student ratio combined with the library, computer facilities and cultural interaction which only a major, comprehensive university can provide. Learning is enhanced by the use of music technology across the curriculum and innovative programs in performance, music education and theory/composition. Students may design a degree plan combining music with virtually all other majors offered by the university. Virginia Tech faculty artists and scholars have performed and lectured at conventions, in music festivals and on concert series throughout the United States and in Canada, Europe, Asia and South America.

Virginia Wesleyan College
Department of Music

1584 Wesleyan Dr.
Norfolk, VA 23502
Lee Jordan-Anders
757-455-3200
E-mail: ljordananders@vwc.edu
www.vwc.edu

BA Arts

Virginia Wesleyan is a small, four-year liberal arts college ideally located for education, travel, internship and employment opportunities as well as extracurricular activities. The Virginia Symphony and Virginia Opera perform within minutes of the campus, and a fine concert series takes place in our very own Hofheimer Theater. The small class sizes and intimate nature of the music department provide a wealth of learning and performing opportunities for music majors.

Washington and Lee University
Department of Music

Lexington, VA 24450
Dymph Alexander
540-458-8852
Fax: 540-463-8104
E-mail: alexanderd@wlu.edu
music.wlu.edu

Population: 6,287,759 (2005 Estimate)
Capital City: Olympia
Bird: Willow Goldfinch
Motto: Alki – Bye and Bye
Flower: Pink Rhododendron
Tree: Western Hemlock
Residents Called: Washingtonians
Origin of Name: Named after George Washington.
Area: 71,303 square miles (18th largest state)
Statehood: November 11, 1889 (42nd state)
Largest Cities: Seattle, Spokan, Tacoma, Vancouver, Bellevue, Everett, Federal Way, Kent, Yakima, Bellingham
College Band Programs: University of Washington, Washington State University

Central Washington University
Department of Music

400 East University Way
Ellensburg, WA 98926
509-963-1858
E-mail: schmidtr@cwu.edu
www.cwu.edu/~music

B.M., B.A., and M.M.

The Music Department provided opportunities for all students to develop into self-sufficient, secure and well-informed musicians and attempts to instill in them an aspiration for continual growth in knowledge and acquisition of skills. Academic coursework, ensemble experience and applied music study are directed to these goals. The department's ensembles are particularly strong, with its major groups being invited consistently to regional and national professional meetings. We have two wind ensembles, orchestras, chamber orchestra, chamber choir, choir, three jazz bands, three jazz choirs and many smaller groups all performing each quarter. Our composition program focuses on cutting edge technology, such as composing with Palm Pilots. The department has about 265 majors, with have being in music education, 75 in performance, 15 each in com-position and music business and 12-14 graduate students. The music faculty is highly active in performance and professional service and takes ride in supporting the needs of each student.

Eastern Washington University
Department of Music

302 Sutton Hall
Cheney, WA 99004
509-359-2345
Fax: 509-359-4338
E-mail: genadvising@mail.ewu.edu
www.ewu.edu

Everett Community College
Department of Music

2000 Tower St.
Everett, WA 98201
425-388-9222
E-mail: admissions@everettcc.edu
www.everettcc.edu

Gonzaga Univeristy
Department of Music

502 East Boone Ave.
Spokane, WA 99258
Robert Spittal
509-323-6733
E-mail: spittal@gonzaga.edu
www.gonzaga.edu

Grays Harbor College
Department of Music

1620 Edward P. Smith Dr.
Aberdeen, WA98520
800-562-4830
Fax: 360-538-4299
www.ghc.ctc.edu

Lower Columbia College
Department of Music

P.O. Box 3010
1600 Maple
Longview, WA 98632
360-442-2311
E-mail: info@lowercolumbia.edu
www.lcc.ctc.edu

Northwest University
Department of Music

5520 108th Ave. NE
Kirkland, WA 98033
425-889-5255
www.northwestu.edu

Olympic College
Department of Music

1600 Chester Ave.
Bremerton, WA 98337-1699
360-478-7118
www.olympic.edu

Pacific Lutheran University
Department of Music

Tacoma, WA 98447-0003
253-535-7602
www.plu.edu/-music

Peninsula College
Department of Music

1502 East Lauridsen Blvd.
Port Angeles, WA 98362-6660
360-452-9277
Fax: 360-457-8100
E-mail: dennisc@pcadmin.ctc.edu
www.pc.ctc.edu

Pierce College
Department of Music

9401 Farwest Dr. SW
Olympic 288
Lakewood, WA 98498
253-964-6572
www.pierce.ctc.edu

Seattle Pacific University
Department of Music

3307 Third Ave. West
Seattle, WA 98119
Kim Gilnett
206-281-2205
Fax: 206-281-2430
E-mail: kgilnett@spu.edu
www.spu.edu

Programs: music major with emphasis in: performance, education, technology, composition, theory, literature, general.

Premier Christian liberal arts education with strong music department. Performance majors include piano, vocal, wind, percussion and string specialties. Music education can include certification as part of a 4 year degree program. Up to date music technology lab with opportunities to record and produce.

Shoreline Community College
Department of Music

16101 Greenwood Ave. North
Shoreline, WA 98133-5696
206-546-4101
www.shoreline.edu

Skagit Valley College
Department of Music

2405 East College Way
Mount Vernon, WA 98273
Diane Johnson
360-416-7655
E-mail: diane.johnson@skagit.edu
www.skagit.edu

Associate in Music

Skagit Valley College offers a 2-yr associate in music degree which is a direct transfer degree to both Western Washington University and Central Washington University. It also transfers easily to most public and private universities. SVC prides itself in small class sizes and personal attention.

Spokane Community College
Department of Music

1810 North Greene St.
Spokane, WA 99217-5399
509-533-7000
www.scc.spokane.edu

Tacoma Community College
Department of Music

6501 South 19th St.

Building 20, Room 27
Tacoma, WA 98466-6139
David Endicott
253-566-5063
E-mail: dendicott@tacomacc.edu
www.tacomacc.edu

University of Puget Sound
School of Music

1500 North Warner
Tacoma, WA 98416
253-879-3100
www.ups.edu

University of Washington
School of Music

Box 353450
Seattle, WA 98195-3450
206-543-1201
Fax: 206-685-9499
www.music.washington.edu

Walla Walla College
Department of Music

204 South College Ave.
College Place, WA 99324
Cassie Ragenovich
509-527-2561
Fax: 509-527-2177
E-mail: jamema@wwc.edu
www.wwe.edu/academics/departments/music

BA, BM in Education, BM in Performance

Small private college-church affiliated. Approximately 1900 students on campus.

Washington State University
Department of Music and Theatre Arts

P.O. Box 641067
Pullman, WA 99164
Gerald Berthiaume
509-335-7757
wsu.edu/MusicandTheatre

WSU music activities are located in beautiful, newly enlarged and remodeled Kimbrough Hall, with multiple performance spaces, state-of-the-art recording studio and world-class music library.

Wenatchee Valley College
Department of Music

1300 5th St.
Wenatchee, WA 98801
509-682-6800
www.wvc.edu

Western Washington University
Department of Music

516 High St.
Bellingham, WA 98225
David Fcingold
360-650-7712
E-mail: guitar@cc.wwu.edu
www.wwu.edu/music

B.A., B.M., and M.M.

The department of music has a heritage which reaches back to the founding of Whatcom Normal School in 1893. For years, its superb faculty of artist-teachers has prepared students with the comprehensive knowledge and skill to meet the demands of artist, teacher, composer, historian, arranger, and scholar. All music majors receive applied study with a large faculty of artist-teachers. At WWU the relationship between scholarly study and performance blends emerging and established talent in a unique environment. The facilities include a 700-seat concert hall, two large rehearsal halls, classrooms, computer assisted instruction lab, electronic music studio, practice rooms, ensemble libraries, faculty offices and the music library.

Whitman College
Department of Music

345 Boyer Ave.
Walla Walla, WA 99362
Robert Bode
509-527-5111
E-mail: boderh@whitman.edu
www.whitman.edu

Whitworth College
Department of Music

300 West Hawthorne Rd.
Spokane, WA 99251
509-777-1000
www.whitworth.edu

Yakima Valley College
Department of Music

P.O. Box 22520
Yakima, WA 98907-2520
509-574-4839
www.yvcc.edu

Population: 1,816,856 (2005 Estimate)
Capital City: Charleston
Music Colleges and Universities: Alderson-Broaddus College, Fairmont State College, Marshall University, Shepherd College, University of Charleston, West Virginia University
Bird: Cardinal
Motto: Montani semper liberi - Mountaineers are always free
Flower: Rhododendron
Tree: Sugar Maple
Residents Called: West Virginians
Origin of Name: Named after England's Queen Elizabeth I, the "Virgin Queen."
Area: 24,231 square miles (41st largest state)
Statehood: June 20, 1863 (35th state)
Largest Cities: Charleston, Huntington, Parkersburg, Wheeling, Morgantown, Weirton, Fairmont, Beckley, Clarksburg, Martinsburg
College Band Programs: Marshall University

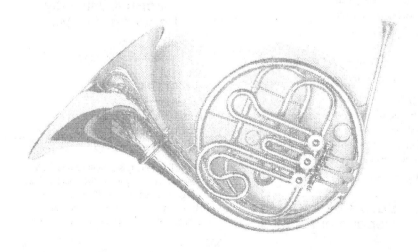

Alderson-Broaddus College
Department of Music

College Hill Rd.
Philippi, WV 26416
304-457-1700
www.ab.edu

Approximately 60 music majors are enrolled in the music programs at Alderson-Broaddus College, a four-year liberal arts institution affiliated with the West Virginia and American Baptist Conventions. There are seven full-time persons and a number of adjunct faculty persons. The music department is located in Wilcox Chapel, which houses a concert/recital hall (also used as a worship venue), classrooms, faculty studios and practice rooms. Students use a well-equipped piano/computer electronic music laboratory. Featured ensembles include a regionally recognized concert choir, The West Virginians (a semi-professional show choir), chapel choir, brass choir, concert band, jazz ensemble and hand bell choir. Auditions are required for entrance. Music scholarships are available.

Bethany College
Department of Music

Bethany, WV 26032
304-892-7831
E-mail: sneel@bethanywv.edu
www.bethanywv.edu

B.A. and minor in music.

Concord College
Department of Music

P.O. Box 1000
Athens, WV 24712-1000
888-384-5249
E-mail: admissions@concord.edu
www.concord.wvnet.edu

B.A. in music.

Davis & Elkins College
Department of Music

100 Campus Dr.
Elkins, WV 26241
Robert D. Psurny
304-637-1201
E-mail: psurnyr@davisandelkins.edu
www.davisandelkins.edu

Fairmont State College
Department of Fine Arts

1201 Locust Ave.
Room 304 Wallman Hall
Fairmont, WV 26554
Peter Lach
304-367-4219
E-mail: plach@fairmontstate.edu
www.fscwv.edu

Glenville State College
Division of Fine Arts

200 High St.
Glenville, WV 26351
Duane Chapman
E-mail: visitor@glenville
www.glenville.edu

Music Education (K-12) major as well as music minor

Marshall University
Department of Music

2 Marshall University
Huntington, WV 25755-2232
Ann Leigh
304-696-3117
Fax: 304-696-4379
E-mail: leigha@marshall.edu
www.marshall.edu/cofa/music

BFA, BA in Mus.Ed., MA, MAT

Marshall University is a multi-campus public university providing innovative undergraduate and graduate education. MU Department of Music is a fully accredited institutional member of NASM, offering programs in music education, performance, theory, composition and history/literature in a caring, student centered environment.

Ohio Valley University
Department of Music

1 Campus View Dr.
Vienna, WV 26105-8000
Laura Hamm
877-446-8668
www.ovc.edu

Minor in music, Associate of Arts Degree.

Shepherd College
Department of Music

Shepherdstown, WV 25443
Mark McCoy
304-876-5223
E-mail: mccoy@shepherd.edu
www.shepherd.edu/musicweb

West Virginia State College
Department of Music

P.O. Box 1000
Institute, WV 25112-1000
800-987-2112
www.wvstateu.edu/music

West Virginia University
Division of Music

P.O. Box 6111
Morgantown, WV 26506
304-293-4841 x3196
Fax: 304-293-7491
www.wvu.edu/music

West Virginia University at Morgantown
Department of Music

P.O. Box 6111
morgantown, WV 26506
304-293-4841 x3196

Fax: 304-293-7491
www.wvu.edu

West Virginia University at Parksburg
Department of Music

300 Campus Dr.
Office #1214
Parkersburg, WV 26104
304-424-8301
www.wvup.edu

West Virginia Wesleyan College
Department of Music

59 College Ave.
Buckhannon, WV 26201
Melody Meadows
304-473-8000
E-mail: meadows@wvwc.edu
www.wvwc.edu

The Bachelor of Music Education degree serves those who are preparing for the teaching profession, and the Bachelor of Arts degree accommodates those pursuing a liberal arts degree or wishing to emphasize a particular aspect of music, such as performance or theory in their study. Various options for a contract major combining music with other disciplines, such as business or Christian education, are possible. All curricula offered provide a strong foundation for graduate study. Minor in music also offered.

Population: 5,536,201 (2005 Estimate)
Capital City: Madison
Bird: Robin
Motto: Forward
Flower: Wood Violet
Tree: Sugar Maple
Residents Called: Wisconsinites
Origin of Name: Based on an Indian word, "Ouisconsin" believed to mean, "grassy place" in the Cheppewa tongue.
Area: 65,503 square miles (23rd largest state)
Statehood: May 29, 1848 (30th state)
Largest Cities: Milwaukee, Madison, Green Bay, Kenosha, Racine, Appleton, Waukesha, Oshkosh, Eau Claire, West Allis
College Band Programs: University of Wisconsin-Eau Claire, University of Wisconsin-Madison

Alverno College
Department of Music

3400 South 43rd St.
P.O. Box 343922
Milwaukee, WI 53234
800-933-3401
E-mail: admissions@alverno.edu
www.alverno.edu

Beloit College
Department of Music

700 College St.
Beloit, WI 53511
608-363-2000
www.beloit.edu

Cardinal Stritch University
Department of Music

6801 North Yates Rd.
Milwaukee, WI 53217
Dennis King
414-410-4349
Fax: 414-410-4239
E-mail: dwking@stritch.edu
www.stritch.edu

Carroll College
Department of Music

100 NE Ave.
Waukesha, WI 53186
Larry Harper
262-547-1211
Fax: 414-524-7139
E-mail: lharper@cc.edu
www.cc.edu

Carthage College
Department of Music

2001 Alford Dr.
Kenosha, WI 53140-1994
James Ripley
262-551-5854
E-mail: jripley@carthage.edu
www.carthage.edu

Lakeland College
Department of Music

P.O. Box 359
Sheboygan, WI 53083-0359
800-569-2166
Fax: 950-565-1206
www.lakeland.edu

Lawrence University
Conservatory

P.O. Box 599
Appleton, WI 54912
920-832-7000
www.lawrence.edu/conservatory

Marian College
Department of Music

45 South National Ave.
Fond Du Lac, WI 54934-4699
David Thompson
800-2-MARIAN
www.mariancollege.edu

Mount Mary College
Department of Music

2900 North Menomonee River Pkwy.
Milwaukee, WI 53222
Sister Rita Schweitzer
414-258-4810
www.mtmary.edu

Mount Mary is a liberal arts college located on a beautiful 80-acre campus. The music department has spacious studios and practice facilities. It is known for its annual Christmas Madrigal Dinner concert, which features madrigal singers, hand bells, string ensemble and recorder consort.

Ripon College
Department of Music

300 Seward St.
P.O. Box 248
Ripon, WI 54971
920-748-8791
E-mail: music@ripon.edu
www.ripon.edu

Silver Lake College
Department of Music

2406 South Alverno Rd.
Manitowoc, WI 54220
920-686-6173
E-mail: abock@silver.sl.edu
www.sl.edu

St. Norbert College
Department of Music

100 Grant St.
De Pere, WI 54115-2099
920-403-3112
Fax: 920-403-4442
E-mail: music@snc.edu
www.snc.edu

St. Norbert College is a small liberal arts college located on the scenic banks of the Fox River. One of the hallmarks of the college is an opportunity for the students to form strong, lasting relationships with the members of the faculty. Since we have developed a remarkably successful placement rate, our graduates have achieved recognition statewide and beyond. Our four-year certification program attracts a growing number of students. St. Norbert College is one of only a few liberal art schools its size, which offers a large number of quality performing ensembles for all students. Our ensembles have toured the U.S., Europe and the South Pacific.

University of Wisconsin at Baraboo
Department of Music

1006 Connie Rd.

Barbaoo, WI 53913
608-356-8351
Fax: 608-356-4074
E-mail: ccaillie@uwc.edu
www.barbaroo.uwc.edu

University of Wisconsin at Barron County
Department of Music

1800 College Dr.
Rice Lake, WI 54868
715-234-8167
Fax: 715-234-1975
E-mail: mhoch@uwc.edu
www.barron.uwc.edu

University of Wisconsin at Eau Claire
Department of Music and Theatre Arts

156 Haas Fine Arts
121 Water St.
Eau Claire, WI 54702
715-836-2284
Fax: 715-836-3952
www.uwec.edu

University of Wisconsin at Fond Du Lac
Department of Music

400 University Dr.
Fond Du Lac, WI 54935
920-929-3600
E-mail: peby@uwc.edu
www.fdl.uwe.edu

University of Wisconsin at Fox Valley
Department of Music

1478 Midway Rd.
Menasha, WI 54952
920-832-2600

Fax: 920-832-2674
E-mail: lzimmerman@uwe.edu
www.uwfox.uwc.edu

University of Wisconsin at Green Bay
Department of Music

Theatre Hall 331
2420 Nicolet Dr.
Green Bay, WI 54311
John Salerno
920-465-2348
E-mail: salernoj@uwgb.edu
www.uwgb.edu

University of Wisconsin at La Crosse
Department of Music

1725 State St.
La Crosse, WI 54601
Gary Walth
608-785-8409
Fax: 608-785-8939
E-mail: walth.gary@uwlax.edu
www.uwlax.edu

Music Education, Performance Emphasis

University of Wisconsin at Madison
School of Music

455 North Park St.
3561 Humanities
Madison, WI 53706
Bonnie Abrams
608-263-1900
E-mail: music@music.wisc.edu
www.wisc.edu/music

The School of Music at the University of Wisconsin-Madison ranked among the top 5% of public music schools, and the University is world-renowned for research and academics.

University of Wisconsin at Marathon
Department of Music

518 South 7th Ave.
Wausau, WI 54401
715-261-6100
www.uwmc.uwc.edu

University of Wisconsin at Marinette
Department of Music

750 West Bay Shore St.
Marinette, WI 54143
David Giebler
7715-735-4316
E-mail: dgiebler@uwc.edu
www.marinette.uwc.edu

University of Wisconsin at Milwaukee
Peck School of the Arts

2400 East Kenwood Blvd.
Milwaukee, WI 53211
414-229-4393
Fax: 414-229-2776
E-mail: mcis@uwm.edu
www3.uwm.edu

University of Wisconsin at Parkside
Department of Music

900 Wood Rd.
P.O. Box 2000
Kenosha, WI 53141
James McKeever
262-595-2562
www.uwp.edu

The UW-Parkside Music Department offers the bachelor of arts in music with degree options in instrumental, choral or general music education, jazz studies, arts management and piano pedagogy and literature. Eight full-time and 15 part-time instructors, who are all active as professional performers or composers, staff the department. Over 200 participate in UW-Parkside Bands, Choirs, Jazz Ensembles, Orchestra and Chamber Ensembles. About 65 concerts are presented annually by students, faculty and guest artists in the Communication Arts Theater and the Union Cinema-Theater. Music major enrollment has risen every year for the past eight years. Seventy-five majors are currently enrolled.

University of Wisconsin at Platteville
Department of Fine Arts

1 University Plaza
Platteville, WI 53818
Daniel Fairchild
608-342-1143
Fax: 608-342-1039
E-mail: fairchig@uwplatt.edu
www.uwplatt.edu

BS & BA Music Education, Music and Businness, Liberal Arts

The UWP music program provides the highest level of specialized music training for students seeking a career in the music profession. Outstanding artist teachers and state of the art facilities combine to provide students with the opportunity to fully develpo there talents as musicians. The UWP music program is an assredited member of the National Association of Schools of Music

University of Wisconsin at River Falls
Department of Music

410 South Third St.
River Falls, WI 54022-5001
715-425-3911
www.uwrf.edu

University of Wisconsin at Rock County
Department of Music

2909 Kellogg Ave.
Jamesville, WI 53546
Jeff Suarez
608-758-6554
E-mail: jeff.suarez@uwc.edu
www.rock.uwc.edu

AAS, core music classes that apply towards four year degree

UW - Rock County is one of thirteen two-year transfer institutions in the UW System...we offer many different ensembles that a student may participate in including concert band, orchestra, stage band, jazz combos, choirs, and small ensemble opportunities. We have the lowest tuition rates in the UW System, and with the guaranteed transfer program, one may transfer to the four-year UW institution of your choosing upon completion of studies at UW-Rock County. Also, UW-Rock County offers a person the chance to be a "star" in a small college setting, complete with small class sizes, instruction from professors (not teaching assistants), and the chance to become part of a close knit and supportive music community.Lastly, there is no audition requirement to study music at UW-Rock County, and if you are a music major, you will receive FREE lessons on your major instrument.

University of Wisconsin at Superior
Department of Music

Belknap and Caitlin
P.O. Box 2000
Superior, WI 54880-4500
715-394-8115
E-mail: music@uwsuper.edu
www.uwsuper.edu

This is a NASM-accredited, quality music program at Wisconsin's Public Liberal Arts College. A highly qualified faculty, excellent facilities and ample performing opportunities are the hallmarks of this program.

University of Wisconsin at Whitewater
Department of Music

Greenhill Center of the Arts
Whitewater, WI 53190
262-472-1310
Fax: 262-472-2808
E-mail: music@uww.edu
www.uww.edu

Viterbo University
Department of Music

900 Viterbo Dr.
La Crosse, WI 54601
Sue Hauser
608-796-3760
E-mail: music@viterbo.edu
www.viterbo.edu

BA in Music; BM in Music Education, Performance/Pedagogy; Music Minor; Church Music Minor Facilities: Main Theatre, Recital Hall

The Viterbo University Music Department prepares vocal and piano students for professional careers in teaching and performing, provides opportunities for the general student to engage in artistic experiences, and encourages students to influence the musical lives of the communities in which they serve.

Wisconsin Conservatory of Music
Department of Music

1584 North Prospect Ave.
Milwaukee, WI 53202
414-276-5760
Fax: 414-276-6076
E-mail: karendeschere@wcmusic.org
www.wcmusic.org

Wisconsin Lutheran College
Department of Musical Arts

8880 West Bluemound Rd.
Milkaukee, WI 53226
Craig Swiontek
414-443-8800
E-mail: craig.swiontek@wlc.edu
www.wlc.edu

Bachelor of Arts, Bachelor of Science

Christian Liberal Arts College

Population: 509,294 (2005 Estimate)
Capital City: Cheyenne
Bird: Western Meadowlark
Motto: Equal rights
Flower: Indian Paintbrush
Tree: Cottonwood
Residents Called: Wyomingites
Origin of Name: Based on an Algonquin or Delaware Indian word meaning "large prairie place."
Area: 97,818 square miles (10th largest state)
Statehood: July 10, 1890 (44th state)
Largest Cities: Cheyenne, Casper, Laramie, Gillette, Rock Springs, Sheridan, Green River, Evanston, Riverton, Cody
College Band Programs: University of Wyoming

Casper College
Department of Music

125 College Dr.
Casper, WY 82601
800-442-2963
www.caspercollege.edu

Associate of Arts Degree Music, Associate of Fine Arts Degree Instrumental Music Performance, Associate of Fine Arts Degree Music Education, Associate of Fine Arts Degree Vocal Music Performance.

Central Wyoming College
Department of Music

2660 Peck Ave.
Riverton, WY 82501
307-855-2213
Fax: 307-855-2090
E-mail: bhussa@cwc.edu
www.cwc.edu

Eastern Wyoming College
Department of Music

3200 West C St.
Torrington, WY 82240
866-327-8996
Fax: 307-532-8222
www.ewc.wy.edu

Laramie County Community College
Department of Music

1400 East College Dr.
Cheyenne, WY 82007
Karen Reynolds
307-778-1158
www.lccc.cc.wy.us

Northwest College
Department of Music

231 West 6th St.
Powell, WY 82435
Neil Hansen
307-754-6427
E-mail: Neil.Hansen@northwestcollege.edu
www.northwestcollege.edu

Sheridan College
Department of Music

P.O. Box 1500
3059 Coffeen Ave.
Sheridan, WY 82801
307-674-6446
www.sc.cc.wy.us

University of Wyoming
Department of Music

Department 3037
1000 East University Ave.
Laramie, WY 82071
307-766-5242
Fax: 307-766-5326
E-mail: musicdpt@uwyo.edu
uwadmnweb.uwyo.edu/Music

Dort College
Department of Music

498 4th Ave. NE
Sioux Center, IA 51250-1606
712-722-6000
E-mail: admissions@dordt.edu
www.dordt.edu